THE
GOLDFISH

by

GEORGE F. HERVEY

and

JACK HEMS

Illustrated with line drawings by
A. Fraser-Brunner, F.Z.S.
and photographs by
Laurence E. Perkins

FABER AND FABER
3 Queen Square
London

First published in 1948
by Batchworth Press Limited
20 Tudor Street London EC4
Revised edition published in 1968
Reprinted 1968 and 1974
by Faber and Faber Limited
3 Queen Square London WC1
Printed in Great Britain
by Unwin Brothers Limited
The Gresham Press Old Woking Surrey

ISBN 0 571 08245 9

CONTENTS

... ab ovo
usque ad mala ...
HORACE *Satires, 1.3*

ILLUSTRATIONS

I can look for a whole day with delight upon a handsome picture, though it be but of an horse.

BROWNE, *Religio Medici*

COLOUR

PLATES

FIGURES

Illustrations

Illustrations

PREFACE

Presumption or meanness are both too often
the only articles to be found in a preface.

CRABBE, *Inebriety*

A Preface, by its very nature, is something of an explanation, an apology for inflicting a book on the reader. It has been said, not perhaps without some degree of truth, that no book needs a preface; for if it is a good book it needs no explanation, and if it is a bad book no explanation will improve it. The logic of this is irrefutable. Yet we find it necessary to write a preface; for this book is one that needs some explanation.

The Goldfish has attracted to itself such a large literature that the reader may be excused if he thinks that here is nothing more than a new variation on a hackneyed theme. It is true that we write for the aquarist—the fancier and breeder—and not for the ichthyologist. That, however, is inevitable; for to the ichthyologist the goldfish can never be more than one species among some twenty thousand. But in particular we write for the experienced aquarist who seeks to break new ground. It was our first intention to appeal as much to the novice-aquarist as to the experienced aquarist, but in the end we reached the conclusion that no one book could satisfy these mutually inconsistent functions, and, since the novice-aquarist is already well catered for, chapter after chapter was revised, torn up, and rewritten, and each time we took the advice that Hamlet gave to his mother: 'O, throw away the worser part of it.' In the end, the well-trodden ground, the hackneyed theme of aquarium and pond-management, was reduced from ten chapters to one; and though Chapter IV has been included mainly for the benefit of the novice-aquarist who may choose to read this book, it contains material that, we think, even the experienced aquarist will welcome; for he who can honestly claim to know all that there is to know about the care of goldfish in aquaria and ponds has yet to be born.

In the main this book differs entirely from its predecessors bearing the same or a similar title, because here, for the first time, the goldfish is treated anatomically, historically, pathologically, and artistically. This, in itself, is something of an achievement. We say it with conscious pride; for those who have made a special study of the species have hardly touched the fringe of the subject. Much work remains to be done, even though we have done much, and here, for the first time in a book addressed to aquarists, describe the anatomy of the goldfish; present an original and authoritative history of the species and the fancy breeds, much of it compiled from ancient Chinese sources; suggest treatments for diseases hitherto unmentioned in English books; and present a unique chapter, the result of many years of patient research, associating the goldfish with the arts. In all this, and much other new material, there is nothing in the pages that follow to cause anyone alarm; for, so far as it has been possible to do so, we have avoided technical language and abstract speculation, and kept the text free of facts that are of interest only to the ichthyologist and limnologist.

Despite the proverb that two heads are better than one, collaboration between authors is notoriously difficult. In this particular case it was more difficult than usual owing to the fact that the book was planned in 1942, and the greater part was written during the years 1943 and 1944. During these three years the Second World War may be said to have been at its worst, and our difficulties were increased because force of circumstances compelled us to discuss almost every detail by correspondence, since we were able to meet only at rare intervals and even then only for short periods at a time. This may explain any errors that still remain in the book: it does not excuse them.

We use the word 'goldfish' in its strict European sense, to mean the Common Goldfish and the numerous fancy breeds that have been developed from it by selective breeding. In the Far East, at all events in China, a marked distinction is made between the wild goldfish and the domestic goldfish. The Wild Goldfish, known in Chinese as the *Chi*, or more correctly as the *Chi-yü*, is a grey fish not much esteemed for ornamental waters, but sold in most Chinese markets as a food-fish. The Domestic Goldfish is a golden-coloured variation of the *Chi-yü*, and is correctly known in Chinese as the *Chin Chi-yü* (literally Golden *Chi*-fish) though in practice it is more usually referred to as the *Chin-yü*. We do not make this distinction, however, because it is contrary to European practice to distinguish between the wild and domesticated fish: both are known as The Goldfish (*Carassius auratus*) with no distinguishing adjective.

The goldfish is a member of the Cyprinidae, or carp family, and, therefore, it is essentially a freshwater species; but it is a remarkably accommodating species—hence its popularity as an aquarium- and pond-fish; and in this connection it is of interest to note that goldfish have adapted themselves to the brackish waters of Bermuda. Although generally regarded solely as an ornamental animal—the pampered pet of the home-aquarium and garden-pond—the goldfish is not without its utilitarian value to man, and it has lent itself to the progress of science. Scientists have discovered a method of testing the efficiency of local anaesthetics, and determining their toxicity, by immersing goldfish in the solution. In the First World War by immersing goldfish in water in which gas-helmets had been washed, the nature of the chemicals used in the manufacture of the gases was determined. Anglers have been known to use it as live-bait. The goldfish, therefore, is not altogether a luxury-fish, even though current inflated prices suggest that it is, and the more grotesque fancy breeds have for long been among the recognized show-pieces of public aquaria. We mention these facts because we know from experience that few aquarists, even among those who have for long kept goldfish in aquaria and ponds, are aware of them. As for the anatomy of the goldfish, its long history, the many diseases to which it may fall a prey, its references in literature, all this, and much more, is as the proverbial sealed book to the great majority of aquarists. It is our aim, in the pages that follow, to open that book, and expose at least the early chapters of an interesting story.

We have to acknowledge a very great debt of gratitude to a large number of authorities who have given us direct and indirect help. The information contained in the following pages is largely the result of our personal experiences, observations and researches, extending over a period of many years; but, partly because we lack certain highly specialized knowledge and partly because it is always desirable to verify debatable points, we found it necessary to consult a number of experts before we could claim this book to be fully authoritative. To those who gave us practical help and advice our thanks are accorded in the immediately following pages. At the end of the book there is a bibliography of the books, monographs and periodicals which we consulted. Our thanks are due also to the authors of these works, not for any practical help, but because in our attempt to produce a comprehensive handbook for the guidance of the aquarist in all branches of the care and culture of the goldfish, it was impossible to avoid covering some old ground, and, with it, quotations from the works of other writers. Lengthy quotations and striking phrases extracted from any of these works, are acknowledged in the text. Since it may be found that here and there we have not scrupled to quote a few short passages with no acknowledgment, we should explain that our aim has been partly to avoid vexing the reader with an excess of references when the information given is common property, and partly to the fact that, along with Montaigne, we quote others mainly in order the better to express ourselves.

We have reduced footnotes to a minimum; for it is our experience that a large number of footnotes, giving sources, references and cross-references, involves the reader in that study which the Preacher tells us is a weariness of the flesh. In the main we have included a footnote only to amplify personal or bibliographical information, to give a geographical direction, or to mention an important fact that cannot be conveniently given in the text; but when we have quoted from a periodical or from an author who has two or more works mentioned in the bibliography, a footnote has been given to direct the reader to the source of the quotation.

So far as it has been possible to do so, we have retained a sequential order, and avoided unnecessary repetitions by omitting from later chapters minor details that have been mentioned in earlier ones. It follows, therefore, that the book is best read as a whole. It is, however, not essential to do so; for the cross-references should prove adequate for all practical purposes, and the complete index should enable the reader to find his way about the book with ease.

Although we have taken every precaution to ensure accuracy we are not so young that we can claim the right of infallibility. So we take full responsibility for any errors that may appear in the text, apologize for them in advance, and attach no blame to other hands.

London and Leicester,   GEORGE HERVEY
1942–8   JACK HEMS

PREFACE TO REVISED EDITION

Exactly twenty years have passed since the first edition of this book was published. In the history of man the species it is no great length of time; in the history of man the individual it is a long time, more than a full quarter of his life expectancy.

The demand for a revised edition of this book, therefore, comes by no means too soon, and all the more so since our original work was written under the stress of total war.

It is unfortunate that during the intervening years the original illustrations have been lost and the blocks destroyed. We have been able to reproduce the line drawings of Mr. Fraser-Brunner but not the plates, and these we have replaced with photographs by Mr. Laurence Perkins. It is no reflection on him, as a first-class photographer of fishes, that historically and artistically his photographs are less interesting than the illustrations, some taken from antique MSS and books, which accompanied the first edition of this book.

We can only hope that our present efforts will be received by critics and readers with the same kindly enthusiasm that they received our first.

1968   G. F. H. & J. H.

TABLES OF EQUIVALENTS

TEMPERATURE

Fahrenheit to Centigrade

$122°F = 50°C$
$119°F = 48·3°C$
$116°F = 46·7°C$
$113°F = 45°C$
$110°F = 43·3°C$
$107°F = 41·7°C$
$104°F = 40°C$
$101°F = 38·3°C$
$98°F = 36·7°C$
$95°F = 35°C$
$92°F = 33·3°C$
$89°F = 31·7°C$
$86°F = 30°C$
$83°F = 28·3°C$
$80°F = 26·7°C$
$77°F = 25°C$
$74°F = 23·3°C$
$71°F = 21·7°C$
$68°F = 20°C$
$65°F = 18·3°C$
$62°F = 16·7°C$
$59°F = 15°C$
$56°F = 13·3°C$
$53°F = 11·7°C$
$50°F = 10°C$

LINEAR MEASURE

Inches and Feet to Centimetres and Metres

$\frac{1}{16}'' = 0·15875$ cm
$\frac{1}{8}'' = 0·3175$ cm
$\frac{1}{4}'' = 0·635$ cm
$\frac{1}{2}'' = 1·270$ cm
$1'' = 2·540$ cm
$2'' = 5·080$ cm
$3'' = 7·620$ cm
$4'' = 10·160$ cm
$5'' = 12·700$ cm
$6'' = 15·240$ cm
$7'' = 17·780$ cm
$8'' = 20·320$ cm
$9'' = 22·860$ cm
$12'' = 1' = 30·480$ cm
$15'' = 38·100$ cm
$18'' = 1\frac{1}{2}' = \frac{1}{2}$ yd $= 45·720$ cm
$21'' = 53·340$ cm
$24'' = 2' = 60·960$ cm
$30'' = 2\frac{1}{2}' = 76·200$ cm
$36'' = 3' = 1$ yd $= 91·440$ cm
$42'' = 3\frac{1}{2}' = 1·0668$ m
$48'' = 4' = 1·2192$ m
$54'' = 4\frac{1}{2}' = 1·3716$ m
$60'' = 5' = 1·5240$ m
$66'' = 5\frac{1}{2}' = 1·6764$ m
$72'' = 6' = 2$ yd $= 1·8288$ m
$84'' = 7' = 2·1336$ m
$96'' = 8' = 2·4384$ m

Tables of Equivalents

LIQUID MEASURE	DRY MEASURE
Pints and Gallons to Litres	Ounces and Pounds to Grammes and Kilogrammes

<table>
<tr><td>

$\frac{1}{4}$ pt = 0·142 lt
$\frac{1}{2}$ pt = 0·284 lt
1 pt = 0·568 lt
2 pt = 1 qt = 1·136 lt
3 pt = 1·705 lt
4 pt = 2 qt = 2·273 lt
8 pt = 4 qt = 1 gal = 4·546 lt
2 gal = 9·092 lt
3 gal = 13·638 lt
4 gal = 18·184 lt
6 gal = 27·276 lt
8 gal = 36·368 lt
10 gal = 45·460 lt
15 gal = 68·189 lt
20 gal = 90·919 lt
25 gal = 113·649 lt

</td><td>

$\frac{1}{8}$ oz = 3·544 gr
$\frac{1}{4}$ oz = 7·087 gr
$\frac{1}{2}$ oz = 14·175 gr
1 oz = 28·350 gr
2 oz = 56·699 gr
4 oz = $\frac{1}{4}$ lb = 113·398 gr
8 oz = $\frac{1}{2}$ lb = 226·796 gr
16 oz = 1 lb = 453·592 gr
2 lb = 907·20 gr
4 lb = 1·814 kg
6 lb = 2·721 kg
8 lb = 3·629 kg
10 lb = 4·536 kg
15 lb = 6·804 kg
20 lb = 9·072 kg

</td></tr>
</table>

ACKNOWLEDGMENTS

The still small voice of gratitude.
GRAY, *The Installation Ode*

The present writers take this opportunity to tender their grateful thanks to all those individuals and firms who have been kind enough to give them practical help and advice, without which, indeed, much of this book could never have been written. In particular to: Mr. Robert J. Affleck, B.SC., M.R.S.T., for giving them the privilege of reading his monograph on the embryology of the goldfish while in MS form; Mr. W. Harold Cotton, F.Z.S., the well-known aquarist and icthyotomist; Mr. L. Cura the well-known commercial pisciculturist; Mr. J. E. Dandy, M.A., for help with the classification of aquatic plants; Professor E. D. Edwards, M.A., D.LIT., of the School of Oriental and African Studies, the University of London; Mr. A. Fraser-Brunner, F.Z.S., of the British Museum (Natural History) for much practical advice and for revising Chapter I; Miss Winifred Frost, D.SC., of the Freshwater Biological Association of the British Empire, for a number of advisory letters; Doctor Gustav Haloun, PH.D., Professor of Chinese at Cambridge University, for research work in connection with Chapters III and X; the Reverend A. C. Moule, LITT.D. for much research work in connection with Chapter III, for translating numerous passages from the Chinese, and for his invaluable and never-failing advice; his brother, the Reverend Henry W. Moule, B.A., for furnishing some interesting information on breeding goldfish in China; Miss Ethelwyn Trewavas, D.SC., of the British Museum (Natural History) for supplying some valuable sources of information and for a number of advisory letters; the Parasitologist of the Zoological Society of London for a number of advisory letters; the Analytical Laboratories of the British Drug Houses Limited for a number of advisory letters on water; Spratt's Patent Limited, manufacturers of foods for dogs, cats, birds, and fishes, for a number of advisory letters; and many others who were good enough to offer practical advice.

In conclusion they are especially grateful to their two illustrators: Mr. Fraser-Brunner for executing the line drawings and Mr. Laurence Perkins for his photographic work.

Chapter I

ANATOMY

There can be no reason given but onely from Anatomy.
CROOKE, *Body of Man*

When a zoologist speaks of a fish he has in mind a definite class of animals, with a skeleton composed mainly of bone, exhibiting certain distinctive structural features, and having gills for the extraction of oxygen from water. By this he excludes sharks, rays, lampreys, lancelets, and the like, which are often loosely spoken of as fishes. Still more, of course, does he exclude cuttle-fish, starfish, shell-fish, and others, which are invertebrates; and whales, dolphins, porpoises, and the like, which are mammals.

Even so, the true fishes are a vast and varied assemblage; for over twenty thousand species are known to zoologists, and some of them are of weird and wonderful appearance. This great class is divided up, or classified, into a number of orders, partly for convenience and partly to show their relationships. One of these orders is called the Ostariophysi, a meaningless word to those who have no Greek, but very apt, since it refers to the anatomical feature which distinguishes all its thousand-odd species from those of any other order, namely the chain of small bones connecting the swim- or air-bladder with the ear.

A good modern classification aims to resemble, as nearly as possible, the family tree of the group it represents, based upon what can be deduced—by the study of structure, life histories, and fossil evidence—about the evolution of the various forms. If the order Ostariophysi is compared to a large limb of the tree, it is seen to divide into two main branches. With one of these, the sub-order Siluroidea that includes all the catfishes, we are not concerned here; but the other branch, the sub-order Cyprinoidea, is of much concern to us; for it divides into two smaller branches —called families—one of which is the Cyprinidae or carp family.

The Cyprinidae is the largest of all fish families and contains about two thousand species. It is characterized by its members having toothless jaws: the only dentition is a set of eight teeth (arranged 4–4) on certain highly modified gill-bones known as pharyngeals. These pharyngeal teeth are of considerable importance in classifying the family; for, of course, this huge family shows within its ranks further lines of divergence, and it is divided into a large number of still smaller branches—called genera—each of which includes several species (rarely only one) the species being the end twigs, so to speak, of the tree.

One of the genera is called *Carassius*: it contains only two species, namely *Carassius carassius* the Crucian Carp, and *Carassius auratus* the Goldfish.

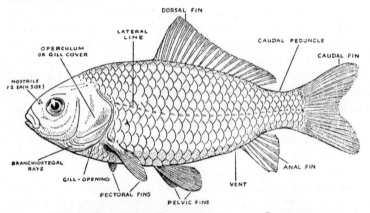

Fig. 1. EXTERNAL FEATURES OF THE GOLDFISH

From this it follows that the systematic position of the goldfish is: *Carassius auratus*, of the family Cyprinidae, of the sub-order Cyprinoidea, of the order Ostariophysi, of the class Osteichthyes. And it is important to note that the goldfish is a distinct species and is not a domesticated variation of the crucian carp, though the two are closely related. Still more is the goldfish not a sport from the Common Carp (*Cyprinus carpio*), though we often see it stated in popular works that it is, and, indeed, many practical men have been led along false paths by this erroneous assumption.

Externally, the carp can be distinguished at a glance from both members of the genus *Carassius* by the presence of a pair of barbels, or feelers, at each corner of the mouth. Internally, the most striking difference is in the arrangement of the pharyngeal teeth;

for in *Cyprinus* they form three rows, whereas in *Carassius* there is only a single row. It is not quite so easy to distinguish the wild form of the goldfish from the crucian carp; for, as we have seen, they are closely related. Perhaps the most obvious difference is in the shape of the dorsal fin and the body. The crucian carp has a deeper body than the goldfish, and the upper margin of the dorsal fin is convex, whereas in the goldfish it is either straight or concave. A more exact method of distinguishing the two species is by counting the scales. The crucian carp has from twenty-eight to thirty-five scales along the lateral line, and from seven to nine scales between the dorsal spine and the lateral line. The wild goldfish has proportionately larger scales, numbering from twenty-eight to thirty-one along the lateral line, and six between the dorsal spine and the lateral line. In domestication, of course, the two species will seldom be confused; for, as a rule, only the highly coloured mutants of the goldfish are encouraged by breeders. A possible source of difficulty, however, and one which has no doubt given rise to confusion in the past, lies in the fact that the two species are so closely related that they hybridize readily.

We began this chapter by making it clear that the goldfish has a bony skeleton. In broad outline, the skeleton consists of a vertebral column, or backbone, supporting a well-developed skull at the anterior end, providing attachment for the limbs and ribs, and giving support to the fins.

The backbone consists of a series of vertebrae, which at first sight appears to number about twenty-eight; but there are some others, curiously modified, that will be mentioned later. Each of these normal vertebrae consists of a short cylindrical bone, or centrum, concave both before and behind. The division of the column into these segments allows flexibility of the body; and in this respect it may be noted that the vertebrae are more disconnected, and therefore more mobile, in the region of the tail.

Each centrum is surmounted above by an arch, formed by the union of a bony element on each side. Through the long avenue of arches, so formed, the main nerve of the body, the spinal cord, passes. From the summit of each of these neural arches rises a neural spine, which serves to support the dorsal fin and the strong muscles of the back.

The first fourteen normal vertebrae bear ribs. The ribs are long and slender, and form a very strong, yet flexible case for the protection of the abdominal organs. The box tapers behind, so that the last two or three pairs of ribs are short and close together; and, whereas they are borne on processes (parapophyses) that jut out from the centra, the first eleven pairs of ribs are attached directly to the vertebrae. Behind the body cavity the parapophyses are joined together at their tips to form arches similar to those above, so that in the tail region each vertebrae has two arches—the neural arch above, and the haemal arch below. The haemal arch is for the protection of the main blood-vessel of the body—the dorsal aorta. Attached to each neural arch above, and lying between the muscles, are two or three small slender bones (epineurals). Similar bones (epihaemals) are found on each haemal spine. No such processes, however, occur on the ribs.

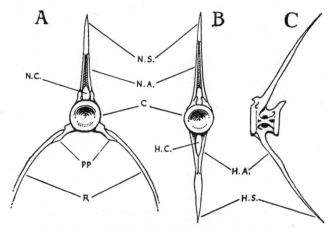

Fig. 2. VERTEBRAE

A. Precaudal (trunk) vertebra, front view.
B. Caudal (tail) vertebra, front view.
C. Side view of caudal vertebra.

(c) Centrum; (h.a.) Haemal Arch; (h.c.) Haemal Canal, through which the main artery passes; (h.s.) Haemal Spine; (n.a.) Neural Arch; (n.c.) Neural Canal, through which the spinal cord passes; (n.s.) Neural Spine; (pp) Parapophyses; (r) Ribs.

The spines of the neural and haemal arches support, above and below, a row of flattened bones that provide attachment for the rays and muscles of the dorsal and anal fins. The end of the vertebral column is turned upwards, and here there is a curious modification; for the centra of the vertebrae are not distinct, but represented by a single rod, while the paired elements of the arches are brought together to form a fan-like structure supporting the principal rays of the caudal fin. Later we shall see that, in the case of certain fancy breeds of goldfish, the divided caudal fin, so highly prized by aquarists, is associated with the separation of these paired bony supports, known as hypurals.

At the head end, the first four vertebrae are so modified and welded together as to appear almost a part of the skull. Certain of their elements on each side are curiously shaped and in contact, to form a chain of little bones, known as the Weberian ossicles,[1] which provide contact between the ear and the air-bladder. The foremost ossicle, the scaphium, encloses a backward extension from the perilymph cavity of the ear, and it is linked by two other ossicles, the intercalarium and the claustrum, to the last one, the tripus, which is inserted into the front part of the air-bladder. The possible functions of this complex apparatus is reserved for discussion later.

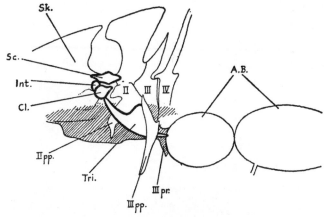

Fig. 3. THE WEBERIAN OSSICLES

(sc.) Scaphium; (int.) Intercalarium, part of first vertebra; (cl.) Claustrum, part of second vertebra; (tri.) Tripus, modified rib of third vertebra. (sk.) Skull; (ii, iii, iv) Vertebrae; (ii pp.) Parapophysis of second vertebra; (iii pp.) Parapophysis of third vertebra; (iiipr.) Process of third vertebra to which air-bladder is attached; (a.b.) Air-bladder.

The skull of the goldfish is made up of at least seventy-two

[1] After E. H. Weber, who first described the mechanism in *De aure et audita homines et animalium* (Leipzig, 1820).

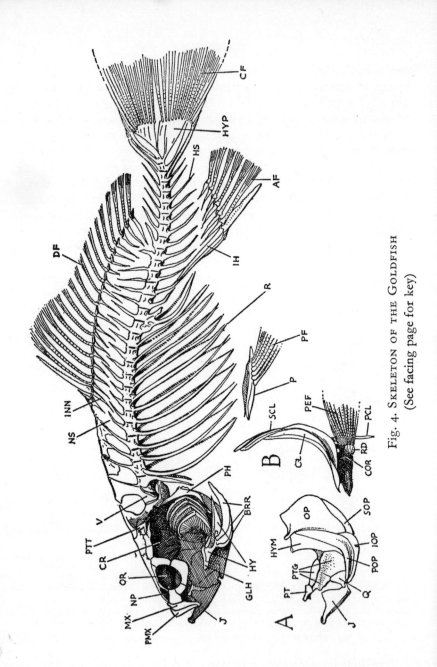

Fig. 4. SKELETON OF THE GOLDFISH
(See facing page for key)

recognizable bony elements. But no useful purpose will be served by describing it here in any great detail; for, from the practical point of view, it is sufficient to be acquainted only with the main functional parts. The cranium, for example, may be considered as a unit, though actually it is composed of many parts. It is a box-like structure in which the brain is housed; and a large aperture at the back (the foramen magnum) allows the spinal cord to pass out backwards through the neural arches. Other apertures allow egress of the nerves to nasal organs and eyes; but the ears are enclosed. The top of the cranium is expanded sideways to form part of the roof of the orbit.

Hanging from each side of the cranium, behind the eyes, is a chain of bones, the suspensorium, and the lower jaw hinges upon the lowest of these bones. The lower jaw is built up of three bones on each side: the upper jaw is composed of four bones—a premaxillary on either side and behind each a maxillary. They move forwards telescope-wise when the lower jaw opens, so that, as every aquarist will have noticed, the mouth forms a short tube. The mouth is toothless, and roofed by flat bones forming the palatine arch.

Surrounding the eyes externally on each side is a ring of circumorbital bones: they contain channels for certain sensory canals. Behind these, movably hinged to the cranium, are the gill-covers, each composed of four flat bones which are plainly visible in the

Fig. 4. SKELETON OF THE GOLDFISH

Part of left side of skull removed (shown below, A) to show position of the gill arches and part of hyoid arch with branchiostegal rays. Pectoral arch (shown below, B).

BONES OF THE SKULL: (brr) Branchiostegal rays; (cr) Cranium; (glh) Glossohyal or 'Tongue'; (hy) Hyoid Bones; (j) Lower Jaw; (mx) Maxillary; (np) Nasal Pit; (or) Orbit; (ph) Pharyngeal Bone; (pmx) Premaxillary; (ptt) Post-temporal, to which pectoral arch is attached.

PARTS REMOVED AS FIG. A ARE: *Bones of Palate:* (pt) Palatine; (ptg) Pterygoids. *Suspensorium:* (hym) Hyomandibular, connected internally by Sympletic (not shown) to (q) Quadrate, on which the lower jaw hinges. *Gill Cover:* (op) Operculum; (pop) Preoperculum; (iop) Interoperculum; (sop) Suboperculum.

BONES OF AXIAL SKELETON: (af) Anal Fin; (cf) Caudal Fin; (df) Dorsal Fin; (hs) Haemal Spine; (hyp) Hypural; (ih) Interhaemal; (inn) Interneural; (ns) Neural Spine; (r) Rib; (v) Vertebra.

BONES OF LIMBS: Pectoral Arch (left half) displaced below as Fig. B; (cl) Cleithrum; (cor) Coracoids; (pcl) Post Cleithrum; (pef) Pectoral Fin; (rd) Radials; (scl) Supracleithrum, which attaches to Post-temporal on skull.

THE PELVIS (shown in position): (p) Pelvis; (pf) Pelvic Fin.

living fish. These bones, which form the operculum, cover the gill-cavities, and are raised and lowered regularly during the process of breathing.

The gill-arches are five in number, though only four support gills. The first is known as the hyoid arch. It consists of rather large flat bones forming a strong frame, or strut, for the gill-cavities. The gill-arches also bear a series of sabre-shaped bones, known as branchiostegal rays, that open like a fan below the gill-covers to protect the gills even when expanded. From the junction of the hyoid arches near the chin, a bone projects forwards into the mouth, to support what may be called the tongue of the fish, while another bone passes backwards, to form a firm connection with the shoulder-girdle. Each gill-arch consists of several slender bones, suspended in a chain from below the cranium, all linked together below. In the last arch, the elements known as the lower pharyngeals are greatly enlarged, almost sickle-shaped, and bear rows of four strong and flattened tooth-like processes, which can be brought together for the purpose of masticating food.

Firmly attached to the back of the skull, on each side, and meeting below, are the pectoral arches, which thus form a complete shoulder-girdle. Each arch consists of several bones joined together, and supports a pectoral fin. The pectoral fins are the fore-limbs of the fish.

Farther back, on the belly, is a pair of pelvic fins, the hind-limbs of the fish. They are supported by two flat pelvic bones, which are not directly attached to any other part of the skeleton.

All the fins are supported by rays, which are built up of short segments of bone, so that they are mostly flexible (not unlike the vertebral column). In the dorsal, caudal, and anal fins, each ray is actually double, and formed by elements from both sides of the body. Most of the rays are branched and very flexible, but in some of the fins the first one to three rays may be stiff and spine-like, the segments being firmly united. This is particularly noticeable in the dorsal and anal fins, where the third rays are very strong and bear sharp thorn-like spikes down the hind edges. Close examination shows that these spines are each borne on one of the closely inter-locked segments of the ray.

The fin-rays are hinged upon their supporting bones, to allow of movement in one or more directions.

Wherever movement is needed, the bones are bound together

by ligaments, and frequently buffered with cartilage to reduce shock.

The muscular system is comparatively simple. Two masses of muscle lie along each side of the central axis, one above and the other below, and each is divided again into an upper and lower part. All the muscle-bands are divided into segments (the flakes seen in cooked cod or haddock) known as myotomes, and corresponding in number to the vertebrae. It is the rhythmic contraction of these segments that enables the body to be flexed from side to side in swimming. The dorsal muscle-mass is attached at its forward end to the back of the skull, and, therefore, extends along the whole body; but the ventral mass is most developed on the tail, and becomes very thin and feeble towards the head. The bony supports of the dorsal and anal fins bear a series of small muscles, whose function is to erect or depress the rays; and, since the elevating muscles are the stronger, the fins are seldom folded in a healthy fish. Similar muscles are concerned with keeping the caudal fin spread, and moving its upper and lower rays from side to side independently, imparting the necessary wavy motion to the fin when the fish is swimming.

The muscles of the pelvic fins are small and serve only to open the fin fan-wise in one direction. Those of the pectoral fins are more complicated and more powerful; for they are in constant use for several purposes. They are attached to the rigid pectoral arches.

The skull, of course, supports a complex of muscles, whose function it is to open and close the mouth, operate the gill-mechanism, move the eyes, and so on.

The energy, which manifests itself as movement of the muscles, is achieved by the combustion of food substances in the muscles themselves. Food taken into the mouth is at once passed backwards; for the mouth is toothless and goldfish have no salivary glands. But at the entrance to the gullet the food is masticated by the eight pharyngeal teeth (four on each side in a single row) which bite against a horny pad on the base of the skull. The food then passes down the gullet (oesophagus) where the first processes of digestion begin, and into the stomach. This appears as a mere distension of the alimentary tract, though the structure of its lining is different. Here, in an acid medium, various enzymes, or ferments, operate, reduce the food to a liquid, and pass it into the long and winding intestine. The final digestive agents now play their part, and the nutritive substances are absorbed through the intestinal walls, to be collected by the blood. Finally, the indigestible matter passes out, as faeces, through an aperture, generally known as the vent, just in front of the anal fin.

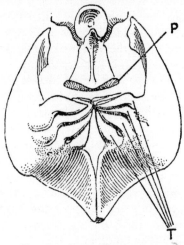

Fig. 5. PHARYNGEAL BONES AND TEETH
(seen from behind)
(p) Bony Pad on base of skull against which (t) Pharyngeal
Teeth bite. (See page 20)

The food substances taken by the goldfish include a large amount of carbohydrates, or starchy foods, obtained from vegetable matter, as well as a quantity of animal proteins, and a small amount of inorganic salts. While it would be unjustified to trace here the complex processes involved in the digestion of all these, it would be of advantage to note briefly the manner in which the energy locked up in carbohydrates is liberated as muscular activity.

This, as we have remarked above, is achieved by combustion, and everyone knows that there can be no combustion without oxygen. It is, therefore, very necessary that the blood shall bring to the tissues a certain amount of oxygen in addition to carbohydrate. This it is able to do by means of the red corpuscles, which, as they pass through the gills, absorb through the thin membranes oxygen from the water that passes through the gill-chambers. Carbohydrates, as the name implies, are composed largely of carbon and hydrogen. When these come together with the oxygen in the tissues of the fish a sudden re-combination, or combustion, takes place, resulting in the liberation of energy for muscular movement, and involving the destruction of a certain amount of muscular tissue. The carbon combines with the oxygen to form carbon dioxide, and the hydrogen combines with more oxygen to form water, while, of course, some heat is produced. The red corpuscles, having lost their oxygen, are now able to take up the carbon dioxide and carry it away to the heart. The water is eventually excreted, with other waste products dissolved in it, by way of the kidneys. The elimination of so much water has necessitated the development of a special renal portal system of veins, so that the blood from the region of the tail, on its way back to the heart, is passed for a second time through the kidneys.

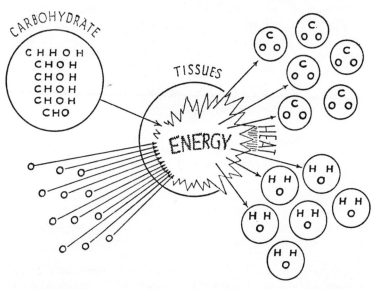

Fig. 6. DIAGRAM TO ILLUSTRATE UTILIZATION OF FOOD AND OXYGEN

Food (carbohydrate) and oxygen (breathed in) on left are passed to tissues where combustion occurs, producing energy and heat, and re-combining the atoms as water (H_2O) and carbon dioxide (CO_2) (later breathed out).

Atoms indicated: (c) Carbon; (h) Hydrogen; (o) Oxygen.

All the blood containing carbon dioxide eventually passes through the veins, and enters the heart through the sinus venosus. The heart lies far forward in the body, below the gullet, in a special chamber—the pericardial cavity. The heart is rather small, compared with the size of the fish, and of simpler structure than in the higher animals. The blood is received into a single auricle, and is pumped out by a single muscular ventricle, so that the heart deals only with venous blood. Given a new impetus, the blood passes along a ventral aorta, through a set of efferent arteries, and is spread out over a very large area in the gills, so that the red corpuscles may discard as much carbon dioxide and take up as much oxygen as possible.

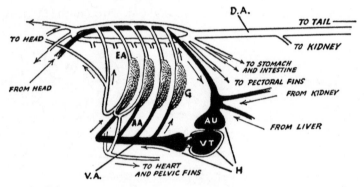

Fig. 7. THE CIRCULATION AND OXYGENATION OF THE BLOOD
(Diagrammatic)

Vessels carrying oxygenated blood shown white, others black. Arrows indicate direction of flow.

(aa) Afferent Arteries; (au) Auricle; (d.a.) Dorsal Aorta; (ea) Efferent Arteries; (g) Gills; (h) Heart; (v.a.) Ventral Aorta; (vt) Ventricle.

The gaseous exchange having taken place, the oxygenated blood is carried off by a set of efferent arteries into the great dorsal aorta, which lies below the vertebral column and gives off branches which supply blood to all parts of the body. In fishes, the blood-temperature is not regulated to remain stable irrespective of the surrounding medium, as it is in the mammals and birds. The temperature of the blood varies with that of the water, and, therefore, it is usually much lower than in human beings. Hence fishes are poikilotherms, popularly called cold-blooded animals, though, of course, a goldfish in water at a temperature of 98° F.[1] (which will not prove fatal for a short period) would have a blood-temperature as high as that of man: higher, in fact; for owing to the heat derived from muscular activity, the blood-temperature is often as much as 2 degrees above that of the surrounding water. From this it follows that every time the temperature of the water in which the fish is living changes, the fish has to undergo a major functional change. The fish must be given time to adapt itself to such change, and if it is not given that time (such as happens if it is suddenly plunged into water ten or more degrees higher or lower than the water in which it has been living) it will, at worst, be killed, and, at best, suffer a serious functional derangement that will result in the premature death of the fish. It is customary to say that a fish that is subject to constant changes of water is given chill after chill and finally succumbs. In the strict sense of the word 'chill' this is not true; for, in theory, a chill can be contracted only by an animal that has a body-temperature of its own. In a loose sense, however, the word 'chill' is applicable to the case in point, since the final result of constantly subjecting a fish to changes of water at a lower temperature than that in which it has been living, is much the same as constantly subjecting a human being, heated by exertion, to an ice-cold bath: in both cases death supervenes if it is done too often. The use of the word 'chill', however, is to be avoided, because it implies that no harm will come if the fish is plunged into much warmer water, and this, as we have seen, is equally harmful to the fish.

Because the red corpuscles (which are oval in shape) are relatively fewer in number than in mammals, the blood does not appear so red, except in the heart and gills where the corpuscles are concentrated. The flow of the blood, too, is comparatively sluggish; this is due to the small size and simple construction of the heart.

A large amount of carbohydrates, in the form of non-soluble sugar, is stored in the liver, to be released and made soluble as required under the control of certain glands in the pancreas. In addition, the liver contains a considerable amount of oil and

---

[1] Since most thermometers sold in England are graded with the Fahrenheit scale, all temperatures mentioned in this book are given in degrees Fahrenheit. The following formulae, however, may be used for converting Fahrenheit into centigrade and Réaumur: C. = 5/9 (F.-32). R. = 4/9 (F.-32).

secretes bile to assist digestion. The bile is stored in a gall-bladder, and passes to the intestine through a bile-duct. Dissection reveals the liver at once; for it is a large and dark red gland lying just behind the shoulder-girdle. The pancreas, on the other hand, is less easy to see; for it is imbedded in the substance of the liver; its duct enters the intestine close to the bile-duct. The goldfish also has a spleen, located near the stomach, and other ductless glands which may be conveniently ignored at this point.

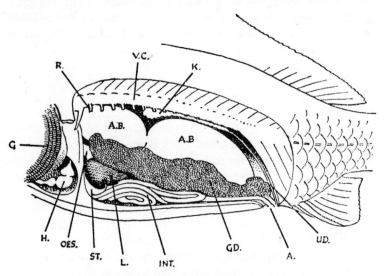

Fig. 8. Dissection of Goldfish

(Showing arrangement of organs in body cavity)

(a.) Anus; (a.b.) Air-bladder; (g) Gills; (gd.) Gonad, female ovary, male testis; (h.) Heart; (int.) Intestine (coiled) (four times the length of the fish when uncoiled); (k.) Kidney; (l.) Liver; (oes) Oesophagus or Gullet; (r.) Ribs (cut); (st.) Stomach; (ud.) Urinary Duct or Ureter; (v.c.) Vertebral Column.

The kidneys are long and thin, deep red in colour, and situated immediately below the vertebral column. Their duct (the ureter) passes down the hind end of the abdominal cavity.

We have already pointed out that the goldfish has to face something of a problem in getting rid of excessive water. It should, therefore, come as no surprise to learn that it does not drink. All the water taken into the mouth (possibly with minute exceptions) passes over the gills and out of the gill-openings. This can be seen quite well if a few drops of some harmless colouring matter, such as cochineal, are taken in a pipette and let free near the mouth of the fish: the coloured water will be sucked in at the mouth, and almost immediately poured out behind the gills.

Now, it puzzles many people how it is that water is prevented from passing into the alimentary canal; and why particles of food do not escape through the gill-openings. The explanation is that when a fish opens its mouth, water is drawn into the pharynx, and at the same time the gill-openings are kept tightly closed. Immediately the fish shuts its mouth, the pharynx is contracted, and the water is driven out through slits in the pharynx and over the gills. No water is swallowed because the gullet, situated immediately behind the last pair of pharyngeal slits, is kept so tightly contracted that no water can enter it and pass down the alimentary canal. The contraction is performed by muscles which Pycraft has likened to the double string which, when pulled, closes the mouth of a bag. When, however, a piece of solid matter, such as a piece of food, touches the closed gullet, no matter how lightly, the muscles relax and the solid matter is pressed down the alimentary canal and into the stomach. Some water may be swallowed, but only a negligible quantity, because the gullet clasps the solid matter very tightly. Pycraft continues the simile by comparing this action to that of a cork being pushed into a bottle with a flexible rubber neck that closes up as the cork passes down. Finally, to lessen the danger of minute particles of food, or grains of sand, passing through the pharyngeal slits and so injuring the gills, double rows of stiff fibres are affixed to the inner margins of the gill-arches; known as gill-rakers, although they do not rake the gills, they serve to strain the water before it reaches the delicate gills. It must be added, however, that the gill-rakers function only so long as the fish keeps its gill-arches close together. We have seen a piece of worm pass through the gill-openings of one of our goldfish, and there are records of two fish being caught on one line in this way. The occurrence is unusual, but not exceptional, and is due to the fact that the gill-arches are quite capable of being separated far enough to permit the passage of a worm.

Thus, the close association between feeding and breathing, not only in physiological processes but also in the arrangement of the structures, will be clear to the reader. We must now touch upon a further extension of this association, which is a striking feature of the anatomy of the goldfish, namely the air-bladder.

Primitively, the air-bladder (or swim-bladder as it is more often called) was developed as an upward distension of the gullet, and served as an accessory breathing organ. It was, in fact, the primitive lung, and from the study of the Lung-fishes of South America, Africa, and Australia we can see how the breathing apparatus of the higher animals came about. It is, therefore, of particular interest to find that in the goldfish the air-bladder is still connected with the oesophagus by a duct, and that fairly recent experiments[1]

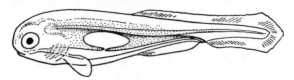

Fig. 9. GOLDFISH EIGHTY HOURS AFTER HATCHING

Showing air bladder as an outgrowth from the gullet.

(Much enlarged.)

show that it may still serve, to some extent, its original purpose.

The air-bladder is a membranous sac lying below the vertebral column at the centre of gravity. It is divided by a constriction into two lobes—the hind lobe being a trifle the larger, at all events in the wild fish. The bladder contains oxygen, nitrogen, and a trace of carbon dioxide, obtained mainly from the atmosphere by the fish gulping air at the surface of the water. In the hind lobe, however, the proportion of oxygen is higher than in atmospheric air, due to excretion and absorption of gases through the walls of the bladder.

Besides serving as a reservoir for oxygen, the air-bladder serves at least two other purposes. In the first place, by the adjustment of its contents the fish is able to alter its total specific gravity, in order that it may float without effort at any desired level in the water. The importance of this hydrostatic function will be illustrated later in our discussion of the changes that occur in the fancy breeds. In the second place, the air-bladder, as we have already said, is firmly attached by its front end to the tripus, the largest

[1] See article 'The Swim-Bladder of Freshwater Fishes' by H. Muir Evans in *The Field* (21st August 1943).

of the Weberian ossicles, and it serves, therefore, as an important adjunct to the organs of hearing (Fig. 3).

Anyone who has kept an aquarium of goldfish in his home will have noticed that they make a characteristic murmuring noise. Precisely how they do this cannot be stated with certainty, but it is believed that the sounds are due to the passage of air through the duct of the air-bladder. Although fishes are incapable of vocal efforts comparable with those of the higher vertebrates, many investigators have come to the conclusion that the deliberate production of sound is not uncommon among them. The investigations of von Fritsch show that most fishes are capable of emitting sounds, though not always of a pitch that can be heard by man. The experiments of Christopher Coates, in the New York Aquarium, with a waterproof microphone connected to an oscillograph, have demonstrated that when fish are excited they emit loud and rapid sounds, while feeding the sounds are loud and steady, and at rest some fishes purr like kittens. These experiments, however, are not altogether convincing: for, of course, it is difficult, if not impossible, to determine whether the sounds are deliberate or accidental. At the same time, we hazard the opinion that it is very possible that the goldfish uses its air-bladder to express itself; for it may be argued that nature would hardly have provided fishes with a hearing apparatus for no good reason.

Yet another supplementary breathing apparatus is furnished by the skin. It is now known that, even when the gills are prevented from functioning, a goldfish can live for some time in an inactive condition by exchanging the necessary gases through its skin. This may be one of the reasons why goldfish can live in conditions that would speedily kill another species.

The main reason why most fishes die when taken from the water is that the gills soon lose their water, and no animal can breathe dry air (the lungs of human beings contain an appreciable amount of water). Most members of the Cyprinidae, however, can live for some time out of their natural element; for the gill-covers are thick and close-fitting, preventing evaporation, and the above-mentioned accessory breathing systems are brought into action. Carp have been known to live for a full two hours out of water, and for a much longer period if their gills are kept moist. Indeed, in Holland, carp were (if they no longer are) fattened for the dinner-table by being suspended in the air in a net containing damp moss, and in this position they were spoon-fed with vegetables and bread steeped in milk. It was not so long ago we read in a London newspaper that a housewife, while cleaning out a grate, found what she thought was a lump of fat covered with soot. A closer inspection revealed that it was a live goldfish, that soon recovered when placed in water. It is presumed that some bird took the fish from a pond and accidentally dropped it down the chimney. Francis Buckland once had a dozen goldfish given to him, which he took home, wrapped in wet moss and a cloth, in a carpet bag. After eighteen hours six of the fish were dead, but the other six were still alive, and when placed in an aquarium soon recovered from the effects of their experience, though at first they rolled about as if drunk.[1]

The nervous system of the goldfish represents the general plan from which that of the higher animals has been elaborated. The main nerve centre is the brain, which is rather elongate in the wild type, its lobes being widely separated. From the front lobe (the prosencephalon) the olfactory nerves pass forward to the nasal organs. On each side is a large optic lobe, giving rise to the optic nerve which makes sight possible. Below this is a lobe (the infundibulum) to which is suspended that important ductless gland, the pituitary body. Behind the optic lobes, on the upper side, is the cerebellum, or hind brain, which is responsible for the co-ordination of muscular activity in response to stimuli received through the senses. Under the cerebellum is the medulla oblongata which passes into the spinal cord as it leaves the cranium. From the region of the medulla arise five cranial nerves on each side, and along the spinal cord a somewhat similar pair of nerves is given off, above and below, at each vertebral segment. The nerves divide and re-divide into branches, becoming finer and finer, to serve all parts of the body in a very complicated manner.

Nerve-fibres are either sensory, conveying stimuli to the brain or other centres; or motor, controlling muscular response. Those concerned with involuntary movements, such as, for example, the rhythmic contractions passing food along the alimentary tract, constitute the sympathetic nervous system.

Whether or not a fish can feel pain is a subject that has given rise to many bitter arguments, with little gain to either side. The

Francis Buckland, *Curiosities of Natural History* (London 1900). Selections edited by L. R. Brightwell, London, 1948.

Anatomy

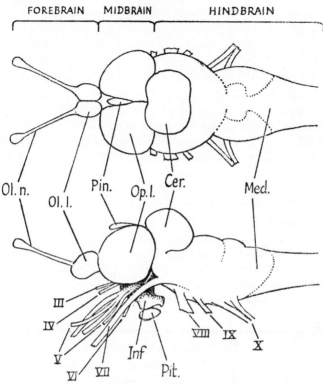

Fig. 10. THE BRAIN, seen from above and from side
(semi-diagrammatic)

(cer.) Cerebellum; (inf.) Infundibulum; (med.) Medulla Oblongata; (ol. l.) Olfactory
Lobe; (ol. n.) Olfactory Nerve; (op. l.) Optic Lobe; (pin.) Pineal Body; (pit.) Pituitary
Gland; (III–X) Cranial Nerves.

angler will insist emphatically that it cannot; the humanitarian will
be equally insistent that it can; and it is hard to convince either.
Pain needs defining. It is a warning of injury conveyed by the
sensory nerves, and generally stimulates the motor nerves to remove the affected part from the site of danger. Pain, in fact, is a
protective device. The mechanism necessary for this reaction
appears fairly early in the scale of evolution, and it is certainly
present in fishes, though admittedly less highly developed than in
the higher vertebrates. The argument of the angler, that a fish does
not feel pain because a fish that has been hooked and has escaped
will promptly return to the bait, will not bear the weight that

37

some have placed upon it; for the behaviour of the fish can be explained by the fact that the roof of the mouth is poorly supplied with nerves. There is little doubt, however, that a fish hooked through the lip feels considerable pain. But the subject is very controversial and bristles with difficulties, because it is necessary to take into consideration many factors, not the least that when pain attains a certain degree of intensity it produces shock, in itself a further protective nervous reaction.

Closely associated with the nervous system are the sensory organs.

The organs of smell are a pair of sac-like bodies, lying in the nasal pits. The linings are ridged; the rooves pierced by two nostrils on each side. Water passes into the first nostril, which is provided with a valve, bathes the olfactory organ, and leaves by the hind nostril.

The fact that most fishes bolt their food, that no salivary glands are developed, and that a tongue, even if present, is not protrusible, leads ichthyologists to the belief that a sense of taste is unknown to most fishes. There is, however, some evidence to show that goldfish may be sensible of taste; for goldfish, and indeed all the Cyprinidae, masticate their food with some considerable care; and it has been pointed out by many writers that the peculiar organ, richly supplied with nerves, found on the palate of the Cyprinids, is perhaps an organ adapted for the perception of this sense. Moreover, observation shows that fishes, at all events the majority of aquarium-fishes, must to some extent be sensible of taste; for in no other way can the fact that they will readily take some foods, but reject others even when hungry, be accounted for. Sight or smell cannot account for it, since the food is taken into the mouth and then rejected. It has been contended that taste in a fish is perceived as the sense of smell is in terrestrial vertebrates. 'The fish', Roule writes, 'need not receive substances that taste in its mouth, on its tongue. They are disseminated in the surrounding water as odours are in the air around us. Taste, in the fish, is from an external, not an internal source.' The contention is ingenious, but we do not think it will bear close examination. It will pass only if a very loose definition of taste is agreed upon. Indeed, of the sense of taste in aquatic animals, Roule writes: 'Theirs is a sense of taste which behaves like a sense of smell. The creature tastes at a distance.' Taste, however, is defined as the sensation produced in the mouth by contact with certain

Anatomy

substances, and the definition holds good whether in terrestrial or aquatic animals; for it will be noticed that a goldfish will reject a piece of distasteful (to it) food only after it has taken the food into its mouth, and, furthermore, will continue to take the same piece of food into its mouth and reject it time after time. In a word, we cannot say that a fish tastes substances disseminated in the surrounding water any more than we can say that a terrestrial vertebrate tastes substances disseminated in the surrounding air. Kyle, in fact, expressly states that 'so long as a fish is alive, its internal constitution, and particularly the composition of its blood, are quite different from those of the surrounding medium. It is self-contained and only takes in the material it wants to take in. This is also the case with the higher vertebrates. . . . In this way we can understand why fishes do not taste salt although they live in salt water, a puzzle to many people.'

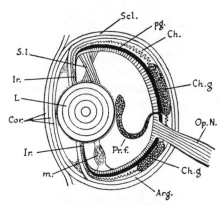

Fig. 11. THE EYE (Diagrammatic)

(arg.) Reflective Layer; (ch.) Choroid; (ch.g.) Choroid Gland; (cor.) Cornea; (ir.) Iris; (l.) Lens; (m.) Muscle; (op.n.) Optic Nerve; (pg.) Pigmented Layer; (pr. f.) Processus Falciformis; (scl.) Sclerotic; (s. l.) Suspensory Ligament.

The eyes are very much like those of man, but somewhat more globular, and with flatter corneas. Since the eyes are placed on each side of the head, it is doubtful whether both can ever be focused upon the same object. The outer wall of the eye is formed, in the eye socket, by a sclerotic coat, and, externally, by the transparent cornea. Behind the cornea, separated by a space filled with aqueous humor, is the iris. Light passes through the central aperture (the pupil) of the iris, to be focused by the globular lens upon the

39

sensitive retina. The stimuli thus formed are collected and conveyed to the brain by the optic nerve. The space between the lens and retina is filled with a jelly-like substance called vitreous humor. Adjustment to varying distances is accomplished by moving the lens, by means of a special muscle, nearer or farther from the retina. The eyelid is represented only by a narrow fold of skin round the eye. There are no tear-glands; nor need there be; for the eye is kept washed by the surrounding water.

Because the eyes of a fish have no lids it was for long believed that fishes never slept. In the 1870's there was a considerable correspondence on this subject in *The Field*, and a correspondent, signing himself 'M.M.', writes: 'I have kept carp, tench, minnows, and goldfish, in an aquarium. Of these all but the goldfish appeared to sleep at certain intervals. . . . The goldfish, on the contrary, appeared to be always in motion, and wide awake; night or day, dark or light, they were moving about like unquiet spirits.' That goldfish do spend a part of the twenty-four hours in a condition closely approaching to sleep in the higher vertebrates is now an established fact. The aquarist can prove this for himself; for he has only to creep into the room in which an aquarium is kept, at a time when all is quiet (the early hours of the morning for preference) and turn on a light suddenly. He will surely find most, if not all, of the fish on the bottom of the aquarium, or suspended in mid-water, in a comatose condition; and it will be some little time before they begin to show any activity. The only noticeable movements of a fish in this condition are those of the breathing apparatus, and the very slow regular motions of the pectoral fins to counteract the forward thrust of the respiratory jets from the gill-openings. We can only conclude that the observation of 'M.M.' was faulty. It is to be added, however, that goldfish do not appear to take their rest at regular and fixed hours, but whenever the mood comes upon them; for goldfish have been observed sometimes resting during the day and at other times during the hours of darkness. A goldfish certainly rests at some period during the twenty-four hours, and though normally it is a diurnal animal, some specimens do appear to be semi-nocturnal in their habits.

The ear is enclosed in a special bony capsule on each side of the skull, and represents only the part known in man as the inner ear. It is a simple membraneous sac, constricted into two lobes, the upper having three semicircular canals. In the lobes are limey con-

Anatomy

cretions known as otoliths. Although called the ear, it is doubtful
if this apparatus by itself would be very effective as an auditory
organ; it seems to be primarily concerned with the sense of balance. Combined with the Weberian ossicles, however (which have
a remarkable similarity to the hammer, anvil and stirrup bones of
the human ear) it no doubt enables the goldfish to hear very well
(Fig. 3).

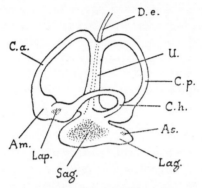

Fig. 12. THE EAR (Diagrammatic)
(am.) Ampulla; (c.a.) Anterior Canal; (c.p.) Posterior Canal; (c.h.) Horizontal Canal;
(d.e.) Duct for Endolymph; (lag.) Lagena; (u.) Utriculus.
The shaded areas represent enclosed otoliths; (as.) Astericus; (lap.) Lapillus; (sag.)
Sagitta.

In the skin there are many sense-cells in close association with
nerve-endings. The most conspicuous are those of the lateral-line
system, which lie in a canal along the middle of each side of the
body. It is a matter of interest that in the embryo this lateral line
and the ear develop from the same rudiment, and both are supplied by the same nerves; for it has long been supposed that the
lateral line is part of the organ of hearing. Perhaps it would be
more correct to say that the ear arose as a specialized part of the
lateral line.

On the whole fishes are mainly creatures of reflex actions, by
which it is meant that the actions of a fish follow sensory stimuli,
resulting in nervous pre-arrangements, and that there is no partici-
pation of the will. Norman writes: 'A fish moves, breathes, feeds,
and reproduces but rarely thinks.' However, in common with
other vertebrates, fishes undoubtedly have sufficient intelligence
to learn by experience. This much may be deduced from the fact

41

that in waters that are much fished the older fish show a remarkable cunning in avoiding the angler's hook; and it is recorded by Kirby that a carp will burrow into the mud in order that the net may pass over it, or, if the bottom is stony, jump over the net. It is pointed out that experience has undoubtedly taught the older fish to be cautious, and observation shows that younger fish are less wary under the same conditions. In writing of instinctive fear in the lower animals, however, we must remember that the instinct is only put into effect by the perception of a natural threat. The angler's hook or net represents an artificial threat, and, in consequence, it would, perhaps, be more accurate to say that experience has taught the older fish that the hook and net are to be classified as dangerous objects, and consequently to be avoided as they would avoid natural enemies. In any case, among all wild animals caution is instinctive, and isolated examples among wild fish prove very little. Caution and timidity among fishes is altogether too apparent to demand special proof.

Though fish are capable of learning by experience, it is more than doubtful that they possess any powers of reasoning. Observation kept on fishes living in aquaria and ponds, such as goldfish, is not very convincing; it is not possible to draw fair deductions from the behaviour of fishes that are living under the artificial conditions of being always in close proximity to man. It will be observed that goldfish living in aquaria and ponds are notoriously punctual at feeding times, and from this it has been deduced that goldfish have the power to think and reason; but it is no proof that an animal possesses the power to reason because hunger drives it to learn. In any case, we need not doubt that fishes learn by experience, at all events to some extent; for goldfish, and other species kept in captivity, soon learn to hide among the aquatic plants when a net is placed in the aquarium or pond, and to take no notice when a harmless (to them) object is placed in the water. The point is to be noted, though we do not care to advance it as proof of high intelligence among fishes.

Many experiments have been conducted to test the intelligence of fishes. Some of the experiments are of doubtful value, and the deductions drawn are not always valid; for, even among men of science, there is a strong tendency to credit an animal with more intelligence than it actually possesses, merely because it reacts to a certain test in the way that man expects it to. The results of elaborate experiments can always be explained by ichthyologists to the satisfaction of other ichthyologists, but not always to the satisfaction of the layman. Simple experiments, more often than not, prove nothing that observation has not already shown to be an established fact. Churchill, for example, conducted a simple experiment from which he was able to deduce that 'Goldfish, although lacking a pallium, are capable of forming a definite habit of a moderate degree of complication and of retaining this habit for some time.' Interesting as the experiment was, it hardly needs special proof to establish the fact that goldfish can learn to find their way about an aquarium or pond. That they can do so is shown by the following extract from a letter published by Francis Buckland: 'Some years ago, I saw a vast number of goldfish in a factory "lodge" at Preston, in Lancashire; at the end of the lodge was a pipe conveying the warm water which had been used in condensing. On Sundays the supply of warm water of course ceases; and the manager of the works told me, that in cold weather, the fish used to be seen every *Monday morning*, waiting for it to flow again, as soon as the engine begins working.'[1] There is nothing startling in this; for, of course, the fish did not appreciate what day of the week it was. But it would be a very unintelligent goldfish that could not find its way about the pond in which it is living, and, since experience had taught the fish that normally one particular part of the pond was warmer than the rest, naturally they would collect there in cold weather.

The goldfish is notoriously undemonstrative, but, if the aquarist can gain the confidence of the fish, it will become very tame and take food from the hand. Yet, even when a goldfish has learnt to take a worm from between the finger and thumb of the aquarist, observe how sometimes the fish will be driven from accepting the tempting food, warned by some unaccustomed circumstance imperceptible to the aquarist. Again, observe how goldfish that have learnt to take a worm from the hand of the aquarist will do so readily, whereas a new-comer in the aquarium or pond will for long only come so far towards the worm and no farther, and fails to profit by the example of the other fish. Moreover, it seems as though some goldfish (indicative, perhaps, of a lesser degree of intelligence rather than of no intelligence) never learn to take food from the hand, even though the other fish in

[1] Francis Buckland, op. cit., p. 36.

the aquarium or pond do so readily. We see in all this how the organs of sense guide, control, and work to the advantage of the fish: we see, in fact, that, to quote Roule, 'the senses of the fish are refined.' Roule adds that the senses of a fish 'stand alone and are not supplemented in any way. The brain is incapable of co-ordinating the sensations and storing them up so as to make a memory. When there is any recollection at all it is often brief and limited.' But this is open to argument, at the very least, since the fact that goldfish can learn by experience (and it is undeniable that they do) is indicative that they possess a memory. We do not know what length of time Roule would define as 'brief and limited', but it is to be noted that the experiment of Churchill (referred to above) showed that the ability of goldfish to thread a simple maze was fairly well retained after thirteen days lapse of practice. Moreover, it is our experience that once goldfish have learnt to take food from the hand they will unhesitatingly come to hand for food even after a discontinuance of the practice for three weeks, sometimes longer.

Our observation and experience lead us to the conclusion that goldfish are largely the creatures of routine and of fixed habits. They appear to be incapable of distinguishing between the aquarist who cares for them and strangers; for once a fish has learnt to take food from the hand it will do so whether the food is offered by the aquarist himself or by a stranger. On the whole, it may be said that the goldfish is largely a slave of its senses, and that its intelligence in general is very low. Yet, it must be added that the fact that a human being can gain the confidence of a fish sufficiently for it to conquer its inherent shyness and learn to take food from the hand, opens up a field of speculation (into which, however, we do not intend to wander) on the possibility of reasoning powers in goldfish not being entirely absent.

The skin is composed of two layers; an inner dermis composed of connective tissue in which are nerve-fibres and blood-vessels, and a thin and cellular outer epidermis. One of the characteristic functions of the skin is the production of mucus, a slimy secretion that covers the body, reducing friction and protecting the fish from diseases and parasites. The scales arise from the dermis: they cover the body (excepting the head) in regular rows corresponding to the muscle-segments underneath. The scales overlap, like the tiles on a roof, the inner part being deeply embedded in pouches in the dermis, the outer edges being free and easily raised with the aid of a pointed instrument.

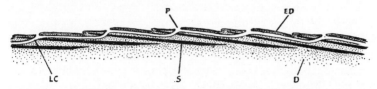

FIG. 13. SECTION THROUGH SKIN ALONG LATERAL LINE
(Showing relationship of sensory canal to scales)
(d) Dermis; (ed) Epidermis; (lc) Lateral-line Canal; (p) Pore to exterior; (s) Scales.
(Much enlarged.)

As stated earlier, the number of scales varies somewhat among individuals. Shisan C. Chen counted them in a large number of goldfish. In domesticated species he found from twenty-two to twenty-eight scales between the head and the end of the tail, from four to six between the front of the dorsal fin and the lateral line, and from seven to nine below the lateral line. The figures for the wild fish were: along the lateral line from twenty-eight to thirty-one, above the lateral line six, and below the lateral line five or six.[1] Since the number of scales remains constant throughout the life of the fish, it is evident that they must grow. This is accomplished by addition at the edges; and as the fish grows more rapidly in spring and summer (when food is plentiful) than at other times, the concentric lines of growth on the scales are wider and more numerous at this time. By examining the zones of slow and rapid growth on a scale it is possible to calculate the age of the fish.[2]

Along each side, the course of the lateral line is marked by a series of short tubes leading from perforations in the scales which cover it.

The scales are formed of a bony substance produced by activity of the skin, and are themselves transparent. Whatever colour a fish possesses is due mainly to pigment cells in the dermis underneath. The pigment cells, known as chromatophores, are disposed in two layers; an outer and an inner, or deeper, layer. They are of

[1] Shisan C. Chen, *Variations in the External Characters of the Goldfish, Carassius auratus*, in *Con. Bio. Lab. Sci. China*, vol. i (Nanking, 1925).
[2] But, of course, not fish kept in an aquarium and fed all the year round so that their growth is constant.

different kinds, according to the kind of colouring matter they contain, and the combination of different sorts produces a variety of effects. In the wild goldfish the dark olive colour on the back is made up of a mixture of black and orange chromatophores crowded together. On the sides, the cells (particularly the black) are less numerous, so that the general colour is paler and more bronze. Loss of the black chromatophores produces the characteristic colour of the domesticated common goldfish. An increase in the black cells (melanism) can produce a black form like the Moor, and absence of all pigment (albinism) a white form. The colour of the individual fish can be changed to some degree; for the chromatophores are able either to concentrate or spread out the pigment within the cell. Consequently, the expansion of cells of one colour and the contraction of those of another will alter the general colour effect of the fish. To some extent this is under the control of the nervous system, and may be influenced by visual stimuli. It is to be noted, for example, that a goldfish kept in a white container will turn pale by virtue of the contraction of the pigment in its cells. Similarly, if a container is illuminated from

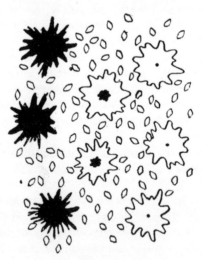

Fig. 14. PIGMENT CELLS
(Chromatophores)

The pigment granules in those on the left are concentrated: in those on the right spread out. (Highly magnified).

Anatomy

below (the opposite to what normally occurs in nature) the fish reverses its coloration, becoming more deeply coloured on the belly than on the back. More frequently, however, the intensity of colour is affected by the secretions of the ductless glands, in particular those associated with the emotions. Fear or anger is accompanied by a sudden paling: pleasurable excitement produces a stronger colour by the general expansion of the pigmentation.

In addition to the chromatophores, the skin contains a large number of opaque plates (iridocytes) which reflect the light and are, therefore, responsible for the bright metallic sheen so well known in the goldfish. Generally speaking, the iridocytes are most abundant where the pigment cells are fewest, though among the fancy breeds of goldfish many different combinations occur.

The pigments, and also the guanin of which the iridocytes are composed, are by-products of the digestive processes, which are secreted in the skin. This does not mean that the coloration of an individual fish can be altered materially by a change of diet, but that, if it differs from its relative, the differences are associated with some deeper physiological change. At the same time, certain black pigments can be utilized as food by reabsorption, and the black cells (melanophores) serve as storage for these materials when food is plentiful, and secretion, therefore, high. This accounts for the black patches which are sometimes seen to come and go in goldfish, much to the surprise of inexperienced aquarists.

The wild stock of eastern Asiatic waters shows a strong tendency to xanthochroism (loss of black pigment and consequent golden colour). Possibly it is due to the mineral content of the local waters; for we have to remember that much of China and the whole of Japan are of recent (geologically speaking) volcanic origin, so that the water of these countries contains a considerable amount of dissolved minerals. It was from these xanthochroous fish that the Chinese were able to develop the numerous fancy breeds, to which we must now turn our attention.

Thus far we have confined our description to the structure which may be termed normal, namely that found on examination of goldfish which approximate to the wild type. It is of interest to see how these structures are modified in the fancy breeds, which are very fully described in the chapter that follows.

Many curious and beautiful fancy goldfish have been developed,

47

though precisely how the various changes were brought about is not very clear. Undoubtedly it is the result of long and careful artificial selection from the sports which arise from time to time among domesticated stock. Geneticists tell us that these sports, or mutants, are produced by changes in the make-up of the chromosomes—such as the suppression of a factor here, the loss of a gene there, or sometimes by the crossing over of factors from one chromosome to another. No doubt these things happen; for the characteristics are hereditary and follow the laws of Mendel.[1] That the early breeders of goldfish made use of the mechanics of heredity (without necessarily understanding them) is certain; for Mitsukuri mentions that, though in general Japanese breeders are men of little education who have obtained all their knowledge from the practical handling of fish, he has heard them talk in a way which reminded him of passages in Darwin's *Origin of Species*. But we are still left to wonder at the fundamental causes for these departures from the normal.[2] The plain truth is that the geneticists only take the problem back a step further; for what they cannot tell us is how the changes in the make-up of the chromosomes are brought about. It is difficult to avoid drawing the conclusion that ultimately we have to look for environmental factors to explain such mutations—remembering, of course, that the physiology of the parent constitutes the environment of the sex-cell containing the chromosomes, this, in turn, being affected by external conditions. If this is true, it is not unreasonable to suppose that some peculiarity of the local waters affected the wild *Carassius* in such a way that black pigment was not deposited in the skin in the normal way, so that a golden variation attracted the attention of the Chinese. Such xanthochroous sports occur every now and then among many species of fishes, and are probably due to a genetical factor becoming recessive. This does not necessarily mean that the factor has a direct control over the pigment cells; probably some more fundamental factor of the physiology is affected, and the pigmentation is only the outward sign of it. Be all this as it may, it is likely that the golden colour was the first striking change in the fish; certainly it is the feature which has

[1] Gregor Mendel (1822–84) an abbot of Brünn (Brno) who established the laws of distributive mechanism of organic inheritance.

[2] Very little work has been done on the genetics of goldfish. A good starting-point for further research is Yoshiichi Matsui 'Genetical Studies on Gold-Fish of Japan', in *Journal of the Imperial Fisheries Institute*, Vol. XXX, No. 1 (Tokyo, 1934).

made the fish popular ever since, and earned for it the familiar name—The Goldfish.

But, despite the name, goldfish of a pure gold colour are very rare. The most usual colours are: pale gold, red-gold (with larger orange chromatophores), yellow (the orange chromatophores numerous and deep in colour: the iridocytes scarcely visible), and white (lacking orange chromatophores, but with a few deep-seated black ones under a layer of iridocytes). Black cells are also present in the so-called silver fish, but lie above the iridocytes. The blue colour, so popular in the Shubunkin (though contrary to popular belief blue is not confined to 'scaleless' fish) is produced by sparse black pigment overlaid with iridocytes: orange cells are absent. All colours involve a greater or lesser reduction in the amount of black pigment. But there has also been developed a black fish, the Moor. In this case the melanophores are more numerous, their rays being short and broad, and heavily laden with pigment. Finally, of course, there are many parti-coloured fish in which these effects are variously combined.

The colours of the goldfish are by no means fixed. Indeed, two distinct processes seem to be involved; for while some specimens are abnormally coloured almost from birth (as one might expect of a mutant) most of them wear their drab ancestral livery for the first part of their lives. In the latter case there is a comparison with the tapirs. Of these mammals there are two species, one native to South America, the other to Malaya; and, although they are differently coloured when adult, the young of both species are remarkably alike in coloration, thus showing that at the time when South America and Malaya were connected they were a single species.

At about the age of six or seven weeks, goldfish-fry gradually darken to greyish-bronze—almost black—and it is only later that they develop the more attractive colours. In point of fact, the coloration of fry depends in part on the chemical content of the water, in part on the food, and in part on the quality of the light reaching them. Fry kept in a shaded aquarium or pond remain dark coloured for much longer than those kept in a well-lighted aquarium or pond, and Yatsu records that Tozawa has shown that if they are kept in darkness decolorization does not take place even four months after hatching. In much the same way fish raised in outdoor ponds in which there is a large quantity of limestone are always brassy in colour, and the rich red colour, so admired by aquarists, can be obtained by transferring the fish for several weeks to a pond with a loam-soil bottom.

Loss of the outer layer of pigment leaves the scales transparent, and as they are often very thin, they are almost invisible when the fish is observed in the aquarium or pond. Such goldfish are known to aquarists as 'scaleless' or calico fish; we prefer calico because specimens actually lacking scales are not found. In extreme cases the scales may be so thin that the ova of the female may be seen through the body wall, and the gill-covers may be so transparent that the gills are clearly visible. Aquarists call these fish transparent or crystal fish: they are highly prized.[1]

The enlargement of certain fins is characteristic of a number of fancy breeds. In the Comet the lobes of the caudal fin are much elongated, and, as the rays (at least in good specimens) remain stiff, the efficiency of this fin as an organ of propulsion is much improved, giving its possessor greater speed. In other breeds the caudal fin may droop, and, in consequence, impair the locomotory effort of the fish. This is particularly true of those breeds in which the caudal fin is divided.

The dividing of the caudal and often the anal fin is a matter of some interest. Like nearly all the structural abnormalities found in goldfish it seems to be connected with the shortening of the body. If we look for genetical causes for the deformities which are prized by aquarists, we shall possibly find only one, namely the one that controls the degree of shortening. However abbreviated and globular a fancy goldfish may be, it still has about the same number of vertebrae, but they are closely crowded one upon another. There is no loss of parts, but a new balance is struck, and the proportions of the parts altered accordingly. This is probably brought about by the fact that in all animals growth proceeds in a very regular manner, according to a law, not yet fully understood. Consequently if a new centre of growth is laid down a balance will be achieved, but it will involve a quite different proportional ratio. When only the hind part of the tail region is

[1] The Goldfish Society of Great Britain deplores the use of such terms as 'scaleless' because they are misleading. They recommend the terms metallic (maximum amount of reflecting tissue), nacreous (intermediate amount of reflecting tissue) and matt (little or no reflecting tissue) as more aptly describing the appearance of the fish.

shortened, a simple enlargement of the caudal fin results. But if there is abbreviation of the whole tail, the number of vertebrae entering into the support of the caudal fin is increased, and the paired elements which would normally come close together to form the fan-like hypural bones, are prevented from so doing by the growth of the ones in front (which develop earlier to protect the main artery). Thus the support of the fin is divided, not doubled, and the same applies to the fin itself (twintail). We have

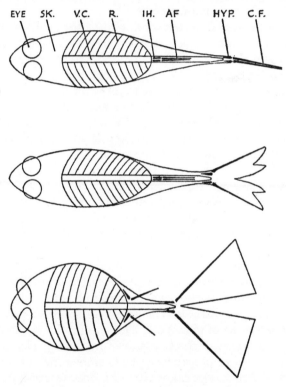

Fig. 15. DIAGRAMS OF GOLDFISH (seen from below) illustrating the effect of shortening upon structure suggested in text.

Top Figure: Common Type.

Centre Figure: Shorter form with 'fan' tail.

Bottom Figure: 'Veiltail' with divided anal fin and telescopic eye.

(af) Anal Fin; (c.f.) Caudal Fin; (hyp.) Hypural Bones; (ih.) Interhaemals; (r.) Ribs; (sk.) Skull; (v.c.) Vertebral Column,

remarked earlier that the rays are composed of elements from each side, and in the divided caudal these elements remain separate; in consequence they are only half-rays, they are less strong, and since they are also prolonged they are very prone to droop. This division of the fin is not, of course, always complete. If only the foremost hypural bones (which support the lower part of the fins) are affected, only the lower lobe is divided, producing the tripod-tail. A further stage divides both lobes, but leaves them united near the base, and the upper rays, therefore, remain stiff and erect, as in good fan-tail types.

If the shortening affects the whole body, a similar division of the anal fin occurs; for it must be remembered that the skeleton is primarily laid down in relation to the soft parts, rather than the reverse, and if the anal bones (interhaemals) are crowded against the internal organs they will have to grow on each side of it. But, of course, it may well be that this apparent relation of parts is not really primary, but the result of a dividing process laid down in the early embryo genetically; for at the present time little is known about the development of the fancy types.

Certainly, in such an extremely shortened form, the abdominal organs are prevented from developing in the axial line. Instead they extend downwards and outwards, accompanied by their protecting ribs, and produce the esteemed globular body.

Similarly, when the head is involved in the shortening process, development of the parts tends to be outwards, and the eyes in particular (which appear to be the central factor in head development) become much enlarged. At first this results in enlargement of the orbits, but, once the bone has become fully formed, the growth can only proceed outwards. This results in the much-prized protuberant (telescope or globe) eye. That this feature is, in fact, due to such an interplay of forces is shown by the considerable variability in the degree of its development among individuals of the same brood. As the bone cannot follow it, the eye is only protected by the thickened sclerotic coat, and an extrusion of the so-called eyelid. In some instances the increased length of the organ results in the lens being so far from the retina that the fish is hypermetropic—long-sighted, and not short-sighted as is stated in many popular works. Now, since the fish cannot see close objects clearly, and water is too dense for distant vision, it is virtually blind,

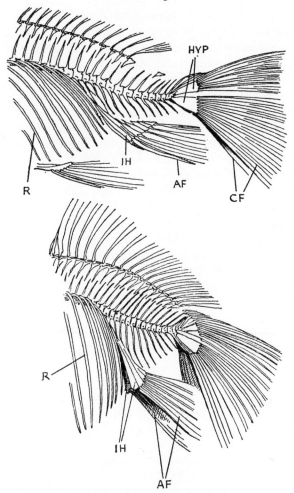

Fig. 16. HIND PART OF SKELETON OF GOLDFISH with divided caudal fin of 'Fan' type (above), and of 'Veiltail' type with divided anal fin (below).

(af) Anal Fin; (cf) Caudal Fin; (hyp) Hypural Bones; (ih) Interhaemal Bones; (r) Ribs.

In 1931 Fraser-Brunner demonstrated to the Zoological Society of London[1] that the changes in the relative proportions of the body of a fancy goldfish were accompanied by similar changes in the relationship between the two lobes of the air-bladder. In the

[1] *Proceedings of the Zoological Society of London* (London, 1931).

normal type the lobes are approximately equal in length, the hind one being pear-shaped. With the shortening of the body, and the enlargement of the caudal fin, the front lobe becomes smaller, and the hind lobe grows larger and more oval. The process continues until we reach the Veiltail (a triumph of the breeder's art in the matter of globular body and a long and divided caudal fin) when the hind lobe of the air-bladder becomes a large sphere, and the front lobe very small indeed. This, of course, is all a part of the adjustment of balance mentioned above. Later, Fraser-Brunner found that a more important modification could be discerned, namely a progressive reduction in the size of the infundibulum of the brain and its attached pituitary body. This is significant; for the secretions of this gland are known to control many processes, including skeletal growth. So it may be that the inherited factor is the size of the pituitary body, and the other changes the result of that. It is possible also that retarded functioning of this gland might account for the late appearance of colour, and other features, noted in these fishes.

Fig. 17. Proportionate Relationship between Lobes of Air-bladder and Body Form
(a) Common Goldfish; (b) Comet; (c) Veiltail.

Some fancy breeds lack a dorsal fin. There is no obvious connection between this loss and the mechanical considerations mentioned above. Possibly, then, this is a distinct mutation. Equally distinct, apparently, is the extraordinary dermal overgrowth (bramble-head), seen in some fancy breeds (e.g., the Lionhead) which, again, does not make its appearance until the fish is well grown.

Owing to the length of time goldfish take to develop, and the comparative infrequency of breeding, much less is known about their heredity than of some tropical species, and there is much uncertainty as to the point where genetical influences cease and environmental factors begin. As long ago as 1842, Sir R. Heron recorded that of those goldfish hatched in his ponds, two out of five lacked a dorsal fin, two in a hundred, or rather more, had a three-lobed tail, and as many had the anal fin paired. All the deformed fish were separated from the others and placed in a pond by themselves, but they did not produce a greater proportion of deformed offspring than did their normal parents.[1] Modern breeders have very much the same experience, and fancy goldfish stock has not been improved, in fact, in many cases it has deteriorated, since its introduction to western breeders.

Efficiency of locomotion is directly related to the shape of the body and fins. Even in the wild state the goldfish is a leisurely fish, though it is capable of short bursts of speed when the need arises. Progress is achieved mainly by flexion of the lateral muscles of the body, particularly by the tail giving a side to side sweep of the caudal fin, which acts rather in the manner of a stern oar. Movement, however, is not entirely from side to side; for it is accompanied by a smaller up and down motion, which, being perfectly timed, or phased, gives a twist to the tail. Since this twist is imparted by both sides of the body, the lobes of the caudal fin act much like the twin screws of a ship, though, in the case of the fish, the two screws are combined in one structure and there is not a complete revolution of the parts. The upper lobe of the fin moves through a gradient in one direction: the lower lobe makes a similar sweep in the opposite direction. It follows, therefore, that the two together have much the same effect as one blade moving in a complete circle. Moreover, the lobes are not flat, but curved, cupping the water to increase its resistance. On completion of the stroke, the 'cups' turn inside out, so to speak, and move in the other direction, so that the whole process is reversed. The fin is reduced between the lobes, forming a sort of notch; for otherwise this part would impede progress by offering resistance

[1] 'On the Breeding of Goldfish in the Author's Menagery' in *Ann. Mag. nat. Hist.* (London, 1842).

to the slip-stream from the sides of the body. A locomotory effort of this nature has a tendency to drive the head of the fish downwards, but this is counteracted by forces farther forward. In the first place, there is jet-propulsion due to the expulsion of water from the gills, which not only corrects the balance but is an important supplementary motive force. In the second place, there are the pelvic fins, which act in much the same way as the elevators of an aeroplane. This alternate screw-like motion has a tendency to roll the fish from side to side, but this is counteracted by the development of the dorsal and anal fins, which act in much the same way as the stabilizing planes of an airship; also, to some extent, by the balancing action of the pelvics.

The pectoral fins play little part in actual progression: they serve mainly as brakes. When the fish is at rest these fins are moved in time with the breathing; as the gill-covers are raised the fins are moved forwards, to counteract the jet-propulsion, and so prevent the fish from moving forward. When moving, the fish can turn to right or left by raising the appropriate pectoral fin, and if it needs to stop suddenly it spreads both fins forward to offer the maximum resistance to the water.

From what has been written, therefore, it will be seen that, with the exception of the caudal fin, the locomotion of a fish is mainly the result of body-motions, the other fins being concerned simply with correction and control.

In the wild fish the body is typically fish-shaped (fusiform) and, though not as streamlined or powerful as a swift species like the mackerel, nevertheless moulded for easy passage through the water. Moreover, as we have said, it is covered with a slimy mucus in part to reduce to a minimum friction with the surrounding water. It need occasion no surprise, therefore, that the considerable changes in body-shape, that occur in the fancy breeds, affect their locomotion. Indeed, it is remarkable that they are not more greatly incapacitated than appears to be the case; but the compensating processes, already noted (e.g., in the case of the air-bladder), serve the fish well. In the case of the Comet, where the body is not shortened to any extent, and the caudal fin is enlarged, greater speed is actually accomplished. In view of what we have said above, it is interesting to note that, mainly, only the lobes are lengthened, and the fin deeply forked. In those breeds in which shortening occurs, the normal flexion of the tail is much decreased, and the fish has to exert considerable effort, throwing the whole of its body from side to side, in order to move forward. In consequence, its progress is slow, its course uncertain, and its journeys never long. Under natural conditions it is at an enormous disadvantage, and it is only the protection afforded it by the aquarist that makes its survival possible.

It is generally believed that most members of the carp family are extremely long-lived. In the gardens of the Palace of Fontaine-bleau[1] there are some carp which are said to be from 150 to 200 years old. Doubtless it gratifies the pious tourist to be told that he is feeding the same fish as were fed by the women of the court of Louis *Quinze*, but there is no evidence to support the theory that carp live to this age. Norman writes that 'although there is good reason for believing that under artificial conditions this fish may attain to a good old age, it is doubtful whether it exceeds fifteen years in a wild state.' Common goldfish kept under good conditions live up to about twenty-five years. We have heard of goldfish reaching the age of thirty. In China specimens have been known to live for over forty years. This may not be exceptional, because the goldfish is a Chinese species so that the water and climate of China would be conducive to its greater longevity. Fancy goldfish usually do not live for so long as common goldfish because they are not so well suited to roughing it. Although some aquarists record that six or seven years is the maximum age to which most fancy goldfish live, we are of the opinion that this is a gross underestimate, and that if properly cared for a fancy goldfish should live for at least twice this length of time. If pampered, by being kept in water that is always at a temperature of about 65° F., and if properly fed and tended, we see no reason why the life of a fancy goldfish should be shorter than that of the common goldfish. Indeed, we have it on the authority of the Reverend Henry W. Moule, who lived in Chekiang between 1880 and 1920, and who took much interest in the culture of fancy goldfish, that in China these breeds live to a considerable age.

The size of a goldfish varies, and depends very much upon the way in which it is kept. A goldfish in a small container rarely grows, but if kept in a large aquarium, and properly fed and cared

---

[1] Built by Francis I, in the earlier half of the sixteenth century, on the site of a fortified chateau in 1162 for Louis VII. Subsequent rulers greatly improved it. The fish-ponds in the gardens are world-famous.

for, it should reach a length of 7 or 8 inches within five years. Dwarfing is fairly general among aquatic animals; and it appears to be largely a case of adaption to environment, since such specimens are not necessarily of poor physique, and frequently enjoy good health and live a normal span of years. There is a record of a goldfish which lived in a 6-gallon aquarium for twenty-five years and measured only 4 inches when it died. If kept under good conditions the common goldfish will eventually reach a length of 12 or more inches. In Portugal and South Africa, where the common goldfish has become naturalized in many lakes and rivers, specimens of 15 inches and longer may be found; large specimens have also been taken from the Seine and its tributaries. In America (U.S.A.), domestic common goldfish, kept in ponds for breeding purposes, have been known to attain a length of 2 feet. The size to which fancy goldfish grow varies with the breed, and is reserved for mention in the chapter which follows.

Chapter II

FANCY GOLDFISH

'Tis beauty truly blent, whose red and white
Nature's own sweet and cunning hand laid on.
SHAKESPEARE, *Twelfth Night*, I. v

The common goldfish, the *Chin-yü* of China, is so well known that a description of it hardly seems necessary. For it is to be seen in almost every pet-shop; regrettably a goldfish in a bowl is a popular prize at fun-fairs, and backdoor hawkers exchanged them for old clothes. Indeed, Robert Lynd is of the opinion that the word 'Gorblimey' was invented precisely to meet the occasion when 'father' discovers that his 'striped trousies' have been exchanged for a goldfish. But those days are on the wane; already the day of the sixpenny goldfish in the sixpenny bowl is over. It is as well; for a goldfish in a bowl may sound an innocent enough ornament, yet, in reality, it compares unfavourably with the Black Hole of Calcutta.

Everyone knows the common goldfish, yet perhaps we ought to add, for the sake of completeness, that the head of a good specimen should be wide and short; the mouth should be small; the eyes should be bright; the body should be arched on back and belly, and the dorsal fin should begin on the peak of the back; the scales should be bright; the caudal fin should be stiff and moderately forked; finally, all the fins should be of moderate size and held stiffly.

In Japan the common goldfish is known as the *Kingyo*. It is the Japanese *kan-on* (Chinese sound) for *chin-yü*. The Japanese name for the common goldfish is given in some European and American books as *Wakin*, but, properly, the Wakin is a cultivated breed of common goldfish in which the caudal and anal fins are divided. Doubtless there is a commercial advantage in attaching a fancy name to a common goldfish that differs slightly from the type; for common goldfish that are yellow in colour are sometimes called

59

Canaries, and white fish are sometimes called Pearls. In the same way, in America common goldfish whose bodies are well spotted and blotched with black are known as Orioles. But all these fancy names really mean very little, and the fish is none the better for them.

Among fishes the goldfish is unique; for Shisan Chen has estimated that from this one common ancestor about one hundred and twenty-six breeds of fancy goldfish have been developed.[1] It is true that the number is largely academic, since nearly every breed has a number of sub-breeds, depending upon whether the fish is scaled or calico, whether it has normal eyes or protuberant eyes, and so on, but, even so, the number of breeds is impressive and it would be impossible to describe them all even if we knew of them, which we do not.

We shall not describe the fancy goldfish in the strict meaning of the word 'describe'; for it occurs to us that a description—however detailed—would in no way help the reader who has never seen a particular breed, and waste the time of the reader who has. It would involve much needless repetition. Instead, we have illustrated this book with drawings and photographs of all the well-known fancy breeds (and some of the rarer breeds, too) and, for the rest, we have set down the main characteristics of each. Together, this should be enough to convey to anyone (even if he has never seen a fancy goldfish in the flesh) precisely what a particular breed looks like, and what its main characteristics are.

So far as British aquarists are concerned, the best known breeds of fancy goldfish are: The Shubunkin, the Comet, the Fantail, the Veiltail, the Telescope, the Moor, the Celestial, the Lionhead, and the Oranda. These, at least, are the names by which the various fancy breeds are usually known; but most have more than one name.

The Shubunkin is sometimes known as the Speckled Goldfish and sometimes as the Harlequin Goldfish. At the same time of the coronation of King George the Sixth dealers advertised it as the Coronation Fish—on account of its variegated colours—but the name was purely a temporary one for advertising purposes. The Shubunkin is sometimes known as the Vermilion Variegated Goldfish, and rightly so, for this is a literal translation of the Japanese *Shubunkin* (*Syubunkin*) from the Chinese *Chu-wên-chin-(-yü)*.

[1] Shisan C. Chen, op. cit., p. 45.

Fancy Goldfish

The Comet and the Fantail have no alternative names.

The name Veiltail was given to the breed by William T. Innes. It is a literal translation of the German *Schleirschwanz*. It is a better name than Fringetail—used by the earlier aquarists—since, as Innes points out, ' "Fringetail" is a word more apt to describe the split and ragged ends of the fins of a fish out of condition'.[1] We have heard this fish called the Ribbontail, the Gauzetail, the Lacetail, the Muslintail, and even the Classtail;[2] but there is no authority for the names, and Veiltail is now the recognized name among modern aquarists, though a few prefer to retain the earlier name of Fringetail. The Veiltail is known to the Japanese as the *Ryukin*, and sometimes as the *Nagasaki*.

The Telescope is sometimes called the Pop-eyed Goldfish. It is known to the Chinese as Dragon Eyes (*Lung chin-yü*). Other popular names for it in China are the Dragon Fish (*Lung-yü*), and the Dragon Head Phoenix Tail (*Lung t'ou fêng wei*).

The Moor is sometimes given the alternative name of the Blackamoor. The Japanese call it the *Demekin*.

The Celestial is known to the Chinese as the Sky-gazer (*Ch'ao-t'ien-yen*), sometimes as the Star-gazer, and sometimes as the Heavenward Dragon. All fish that lack a dorsal fin are called Dragon-back in China. In Japan it is known as the *Deme-ranchu*, a name that is sometimes given to a Lionhead with protuberant eyes.

The Lionhead has the alternative name of the Hooded Goldfish. It is known to the Americans as the Buffalo-head. In Germany one of the names is the not inappropriate one of the Tomato-head (*Tomatenkopf*). The Japanese first give the fish the name of *Ranchu* (*Rantyu*), but, later, after the excrescences have developed, it is known as the *Shishigashira* or *Shishigashira-ranchu*. Mitsukuri, writing in 1904, gives it the alternative name of the Chosen, or Korean Goldfish. This may be an error; for a genealogy of goldfish breeds, prepared by Yatsu in 1937, shows that the Lionhead is not identical with the Korean Goldfish, but developed from it, and, according to Yatsu, the Korean Goldfish is now extinct in Japan though the Lionhead is not.

[1] William T. Innes, *Goldfish Varieties and Water Gardens* (Philadelphia, 1947).

[2] Franz Kuhn uses *Klasseschwanz* (Classtail) as an equivalent of Veiltail. It is an exact translation of a phrase in T'u Lung's *K'ao P'an Yü Shih*, but classtail conveys no meaning in Chinese, German or English, and the equivalence with veiltail is not self-evident.

The Goldfish

The Oranda is known to the Japanese as the *Oranda Shishigashira*. The name may be translated as Dutch Lionhead, but the adjective 'Dutch' has here the same belittling or derisive application as in our own 'Dutch uncle' and 'Dutch courage'. It is not indicative of the country of origin. The Oranda, in fact, is a Japanese fish. The Chinese give it the special and appropriate name of the Goose-head: in North China it is known as the Frog-head.

The Shubunkin and the Comet are hardy fish and may be kept in a pond throughout the year. The other breeds (with the possible exception of the Moor, which can certainly endure a temperature as low as 40° F., and has been known to survive being frozen in ponds, though we do not recommend the practice of wintering Moors outdoors) are not hardy, and normally they cannot be kept in ponds except during the summer months. Essentially they are sub-tropical breeds that should be kept in water at a temperature of at least 65 degrees. They will not die if kept in water at a lower temperature, but it is very unwise to allow the temperature to fall below 60 degrees; for, for one thing, derangement of the air-bladder may occur if they are kept for too long in cold water.

The Moor is always a scaled fish. The Shubunkin is always a calico fish. The other breeds are sometimes scaled and sometimes calico, though calico Lionheads are rather rare, and calico Comets are no longer recognized as show-fish.

In calico fish the colours should be as variegated as possible: they should include blue, violet, red, brown, and yellow, and a mottling of black spots. The most valued fish are those that show blue or violet, and self-coloured specimens (selfs) are the most esteemed by aquarists. The blue should not be a slate-blue, which, in fact, is very common, but a bright forget-me-not blue (known to the Chinese as kingfisher blue) which is very rare.

In spotted fish the usual combinations are black and orange, black and white, and blue and white. Orange, white and black is sometimes found, but brown and black, brown and orange, brown and white, and brown and blue, never.

In dappled fish small spots of black, orange, and blue, are present in an approximately equal degree, intermingled and distributed over the body in tiny spots.

The colours of the scaled breeds vary. The most usual colour of the Comet is deep red, but all-yellow specimens are more highly valued and comparatively rare. A strain of Comet of deep ox-blood colour (the most admired of all colours) was bred in America before the First World War, but, we believe, has since been lost. In the Fantail, Veiltail, and Telescope, the usual colours are found, but all-gold fish are the most prized by aquarists. The most beautiful fish are those in which the fins are hyaline, or of a pearly-white colour. In the Moor the most desired colour is jet-black. The jet-black colouring is difficult to obtain, and still more difficult to fix; for there is a tendency for the colours of fishes to lighten with age, and many Moors, therefore, change to a deep bronze as they grow older. Bronze-coloured Moors are not greatly admired by aquarists. Celestials are usually pink to pinky-white, with red patches. Other colours, however, have been developed. In China, the usual colour is bright gold, sometimes white, and sometimes white with red patches. An all-black type is known to the Chinese, but it is very rare. Lionheads, like Celestials, are usually pink to pinky-white, with red patches; but other colours are found. The most usual colour of the Oranda is red and white, but other colours have been developed, including an all-black fish, and a red fish with a yellow belly.

In shape of body the Shubunkin and the Comet are much the same as the common goldfish, but rather slimmer. The other breeds have deep rounded bodies (at least the best specimens have) the depth of the body being equal almost to its length.

The Shubunkin and the Comet have their full complement of fins, but these are somewhat larger (in proportion to the size of the fish) than in the common goldfish. In the Shubunkin the lobes of the fins are rounded: in the best specimens of Comet they are pointed. Naturally, therefore, Shubunkins and Comets are fast swimmers, and if kept in an aquarium it should be a large one.

In the other breeds the complement of fins varies.

The Fantail has a divided caudal fin of medium length. The Veiltail has a divided caudal fin that is so long and full that it hangs down in graceful folds. In the best specimens the fins are not bifurcated. A type of Veiltail with a single caudal fin goes by the special name of the Nymph. British breeders do not think highly of it, and Chinese breeders think even less of it than British breeders. The Telescope has a divided caudal fin, usually slightly smaller than that of the Fantail. The Moor has a divided

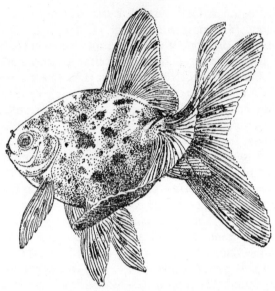

Fig. 18. THE CALICO FANTAIL

caudal fin, sometimes fan-tail, sometimes veil-tail. The Celestial has a divided caudal fin, usually deeply forked. The Lionhead has a divided caudal fin, well spread out, held stiffly, and of medium length, but a type with a veil-tail, known to the Japanese as the *Shukin (Syukin)* was first developed at Tokio in 1897, and about the same time, independently, at Osaka. The Oranda has a divided caudal fin, following the veil-tail type. In all breeds with a divided caudal fin the fins should be separated along the upper margins. In some specimens the caudal fins are sometimes united along the upper margins (web-tail) and sometimes the upper lobe is single and the lower double (tripod-tail): aquarists consider such specimens inferior. The best specimens of fish with a divided caudal fin also have a divided anal fin. The bases of the divided anal fins are usually close together in small fish, but separated by a row of scales in large fish. Like the caudal fins, the anal fins should be separated from each other: in inferior specimens the anal fins are united along the upper or lower margins. The absence of an anal fin is considered a defect.

The Fantail, Veiltail, Moor, and Oranda, have a high dorsal fin. The Telescope has a dorsal fin of medium height. The Celestial and

Lionhead lack the dorsal fin. In specimens that lack the dorsal fin, the back should be round, smooth, and sloping gradually towards the caudal peduncle. In inferior specimens there may be one or more protruberances on the back, indicating that a bone is trying to project: these fish are of no value to the aquarist. Also of no value are those specimens in which the dorsal fin is only partly developed (spike-fin). Usually the front part of the fin is fully developed (the middle and rear parts lacking); but sometimes the rear part is fully developed (the front and middle parts lacking) and sometimes the middle part is fully developed (the front and rear parts lacking). Exceptionally the front and rear parts are fully developed (the middle part lacking).

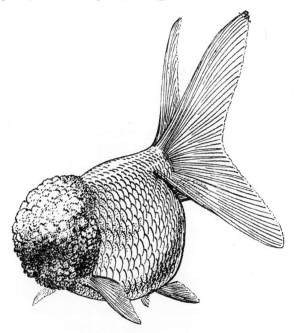

Fig. 19. THE LIONHEAD

The Shubunkin, Comet, Fantail, Veiltail, Telescope, Moor, and Celestial have a normal head. The Lionhead and Oranda have a decorated, or embellished head. The Lionhead is characterized by wart-like excrescences, known as a hood, which first develop on the top of the head, and then gradually spread over the head,

E

The Goldfish

cheeks, and gill-covers, leaving only a small area under the mouth to the throat comparatively free. These excrescences, however, do not develop until the fish is three or four years old, and sometimes they never develop. The excrescences are soft to the touch, and usually red, pink, or white in colour. In the best specimens every excrescence is about the same size, and the fish has been aptly described as having an unripe raspberry for a head. The Oranda also develops soft excrescences on its head (they may be white, pink, vermilion, orange-red or variegated) but they develop better on the top of the head than on the sides as in the Lionhead.

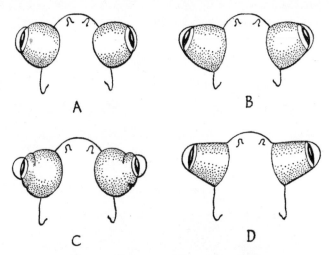

Fig. 20. TYPES OF TELESCOPE EYE
A. Spherical; B. Ovoid; C. Segmented Sphere; D. Truncated Cone.

The Shubunkin and Comet always have normal eyes. The Celestial has protruberant eyes set on the top of the head. The Telescope and Moor always have protruberant eyes that usually point in the same direction as normal eyes (telescope eyes) though exceptionally they point forwards. In a few very rare cases the eyes point downwards. The Fantail, Veiltail, Lionhead, and Oranda sometimes have normal eyes and sometimes telescope eyes. Protruberant eyes (telescope or upturned) should be large, of equal size and shape, and with well-rounded, and not flat, corneas. Four distinct shapes of protruberant eyes may be distinguished: spherical, ovoid, truncated cone, and segmented

66

sphere. Protruberant eyes do not show themselves in fry, and, though development usually occurs when the fish is from three to six months old, development may be delayed for several years. Moreover, sometimes only one eye develops in this way (the other eye remaining normal throughout the life of the fish) but, of course, such a fish is of no value to the aquarist. It is of interest to note also that, although a fish may have protruberant eyes of equal size, it is not uncommon for one of them to become suddenly enlarged for no apparent reason. As we have seen, in the previous chapter, fish with protruberant eyes are almost blind, but, contrary to popular belief, the fish are not greatly handicapped in their search for food; for they are compensated by an extremely acute sense of smell.

Fancy goldfish do not as a rule grow to the same size as the common goldfish. The Shubunkin grows to an average length of 6 in. The Veiltail is a comparatively small fish; for it rarely exceeds a length of $7\frac{1}{2}$ in. or 8 in., and about a half of this is taken up by the caudal fin. The Telescope is a small fish; a body length of 5 in. being exceptional. The Lionhead, when fully developed, reaches a length of about 4 in. or 5 in. (including the paired caudal fin), but specimens have been known to reach a length of 8 in. Orandas usually reach a length of 4 in. or 5 in. (excluding the paired caudal fin), but specimens 6 in. long, with the caudal fins equally as long, have been recorded.

We have now considered, at some length, the better known breeds of fancy goldfish. Among the lesser known fancy breeds we may mention the Pompon (sometimes erroneously called the Pom-pom), the Egg-fish, the Brocade, the Watonai, and the Blue Fish. Few British aquarists know these five breeds, and many more, because, up to the present time, they have been seen in Europe only occasionally, and then mainly in the collections of specialists.

The Pompon derives its name from the fact that the narial septa, which divide the two nostrils, are abnormally developed into bunches of fleshy lobes (called narial bouquets), usually, but not necessarily, of the same colour as the body of the fish. The Chinese have named the fish the *Jung ch'iu* (Velvet Ball). In the best specimens the two narial septa are equally developed; but inferior fish sometimes have only one septum abnormally developed, the other remaining normal. Indeed, once we had such a fish ourselves. In rare cases there are two bouquets over each nostril. The bouquets are sometimes no bigger than the normal eye of a fish, but sometimes they are as large as one-third of the size of the head. In most specimens the bouquets float in front of the eyes when the fish is swimming but in some specimens, more grotesquely, they are sucked into the mouth every time that the fish draws in water. In shape of body the Pompon resembles the Fantail. The best specimens have a divided caudal fin. There is a breed that lacks a dorsal fin; and there is a calico breed. The most usual colour of the scaled breeds is a combination of bright red (orange) and white, but all-red and all-white fish are known.

We do not know when the Pompon was first developed. It is, however, by no means a novelty in the Far East; for, under the name of the *Hiroshima*, it is referred to by Kishinouye as long ago as 1898. It appears to be no longer bred in Japan, because Yatsu, writing in 1937, records that it is extinct in Japan, but flourishing in China. Although the breed is rare outside of China, it is known to experienced European aquarists. In the autumn of 1936 some specimens reached England from Shanghai, and at about the same time some specimens were exhibited in the aquarium of the Muséum des Colonies, in Paris.

The Egg-fish is so called because its two main features are no dorsal fin and a short and round body. The Reverend Henry W. Moule, in a letter to the present writers, says that it is very popular in China where it is known as the *Ya-tan-yü*. He adds that, apart from no dorsal fin and an egg-like body, the best specimens have normal eyes in a narrow pointed head, and a stiff and divided caudal fin. The usual colour is bright gold, but some specimens are white, or white with bright (not gold) patches. Jet-black specimens are known, but they are very rare. Even more rare are specimens that lack a caudal fin as well as a dorsal fin; only the pectoral, ventral, and anal fins being present. A few specimens reached England from Japan in 1939 but were lost when London was bombed in the following year.

In Japan the Egg-fish is known as the *Maruko*. But the name means 'round fish', and it is, therefore, indifferently applied to any breed that has a short round body and no dorsal fin, such as the Lionhead before the excrescences develop, and the type of Pompon that lacks a dorsal fin.

The Brocade, the *Kinrashi* (*Kinransi*) of Japan, is mottled with red, black, and white, in varying proportions. In shape of body it is similar to the common goldfish, but lacks a dorsal fin.

It is a Japanese breed, and was first bred by Akiyama Kichigoro of Tokyo about 1905.

The Watonai arose as a cross between the common goldfish and the Veiltail. Broadly speaking, the shape of the fish is similar to that of the common goldfish, but the body is shorter, thicker, and rather deeper. All the fins are larger than those of the common goldfish, and the caudal fin is the same as that of the Veiltail. The usual colours are red and white variegated. In 1946 there was a specimen, although not a very good one, on show in a well-known London departmental store.

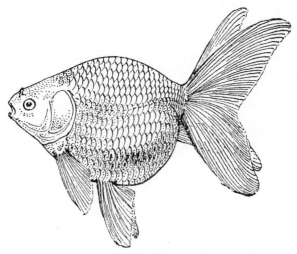

Fig. 21. THE EGG-FISH

Matsubara records that the first specimen to be seen was one exhibited at the Fisheries Exhibition, held at Tokyo in 1883.

The Blue Fish is known in China as the *Lan-yü*. It is an all-blue, not mottled, fish of dark blue colour. The evidence of Mulertt shows that it was known in America as early as 1883. We have never heard of it in England: indeed, for long it has been the aim of British breeders to produce an all-blue fish. We are told that Arthur Derham succeeded in producing a few all-blue fish about the middle of the 1930's, but we have no further information, and do not know whether they reached maturity or not, or whether they were bred from the Chinese *Lan-yü*. Probably not: for we are under the impression that Derham's fish were calicoes, and, from a plate that accompanies a monograph by Shisan C. Chen.[1] the Blue Fish appears to differ from the Moor only in coloration, and, therefore, is a scaled fish.

There remains to be noticed a selection of breeds well-known to oriental breeders and fanciers but which, so far as we know, are only very rarely to be seen in England and America.

The Tumbler is known to the Chinese as the *Chin-t'ou-yü*, and several specimens are depicted on a scroll sent from Peking to Paris in 1772.[2] Under the name of *Le Cabrioleur* (The Caperer) it is mentioned in the *Mémoire*, that accompanied the scroll, as dating from about fifteen years earlier, when a number of specimens were given to the Emperor of China. The fish takes its name from the peculiarity that, owing to a curvature of the spine, it turns perpetual somersaults in the water. Innes[3] records that it has been seen in America.

The Meteor is a breed remarkable for having no caudal fin, but whose fins are so well developed that it makes quite a streaming effect passing through the water. We have no acquaintance with this breed, and it may be connected with the remarkable Egg-fish, mentioned on page 68, as lacking the caudal as well as the dorsal fin.

The Lion Fish is known in Japan as the *Shishi*. Although the Japanese breeders consider that it is a sub-breed of the Oranda, Hugh Smith considers that it has a right to be considered as a distinct breed. Its chief peculiarities are two short caudal fins and a brassy colour.

The Water-bubble-eye obtains its name from the fact that, although the eyeballs are normal, their orbits are as large, or almost as large, as in breeds with protruberant eyes. The eyeballs are situated near the top of the head; below is a gelatinous substance in the form of a bubble, that is sometimes very large and protrudes conspicuously from the socket. The breed is well

---

[1] Shisan C. Chen, 'The Inheritance of Blue and Brown Colours in the Goldfish, *Carassius auratus*' in *Journal of Genetics*, Vol. XXXIX (Cambridge, 1934).

[2] The original scroll is preserved in the Muséum National d'Histoire Naturelle, in Paris. There is an excellent photograph of it in the British Museum (Natural History).

[3] William T. Innes, *Goldfish Varieties and Tropical Aquarium Fishes* (Philadelphia, 1917).

known to the Chinese, and it is particularly prized in the province of Kwangtung.

The Outfolded Operculum (*Fan ssü*) is a Chinese breed that obtains its name from the fact that the gill-covers are upturned, sometimes to expose the gills. It is highly prized in North China, but in South China it is not favoured, owing to the fact that it is a very delicate fish.

Fig. 22. The Meteor

The Pearl Scale (*Chu lin*) is common in the Chinese province of Kwangtung (the best specimens are bred at Tai-lung) but rare elsewhere. The scales are more convex than ordinary ones, and the outer margins are darker than the inner surfaces. It is of interest to note that if one of the scales is lost, it will be replaced by a normal scale: the 'pearl' scale never growing a second time. Innes records that, in 1897, a new breed reached America from Japan. The main feature of the fish was the scales, 'which are raised sharply in the centre to present a line of dots along the sides of the fish'.[1] The fish was named the Barnacle, and it soon disappeared from view. We have reason to believe that the Barnacle was an inferior specimen of the Chinese Pearl Scale Fish.

[1] William T. Innes, op. cit., p. 70.

71

The Goldfish

The Brown Fish is known to the Chinese as the *Tsê-yü*. It differs from the Moor only in coloration. The Brown Fish is widely distributed in China, but is unknown in Japan, Europe, and America. It is important to note that the fish is a distinct breed not to be confused with the bronze-coloured fish, which is merely an inferior type of Moor and very common everywhere.

Finally, mention must be made of the fact that on the scroll of 1772 a number of fish bearing the name of *Shui-yü* (The Sleeper) are depicted belly upwards. The author of the accompanying *Mémoire* gives their approximate date of origin and provenance. This is remarkable; for the description of the fish leaves no doubt that it was not a distinct breed, but a fish suffering from a deranged air-bladder. What is of doubt is whether the Chinese of the eighteenth century, knowing little of ichthyopathology, believed that these fish were a distinct breed, or whether it was a hoax. Certainly, if it was a hoax, it was a successful one; for Valenciennes,[1] among others, was deceived, and Chinese fanciers thought highly of it.

Many more breeds might be mentioned, but we must not allow our enthusiasm to run away with us. We have to remember that many of the fancy goldfish bred in the far east may never be seen outside their country of origin, being too delicate to withstand a long journey. Modern improved methods of transport might overcome this difficulty (if not now, at all events in the future) but, even so, the trouble and expense of importing ultra-grotesque breeds into Europe would never be worth while; for such fish are unlikely to appeal to European aquarists in general, and would find favour only among a few seekers after the novel and unusual. For a time the Tumbler and Meteor might make amusing pets to show to one's friends, but we think that their antics would soon pall. In any event, we doubt the wisdom of encouraging insults in the sight of man and nature; and it is no longer possible to pass off ailing fish as a new breed.

[1] Georges Cuvier and Achille Valenciennes, *Histoire Naturelle des Poissons*, Vol. XVI (Paris, 1842).

Chapter III

HISTORY

In its early stages the earth was very hot—a sort of smelting furnace. The comparison is a fair one; for just as in the process of purifying iron by puddling the iron forms into a round solid mass of hot metal, while the various stony impurities collect about it as a sort of scum, so the earth, as we now know it, consists of a hot central metallic core (the barysphere) and a rocky outer crust (the lithosphere) which was the first to harden as the planet cooled.

But there is a significant distinction in the composition of the lithosphere. Over the hot barysphere lies a universal layer of dark, fine-grained, heavy basalt (commonly known as sima) and the land masses are built up over the sima on a lighter granite material (commonly known as sial).

There is a theory—first presented to the world as a scientific hypothesis by Alfred Wegener in 1910—that the sial was originally continuous over the whole earth, but in very early geological times the sial of the eastern hemisphere was ruptured and contracted into a continental mass centred about South Africa in the western hemisphere. He conceived this land mass as a comparatively thin raft of sial floating, as it were, on the underlying sima. Through the operation of astronomical forces this mass split up, and its parts gradually drifted away to their present positions. As the masses drifted the leading edges were crumpled by pressure to form mountain ranges with much volcanic disturbance, while the rear edges trailed out into chains of islands. This theory of Continental Drift (or Floating Continents) is remarkably interesting. It may not be the whole truth, yet its fundamental truth can hardly be questioned; for a study of the great mountain ranges, volcanoes, and islands does much to confirm it, and during the

73

past few years much evidence has been produced in its favour. Certainly it provides the only solution to many problems concerning fishes; and the distribution of fishes—particularly freshwater species—does much to support the theory.

For although all this took place very slowly over hundreds of millions of years, fishes, the earliest vertebrates, were even then evolving. Now, the goldfish, as we have pointed out, is a member of the huge order of Ostariophysi, which includes the majority of the freshwater fishes of the world. The ancestors of this order began seemingly before any extensive drifting had occurred (though the evidence shows that Australia was isolated and India already adrift) and there is reason to believe that they resembled the primitive Osteoglossidae (a few members of which exist today in widely separated, but equatorial parts of the world) and the distinctive Weberian mechanism must already have been evolved.

The division of the land mass into a northern continent (Laurasia) and a southern continent (Gondwana-land or Lemuria) caused the Ostariophysi to develop along two distinct lines: the Cyprinidae and Cobitidae in the north, and the Characidae and Siluridae in the south. In course of time, however, North America drifted away from Europe taking the Cyprinidae with it, and South America drifted away from Africa taking the Characidae with it. And since, geologically speaking, it is only recently that the Americas have become joined at Panama, to this day the American Cyprinidae are confined to North America, and the American Characidae to South America (though a few species have since found their way as far north as Mexico). Meanwhile, India drifted northwards, collided with Asia, and crumpled up at the point of impact to form the Himalayas; while Africa drifted northwards, towards Europe, and, indeed, overrode it at the line marked by the Pyrenees, Alps, and Caucasus. As a result the Cyprinidae found their way into India and Africa, to mingle with the Characidae of Africa, while the Siluridae found their way northwards.

It is beyond the scope of this work to pursue the matter further, the more so as the geological history of fishes is far from complete. The point at issue is that the peculiar distribution of the Ostariophysi (and, we may add, of others, e.g. the Cichlids and Perches) can be explained only if we accept this important and far-reaching geological theory.

At the time of the juncture of India and Asia it would seem that there was in existence an ancestral form of *Carassius*, of which the population in South China became separated from that of the Caspian area, the former to evolve into the goldfish, the latter into the crucian carp. At all events, there is no evidence to show that the goldfish was ever found wild to the west of the Tibetan plateau, and it is as a Chinese species that it makes its bow in recorded history.

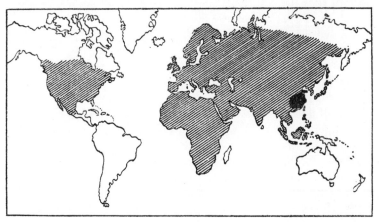

Fig. 23. MAP SHOWING PRESENT-DAY DISTRIBUTION OF CYPRINI-DAE (shaded) AND THE ORIGINAL HABITAT OF THE GOLDFISH (black)

But the precise date we do not know. The story, recorded in a number of modern books, that goldfish were originally confined to a lake near the mountain Ch'ien-ch'ing in the Chinese province of Chekiang, is nonsense, and clearly due to a misunderstanding of a passage in Du Halde's *Description . . . de la Chine* (1735). And the colourful Chinese story, told in the *Shu I Chi* (*Record of Stories of Marvels*), 'In Shensi there was a Goldfish God. In the second year of the reign of the Emperor P'ing [769 B.C.] of the Chou Dynasty, no rain fell for one hundred days, and while sacrifices were being made to appease the gods, suddenly a bubbling well appeared, a goldfish leapt out, and the rain fell,' was never intended by the Chinese to account for the origin of goldfish. For the Chinese themselves have preserved the earliest notices of gold-fish being observed in natural waters. In the same *Shu I Chi* we read that 'Huan Ch'ung [328–84] of the Chin Dynasty [265–420] visiting Mount Lu saw that in the lake there were fish with red scales'; and in the *Pao P'o Tzu*, written by Ko Hung in the fourth century, we read: 'The Red River rises in the Chung-ling Hill in the Shang-lo District of the Metropolis [Shensi] and flows into the Cho River. Red fish are produced in it.' But, of course, these red-scaled fish, first observed by the Chinese in natural waters about sixteen hundred years ago, were wild fish, and it is not until many years later that we find records of them being domesticated under the name of *Chin Chi-yü*, or Goldfish.

We have no means of knowing when the goldfish was first domesticated by the Chinese. A number of western writers have recorded that goldfish were known as domestic pets to the Chinese of the T'ang Dynasty (618–907). We are unconvinced; for, though there are a number of references to goldfish in the literature of the T'ang, many of them refer to goldenfish-shaped badges of office, a very different story. So far as we have been able to ascertain, the literature of the T'ang contains only two references to actual goldfish, and both are obscure and rather uncertain.

The first reference is to be found in the *Yün Yü Yang Ch'iu* of Kê Li-fang, in which we read of a monastery at Hu-chou: 'The three gates are a hundred feet high, and are called the Three Excellences. Moreover in the pool are Golden *Chi* which are seen once in several years. So the poems of Po Lo-t'ien [772–846] contain the sentence: "Now there is the Shang-ch'iang ching-shê Monastery, a place most worthy of a visit which I have not visited" referring namely to this.' We find this reference very far from being conclusive; for, though Kê Li-fang assumes that Po Lo-t'ien thought the monastery worth visiting on account of its pool of goldfish, there is no positive evidence to show that Po Lo-t'ien had the pool of goldfish in mind when he wrote his poem.

The second reference is rather more positive, but by no means conclusive. In the *Description of the Hsiu-shui District* we read that the magistrate Ting Yen-tsan of the T'ang Dynasty found a gold-fish in a pond in Hsiu-shui. He returned it to the pond, which thereafter became known as the Goldfish Pond. Ting-pong Koh, a modern Chinese ichthyologist, dates the history of the domestication of the goldfish from this event. But we are not convinced that he is justified in doing so. The evidence is not confirmed by the *T'u Shu*[1] or by any other Chinese book, and, though this may not count for much, it is to be noted that nothing more is known of the magistrate Ting, and no trace can be found of the so-called Goldfish Pond.

On the whole, therefore, the evidence for assuming that goldfish were domesticated as early as the T'ang is very scanty, and it is of importance to observe that T'u Lung (a very careful writer of the late-sixteenth century) informs us in the *K'ao P'an Yü Shih* that once when he was puzzled about the variety of colour in goldfish, he made a thorough examination of the passages on fish, and found that no mention of them was made in the *I Wu Chih* written by Shên Ju-yün, himself of the T'ang Dynasty.

It is, in fact, only when we come to the early days of the Sung Dynasty (960–1279) that we are on safe ground. The goldfish as a pet appears to have been known to the Chinese by the year 960; for its domestication is recorded by three writers. In the *Pên Ts'ao Kang Mu (Materia Medica)* of Li Shih-chên we read: 'Formerly in ancient times they [goldfish] were little known. . . .No-one kept them domesticated before the Sung.' In the *Ch'ien T'ang Hsien Chih (Description of the District of Ch'ien-t'ang)* we read: 'Only since the Sung have there been breeders [of goldfish].' Finally, and most important of all, in the *Wu Lei Hsiang Chih (Account of the Mutual Influence of Things)*, once doubtfully ascribed to the poet Su Tung-p'o (1036–1101) but now ascribed without query to the monk (Kao) Tsan-ning (918–999), we read: 'If goldfish eat the refuse of olives or soapy water then they die; if they have poplar bark they do not breed lice.' This passage suggests, very strongly, that at this period goldfish were being kept and cared for as domestic pets.

About thirty years after the death of Tsan-ning we find the first reference to goldfish in the literature of the world (see Chapter X). Thereafter the literature of the Sung contains many references to goldfish, thus proving that from the eleventh century onwards it was a popular household pet.

By the middle of the Sung the keeping of goldfish as pets appears to have been well established. In the *T'ing Shih* of Yo K'o

[1] The *Ch'in Ting Ku Chin T'u Shu Chi Ch'êng*, or *Imperial Encyclopædia*, is usually known to Europeans by the abbreviated *T'u Shu*. It was published in 1726 by order of the Emperor Kang-hsi. It is in 10,000 volumes, and the copy in the British Museum occupies 60 yards of shelving.

(1173–1240) we read: 'At the present time there are fish breeders in Chung-tu [Peking] who can change the colour of fish to gold. The *Chi* [goldfish] is the most prized for keeping, and the *Li* [carp] comes next. Most people scoop out stone to make a pool, and place them between the eaves and the lattice [i.e., on the verandah] to provide amusement.' We have it on the authority of the *Ti Ching Ching Wu Lüeh* of Liu T'ung and Yü I-chêng that the Fish-weed Pool (later renamed the Goldfish Pool) at Peking existed as early as the second Chin Dynasty (1115–1234) and that at this period goldfish were bred in it in profitable numbers. Finally, the evidence of the *Mêng Liang Lu* goes to show that before the end of the thirteenth century (1276) gold, silver, red, black, and mottled fish were being bred and sold in Hangchow. More than this cannot be said without the danger of crossing the border-line between fact and fiction.

Not for another two and a quarter centuries did the goldfish find its way to neighbouring Japan; for the goldfish was not introduced there until about the year 1500. This is admitted by several Japanese ichthyologists, notably by Mitsukuri. Writing in 1904 he says: 'There is a record that about four hundred years ago— that is to say about the year 1500—some common goldfish were brought from China to Sakai, a town near Osaka.' A further two hundred years elapsed before the Japanese took up the breeding of goldfish. There is a tradition, and no more, that the first breeder of goldfish was Sato Sanzaemon, who set up in business at Koriyama during the Hoyei Era (1704–1710) and that the business he established has been continuous ever since.

At what precise dates the goldfish first reached other eastern countries must remain a matter of speculation. History is silent on the subject. They were certainly widespread in the east by the end of the seventeenth century; for Engelbert Kämpfer, who visited the far east in 1691 and 1692, writes: 'In China and Japan, and almost all over the Indies, this fish is kept in ponds, and fed with flies before their wings come out.'[1] That is about all we know. In the *Arabian Nights* there is mention of white, red, blue and yellow fish in a lake, but as evidence that goldfish were known in western Asia at an early date this is quite worthless. We mention it only

---

[1] *History of Japan* published in an English translation in 1728. The original unpublished German version, *Heutiges Japan*, is based on his notes made in the far east in 1691 and 1692. It is now in the British Museum.

because one modern writer has accepted the evidence of Scheherazade to suggest that Persia may have been the original home of the goldfish. It is patently ridiculous.

To return to firm ground. Europe followed in the wake of Japan. Bloch, in his *Oeconomische Naturgeschichte der Fische Deutschlands* (1784), records that goldfish were introduced into England in 1611, and he cites Pennant's *British Zoology* as his authority. But, as Pennant gives the year as 1691 it is clear the Bloch's 1611 is a misprint, even if we did not know that misprints were very common in eighteenth-century books. The year 1691 is usually regarded as the year when goldfish were first introduced into England. We think this is an error. Edward writes: 'The first account of these fishes being brought to England may be seen in Petiver's works, published about *anno* 1691.'[1] The work referred to by Edwards is a catalogue in Petiver's *Gazophylacii Naturæ et Artis*, in which reference is made to two goldfish brought alive from China. But Petiver's catalogue is not dated 1691 but MDCCXI (1711). We cannot offer conclusive proof, but the only explanation that fits the facts is that Edwards made the simple mistake of transposing the 'x' and 'c', to produce MDCXCI (1691).[2] Petiver reproduces drawings of two goldfish, and there is some evidence to show that the drawings were executed in 1705, and certainly not later than 1706; for the plate was for sale in 1706. With no further positive evidence, the best that can be said is that goldfish were first known to British naturalists in the early years of the eighteenth century, or perhaps late in the seventeenth century. There is some indirect evidence to show that goldfish were on board a ship that left Macao in September 1691, and reached London in 1692. A few isolated specimens may even have been brought to England by travellers or sailors in the middle of the seventeenth century. Samuel Pepys writes in his *Diary*, 28th May 1665: 'Thence home and to see my Lady Pen; where my wife and I were shown a fine rarity: of fishes kept in a glass of water, that will live so for ever, and finely marked they are being foreign.' It is unlikely that these fish were goldfish, and Dr. C. W. Coates, of the New York Zoological Society, has expressed what he calls the 'educated guess' that the fish were Paradise Fish (*Macropodus opercularis*), which is finely marked in the sense that the word

[1] George Edwards, *A Natural History of Birds* (London, 1751).
[2] First drawn attention to by G.F.H. in *The Aquarist* (December 1946).

'finely' would be used by a seventeenth-century writer, and which by reason of its supplementary breathing organ, would be able to live for a very long time in a small container. Certainly, at this time, goldfish were not generally known in England; for Willughby (1635–72), old Izaak Walton (1593–1683), and others do not mention them, especially, they are not mentioned by John Ray (1627–1705) in his *Synopsis Methodica Piscium*, posthumously published in 1710.

At some time in the third decade of the eighteenth century a large number of goldfish were imported into England. Edwards and Baster mention that some goldfish were brought to England from Saint Helena (having been previously taken there from China) by Philip Worth, captain of *The Houghton*, belonging to the East-India Company. They were given by him to Sir Matthew Decker, a director of the East-India Company and sheriff of the county of Surrey. Edwards and Baster give the year as 1728, but they may be mistaken; for the records show that *The Houghton* sailed from England only at the end of 1728 and did not return until 1730. At all events, whatever the precise date, Baster records that the fish 'were placed in fish-ponds in England, and were increased, so that, sent into other parts of Europe, they became well known'. In fact, by the middle of the eighteenth century goldfish were widespread in England. Horace Walpole (1717–97) was constantly giving them to his friends. In a letter to Henry Fox, dated 19th July 1746, he mentions the goldfish in the 'purling basons' at Vauxhall. Edwards, writing in 1751, mentions that the Duke of Richmond (Charles Lennox, 1701–50) had a large Chinese earthen vessel full of goldfish brought alive to England.[1] There are also many other references.

The goldfish was introduced into France during the last days of the French monarchy. Billardon de Sauvigny records that the first specimens to reach France arrived at the port of Lorient about the year 1750. They were imported by the French East-India Company. There is a story that some of the fish were given to the Pompadour,[2] who thought very highly of them. About thirty

[1] George Edwards, op. cit., p. 79.
[2] Jeanne Antoinette Poisson (1721–64) of obscure parents attracted the attention of Louis XV, and in 1745 appeared at his court as the Marquise de Pompadour. The gift of goldfish to her may be apocryphal. It is mentioned by Vallot (1837) but we have been unable to find an earlier reference. The story may have arisen as a pun on her name.

I. Common Goldfish. Fish such as these were domesticated by the Chinese at least 1,000 years ago, and later, through the agency of man, spread to most countries of the world. It is from fish like these that the many fancy breeds known today have been developed.

II. The Comet. An elementary fancy breed characterized by its high dorsal fin, slender body and long deeply-forked tail fin. In the best specimens the lobes of the fins are pointed rather than rounded.

III. The Shubunkin (London Type). Similar in shape to the Common Goldfish (*see* Plate I) but of the so-called 'scaleless' type. The colour is variegated, and those fish that show most blue are the most esteemed by aquarists.

IV. The Shubunkin (Bristol Type). Very similar to the London Type (*see* Plate III) but has bigger fins. The most prominent feature is a large, deeply-forked tail fin with well-rounded lobes.

years later, in 1780 to be precise, their popularity was still further increased. In that year Billardon de Sauvigny published his beautifully illustrated and remarkably interesting *Histoire Naturelle des Dorades de la Chine*. His book is usually credited with being the first written about goldfish in a European language. This, however, is true only within limitations; for many years earlier Linné (Linnaeus) mentioned goldfish in his *Systema Naturæ*, published an illustrated article in a Swedish periodical; and, in 1765, Job Baster, of Haarlem, devoted the final article of the second volume of his *Opuscula Subseciva* to the goldfish. But, whatever the merits of the work of Linné and Baster from an historical and technical point of view, it was due far more to de Sauvigny's book and its illustrations (copied by F. M. Martinet from the Chinese scroll sent from Peking to Paris in 1772) that the species became popular throughout Europe.

At about the same time that goldfish were being admired by the Pompadour in France (if they were) they were known in Italy. On 6th May 1755, Horace Walpole wrote to Richard Bentley: 'I have lately given Count Perron some goldfish, which he has carried in his post-chaise to Turin: he has already carried some before. The Russian minister has asked me for some too, but I doubt their succeeding there.'

The first goldfish reached the Netherlands in 1753 or 1754. They were introduced into the ponds on the estate of Count Clifford and that of the Lord of Rhoon,[1] but these fish had not bred by 1765. The first goldfish to breed in Holland were sixteen fish, imported from England in the winter of 1759–60 which Job Baster introduced into his two ponds in Zeeland. It was on the Ides (13th) of June 1760, that Baster notices with great delight 'some little fish four to six lines long, and of a blackish or swarthy colour. About six weeks later most of them developed silvery or white spots between the dorsal fin and the tail.'

The goldfish was certainly known in the Scandinavian countries in the first half of the eighteenth century, because, in 1740, Linné, then at Stockholm, received a specimen from the Swedish Ambassador at the Danish Court. It was this fish that formed the subject of Linné's article, already mentioned, and Baster records that in September of the same year he preserved it in alcohol and gave it to the Swedish Academy 'because of its rarity'.

---

[1] Very probably, but not certainly, Count Bentinck.

The Goldfish

The first goldfish reached Germany about the year 1780, Bloch writing in 1784, says that the first goldfish reached Germany a few years before. They were taken to Berlin from Holland by the Count of Heyden, the German envoy to Holland. The fish were greeted with great delight, and the Countess von Goes of Carinthia, Herr Oelrichs the Burgomaster of Bremen, and Herr Grewe, a merchant living in Hamburg, introduced specimens into specially constructed ponds.

Despite the doubt of Walpole, the goldfish was flourishing in Russia before the end of the eighteenth century. On 1st April 1791, Prince Potemkin[1] gave a banquet to Catherine II, and goldfish in bowls were part of the lavish decorations of Potemkin's magnificent Winter Garden, in which the banquet was held.

America was very late in the field; not until the nineteenth century were goldfish known there. The first concrete evidence of goldfish being known in America occurs in Arthur M. Edwards's *Life Beneath the Waters, or The Aquarium in America*, published in 1859. 'The gold carp (*Cyprinus auratus*)', he writes, 'is one of the handsomest fish for an *Aquarium*, and at the same time it is easy of domestication. This beautiful creature is a native of China. . . . It is now to be caught in the Schuykill River, . . . into which stream it has escaped from some pond, and increased greatly in numbers, size, and beauty—fish which breed in a semi-wild state always being of more brilliant color than those reared in confinement.' In fact the very opposite is true, which has led Dr. James W. Atz (to whom we are indebted for this reference) to point out that it seems likely goldfish were a recent introduction. Be this as it may, by 1889 a goldfish farm had been established in Maryland, and by the beginning of the present century most of the fancy breeds of goldfish were known to American aquarists.

So much, then, for the history of the common goldfish. We must now turn our attention to the history, or more correctly the development, of the fancy breeds.

The goldfish is a very plastic species, as witness the fact that when they are transferred from aquaria and ponds to natural waters they usually revert to their ancestral coloration. It is probable, therefore, that some of the fancy breeds were developed almost simultaneously with the common goldfish. Roughley

[1] Gregory Alexandrovitch, Prince Potemkin (1739–91), the acknowledged favourite of Catherine II.

writes: 'The Chinese long ago found that even in its natural state the goldfish is subject to considerable variations. . . . Some individuals would appear with abnormally formed bodies, scales, fins, or eyes, or perhaps with marked colour variations, and with much foresight the Chinese conceived the idea of interbreeding such abnormally formed fish. . . . This careful breeding has been going on for centuries in China.' Indeed, as early as the late sixteenth century T'u Lung expresses the opinion that monstrosities are the result of the breeder's art. In the *K'ao P'an Yü Shih*, published about 1590, he writes: 'We observe that the variations include distortions, and it is said that the skill [to produce these] is with the breeders; nor may this be completely rejected.' T'u Lung, in fact, is not prepared to deny that the distortions may be artificially produced.

Unfortunately there is no positive evidence to tell us when fancy goldfish were first developed from common goldfish. All that we can say, with any degree of certainty, is that the first reference to anything approaching a fancy goldfish dates from about the year 1200. In the *T'ing Shih* of Yo K'o (1173–1240) reference is made to goldfish with 'snow-white bodies with black spots, quite lustrous like varnish and called Tortoiseshell Fish, whose markings are especially beautiful.' Ting-pong Koh quotes a paragraph from the *Sung Shih* (*History of the Sung Dynasty*) which records that, in May 1189, a spotted, multi-coloured goldfish was found in the Ch'ien-t'ang river, near Hangchow. At first sight it would seem that the Tortoiseshell Fish mentioned by Yo K'o is connected with the fish found in the Ch'ien-t'ang River. We do not think that this is so: and, in truth, there is some doubt about the authenticity of the fish found in the Ch'ien-t'ang River, because, as it is a violently tidal river and about a mile wide thirty miles from its mouth, it is not the sort of river in which a fancy goldfish is likely to be found. In the *Mêng Liang Lu* of Wu Tzü-mu, published about the year 1276, there is mention of the Tortoiseshell Fish being bred and sold at Hangchow, along with gold, silver and other coloured fish; but, after the thirteenth century, nothing more is mentioned of anything approaching a fancy goldfish until late in the Ming Dynasty (1368–1644). By the late-Ming a large number of multi-coloured fish appear to have been developed. T'u Lung, writing about the year 1590, refers to fish of various colours. 'First', he writes, 'they prized pure red and pure white;

afterwards they have prized Golden Helmets, Golden Saddles, Embroidered Coverlets. . . .' Later he mentions fish that bore such picturesque names as Piled-up Gold, Inlaid Jade, Falling Flowers, Flowing Water, Lotus Terrace, Eight Melon Seeds; variations without number. T'u Lung adds: 'In fact men have decreed names according to their fancy, following the varying appearances.' In the contemporary *Pên Ts'ao Kang Mu* reference is made to fish 'which are mottled red, white, and black, not always the same'. In the *Shan T'ang Ssu K'ao*, dated 1595, we find that much the same story is told. The author, P'êng Ta-i, writes: 'The bodies of goldfish are like gold; one name is Fire Fish. There are those with the whole body red, there are those with half the body red, there are those with irregular red spots, there are those with red lines on the back forming the pattern of the Diagrams, there are those with the head red and the tail white . . . colours and shapes everyone different.' Special mention is made of the Gold Thread Fish found in the cave of the Pi-chi Hill, and of the Tortoiseshell Fish found at Peking. A year later Chang Ch'ien-tê, in *The Book of Vermilion Fish* (1596), writes: 'It is only in Wu [Soochow] that Vermilion Fish are at their best.'

The sixteenth century saw the beginning of the Fantails and Veiltails. In the *K'ao P'an Yü Shih* of T'u Lung, published about 1590, we read of fish with three tails and four tails (the Chinese counted each lobe as a tail). But, more important still, in the *Hang Chou Fu Chih* (*circa* 1600) we read: 'There are those with three tails, five tails, even as many as seven tails. . . . When it comes to those which have three tails or five tails, these are all what have been produced by fanciers in recent times. In the Hung-ch'ih reign [1485–1505] they did not exist.' The evidence, therefore, goes to show that Fantails and Veiltails were first developed at some time during the sixteenth century.

We have no evidence to show when Fantails and Veiltails were first known in Japan, but they were certainly known there at an early date, because representations of fish with divided caudal fins are to be seen on fairly early Japanese pictures. The fish appear to have been introduced into Japan from China by way of the Ryukyu (Loochoo) Islands,[1] and first landed at the port of Nagasaki; for the Japanese give to the Veiltail the names of the *Ryukin* and the Nagasaki Fish. Fish with divided caudal fins were

---

[1] The group of islands between Formosa and Japan.

known in Europe as early as the middle of the eighteenth century. Edwards mentions a fish with two anal fins and a caudal fin partly double,[1] and among the specimens that Baster (1765) records having seen was a fish 'with two anal fins, and two caudal fins separated one from another.' He also records that he kept in a jar a fish 'whose two caudal fins were only a little joined and that towards the body or trunk'. Pouchet records that thirty-six Fantails left China in February 1870, but thirty-three of them died before the ship reached France. One died at Marseilles, and the other two reached Paris but died a few days later. Pouchet implies that these were the first Fantails to be seen in France, but Fantails, and possibly Veiltails, must have been fairly common throughout Europe at a far earlier date, since, as we have said, Baster records Fantails in the Netherlands a full century before. It is possible that fish with divided caudal fins were among the first specimens to reach Europe, and it is certain that fish with tripod tails and divided anal fins were: indeed, it was such a fish that was given to Linné in 1740; and the two fish depicted by Petiver at the beginning of the eighteenth century had tripod tails; also no anal fins, but this may be an error of draughtsmanship. Pierre Carbonnier was breeding Veiltails in France in 1873, and about ten years later they were being bred in Germany.

The sixteenth century probably saw the beginning of the Egg-Fish. Chang Ch'ien-tê, in *The Book of Vermilion Fish* (1596), after mentioning the various colours of the different breeds of fish, and the different types of caudal fins, writes: 'The body whether long or short must be fat and strong, and it is only the well-developed that can be classed.' And in the contemporary *K'ao P'an Yü Shih* of T'u Lung we read: 'As for the three-tailed, four-tailed, and many-tailed fish . . . their bodies are compact and stunted. . . .' From this we deduce that it was just about this time that the breeders were beginning to develop the round-bodied fish as an advance on the typical long-bodied fish. The quotation from *The Book of Vermilion Fish* is of particular value; for Chang Ch'ien-tê not only kept fish but bred them in a big way, and he tells us that the fanciers in Wu swarmed like ants in their eagerness to seek his advice and to admire. Thus, he may well have set the fashion.

The Telescope Goldfish may also have been known as early as the sixteenth century. In the *K'ao P'an Yü Shih* (*circa* 1590) refer-

[1] George Edwards, *Gleanings of Natural History* (London, 1760).

ence is made to fish with eyes ink-black, snow-white, scarlet, purple, agate and amber; and later to 'red protuberant'. But the passage is uncertain, and although a number of writers have taken the words 'red protuberant' to refer to telescope eyes, we have it on the authority of two eminent sinologues that there should be a full stop after 'red' and that 'protuberant' begins a new sentence unconnected with eyes. T'u Lung, the author of the *K'ao P'an Yü Shih*, also mentions 'gold tubes and silver tubes', and, although at first sight, 'tube' appears to be the origin of the English 'telescope', this is not so; for either T'u Lung or a first-class editor has been very careful to point out that 'tube' means 'tail'. It is all rather confusing because several other explanations of 'tube' have been offered. The best appears to be that given by the authors of the *Ti Ching Ching Wu Lüeh* (see page 87). But the meaning of 'tube' must remain in doubt, and the only certain thing about it is that it does not refer to telescope eyes. The Telescope Goldfish was certainly known to the Chinese of the mid-eighteenth century, because on the scroll sent from Peking to Paris, in 1772, many fish with well-developed telescope eyes are depicted. The Telescope was probably known in Europe about the same time. Baster (1765) records a number of variations that he examined, and though he does not specially mention having seen a fish with telescope eyes, he does say that the eyes of goldfish are bulging 'unusually so in some specimens'. There is indirect evidence showing that Telescopes were among the fish imported into France about 1750. A century later the Telescope was well-known throughout Europe; and in 1872 Carbonnier wrote a paper entitled *Sur la Reproduction et le Développment du Poisson Télescope*, and other writers, English, French, and German, followed almost immediately. Indeed, between 1872 and 1900 the breed seems to have attracted to itself a considerable literature. There is, perhaps, nothing remarkable in all this; but what is remarkable is the fact that the Telescope was unknown in Japan until about seventy years ago. This is almost unbelievable, but it is authenticated by Mitsukuri who writes: 'Contrary to what is stated in many American and European books . . . it was brought to Japan at the end of the late Japan–China war—1894–1895.'

By the seventeenth century, goldfish of many different colours were being bred by the Chinese in large quantities. In the *Ti Ching Ching Wu Lüeh* there is an account of the Fish-weed Pool, dating from the second Chin Dynasty. In 1635, when the *Ti Ching Ching Wu Lüeh* was written, the pool was called, as it still may be, the Goldfish Pool. The authors, Liu Tung and Yü I-cheng, write: 'The pool is deep. The inhabitants have bounded it with a bank; willows droop over it. The yearly breeding of goldfish has been made a trade. The breeds of fish: the deep red are called Gold; the lustrous white are called Silver; snow-white bodies with ink spots, or red bodies with yellow spots, are called Tortoiseshell. If the fish is Gold, they prefer silver to encircle it; if the fish is Silver, they prefer gold to encircle it. And they distinguish between bands [tubes] and hoops: a band [tube], below the fins and above the tail, is that which encircles the body; a hoop, not reaching the fins, is that which encircles the tail. . . . White with vermilion on the brow is called Crane Pearl; vermilion body with white on the spine is called Silver Saddle; vermilion on the spine with seven white spots is called Seven Stars; white spine with eight red lines is called Eight Diagrams. . . . When the sky is about to rain the fish come up to the surface with a smacking sound, and the bottom of the water steams like hot soup. Every year after the Cereal Rain [mid-April] the fish are sold. The larger go to other pools or ponds, the smaller go to bowls or basins or glass jars, and can swim about actively all day.' In the *Pi Ch'uan Hua Ching* (*Mirror of Flowers*) published in 1688, Ch'ên Hao-tzu tells us of the many-coloured variegated fish bred in the Phoenix Well, east of the Fêng-Chên Kuan Temple, in the city of Hsin-fêng Hsien, in Kangsi; in the Yü Ch'üan[1] by the West Lake in Chekiang; in the Great Well, north of the Wu Shan, in the city of Hangchow; and in the Dragon Well which rises in Ch'ang-hua, near Hangchow.

From this time we may certainly date the calico or 'scaleless' breeds; for in the same *Pi Ch'uan Hua Ching* (1688) we read: 'Fish with three tails or five tails, without scales . . . are valued.' This is important; for the Shubunkin is virtually a 'scaleless' common goldfish and the Japanese claim that they were the first to produce the Shubunkin about the year 1900.

We do not intend to press this point, and if we are flatly contra-

---

[1] The Yü Ch'üan (Jade Spring) dates from the fifth century, though the buildings surrounding it are quite modern. An inscription overhanging the pond reads 'Garden of the Fishes' Joy' in allusion to Chuang-tzu's 'If one is not a fish he knows not a fish's joy.' It is one of the sights of modern Hangchow.

dicted we shall not argue, but the evidence seems to point to the fact that the Chinese knew of an early type of Shubunkin (even if they did not call it by that name) at least two hundred years before the Japanese fathered Shubunkins on an admiring world.

So far as we know, calico fish were unknown in Europe before the present century. The Shubunkin, in fact, was not introduced into Europe until after the First World War, though it was known in America before then. To Doctor H. B. Jones must be given the credit of introducing Shubunkins into Europe, but at about the same time L. B. Katterns lent a number of specimens to Arthur Derham, to breed from them in his heated ponds at Watford, and Katterns and Derham were the first to put Shubunkins on the British market in quantity. It appears that the Shubunkin was unknown in Germany until as recently as 1929. The fact would surprise us, if it were not that the history of goldfish is full of surprises.

The early years of the eighteenth century saw the preparation of the *T'u Shu*. It was published in 1726. A frontispiece to the sub-head 'Goldfish', though it has no scientific, and less artistic, merit, at least reveals that fish with no dorsal fin were known to the Chinese of the early eighteenth century. There is some evidence to show that fish with no dorsal fin were developed during the seventeenth century. The illustration of Goldfish in the *San Ts'ai T'u Hui* (*Illustrated Encyclopædia*), designed no later than 1607, reveals three fish all with a dorsal fin, though we must add the reservation that the fact that a certain characteristic is not depicted is not positive proof that it did not exist. Fish with no dorsal fin were known in Europe by the middle of the eighteenth century. Edwards refers to fish with 'little risings on the middle of the back in the place where the fins generally are', and he gives an illustration of such a fish which he drew from life in 1758;[1] and Baster mentions that the dorsal fin is often very short and often lacking altogether, and he, too, gives an illustration of a fish with no dorsal fin. Such fish are not mentioned in earlier European works. The fish with no dorsal fin illustrated in the *T'u Shu* and by Edwards and Baster are of the long-bodied type, but the true Egg-fish (round body and no dorsal fin) had certainly been brought by the Chinese of the eighteenth century to a high state of perfection. On the scroll sent from Peking to Paris, in

[1] George Edwards, op. cit., p. 85.

1772, several of the fish depicted are markedly round, fat, and short in body, and lack the dorsal fin.

Still in the eighteenth century we see the first glimmerings of the Celestial, though we would not care to dogmatize, because the Celestial has such a very obscure history. Indeed, the only certain thing about the Celestial is that it is not a Japanese fish. Mitsukuri, writing in 1904, says: 'This breed is not yet naturalized in Japan, having been imported from China only within the last two or three years.' Yet it was well known to the Chinese in 1882, because we have it on the word of Doctor A. C. Moule that he saw them in China in that year and they were then no novelty. But the Celestial seems to have been known in China a full century earlier; for at least one of the fish depicted on the scroll of 1772 has up-turned eyes and no dorsal fin. It is, however, by no means certain that the Celestial is a Chinese fish, and there is a well-known story that it originated in Korea and was held in veneration by the Koreans, who kept the fish in tanks in their temples and jealously guarded them from foreign collectors. We have been unable to trace any confirmation of this story, which has never yet been denied by a competent writer. On the whole, therefore, it is a story that every man may take as he will. If Celestial Goldfish have been noticed in tanks in Korean temples, their presence was probably not so much a matter of veneration, and connected as some writers have suggested, with the perpetual heavenward gaze, but rather connected with the Buddhist practice of earning merit by liberating living creatures; their liberation in sacred precincts being considered especially meritorious. The profane may argue that it is scarcely liberation to confine a fish in a temple-tank. One thing we can be sure about: if Celestials were originally confined to Korean temples, the popular story that the first specimens to leave Korea were obtained by stealth and bribery, and smuggled out of the country by an adventurous sailor, may be discredited. The evidence, such as it is, seems to show that the Celestial was first developed by the Chinese, or introduced into China from Korea, at some time in the middle of the eighteenth century. The fact that only one fish on the scroll shows the characteristics of the Celestial suggests that it was a rarity in China at the time; the more so as no attempt is made to distinguish Celestials from Telescopes. The *Mémoire* and scroll of 1772 throw a little light on the possible origin of the Celestial. Doctor Moule draws our attention to the fact that the *Mémoire* (though it admits that some Egg-fish have no dorsal fin) specifies as Egg-fish those fish that on the scroll are depicted with a dorsal fin, a short and fat body and normal eyes; and it specifies as Telescopes fish that on the scroll have protruberant eyes and even though they lack the dorsal fin. If this proves anything, surely it is that originally the name of 'Egg-fish' referred to a fish with an egg-like body unbroken by protuberant eyes, and that it is only since 1772 that no dorsal fin has become an invariable feature of the Egg-fish; while the Telescope with no dorsal fin developed into the Celestial.

The nineteenth century saw the decline of the Ch'ing, or Manchu Dynasty (1644–1912), and with foreign wars and internal rebellions there was a marked deterioration in the 'luxury' arts and crafts of China. Inevitably the development of new breeds passed out of the hands of the Chinese and mainly into the hands of the Japanese.

There need exist no doubt that the Lionhead was first developed by the Japanese in the nineteenth century. For though in the *K'ao P'an Yü Shih* of T'u Lung, published about 1590, there is a reference to fish with 'wrapped heads red', which might be taken as a reference to the Lionhead, Shisan C. Chen, who has made an exhaustive study of goldfish in China, writes: 'Lionhead Goldfish are rare and highly prized in China.'[1] Chen was writing in 1925. The Lionhead is such a grotesque fish, and grotesqueness is so much admired by the Chinese, that it is impossible to believe that if the Chinese of the sixteenth century had developed the Lionhead they would have allowed it almost to die out. On the contrary, by 1925 it would have been widespread in China. As contributory evidence it is to be noted that the Lionhead is not depicted on the scroll of 1772, nor is it mentioned in the accompanying *Mémoire*. It is known that the several types of Lionhead were all developed by the Japanese late in the nineteenth century. Ting-pong Koh gives it as his opinion that the Lionhead was probably first developed at some time during the early decades of that century. Koh gives no reason for his statement, but it is probably right, because the Oranda was first bred at Koriyama or Osaka about 1840, and was produced by crossing a Veiltail with a Lionhead.

By the end of the nineteenth century, and beginning of the

---

[1] Shisan C. Chen, op. cit., p. 45.

History

twentieth, a number of new breeds had been developed, mostly by crossing existing breeds. Few of these breeds are known to British aquarists, except by name, and they have little, if any history behind them. What little is known of them has been touched upon in the previous chapter, and only the Comet calls for more than a passing mention.

The Comet is usually regarded as an American fish, developed in the early 1880's. The credit for developing it is sometimes given to the Government Fishery at Washington, and sometimes to Hugo Mulertt, a private breeder. But in his book, *The Goldfish and its Systematic Culture* (1883), Mulertt actually catalogues the Comet as a Japanese breed. On the other hand, Kishinouye, Matsubara, Mitsukuri, Watase, and in fact all the contemporary Japanese writers, make no claim to the Comet. It is now generally accepted that at some time between 1880 and 1883 the Americans developed the Comet from imported Japanese stock, and that Mulertt, despite his tacit denial, was the first to put Comets on the market in quantity. Be that as it may, the Comet is nothing out of the ordinary, and it is worth noting that as early as 1834 Valenciennes[1] mentions a fish that he received from Macao, near Hong Kong, and his description of it shows that it was virtually a Comet.

From all that we have written, it will be seen that our knowledge of the history of goldfish is limited. Yet it is not altogether an incoherent story, and we doubt whether the history of any other animal—wild or domestic—can claim so complete a record as that of the goldfish. With a few gaps here and there it has, after all, a documented pedigree taking us back almost exactly 1,000 years. For that alone it merits our respect, if only because it is more than most of us can boast for ourselves.

[1] Cuvier and Valenciennes, op. cit., p. 72.

Chapter IV

ENVIRONMENT

Tout se fit ombre et aquarium ardent.

RIMBAUD, 'Bottom' from *Les Illuminations*

It may seem that this chapter is in its wrong place. Surely, it will be argued, before a person wants to know how to look after goldfish he must buy them and carry them home; therefore this chapter should follow, not precede, the chapter on selecting and transporting goldfish. In fact, this chapter is in its right place because the high rate of mortality among goldfish is mainly due to the fact that far too many people who take a sudden liking to a goldfish in the window of a pet-shop, buy it, take it home, and then have no notion of what to do with it. We have recollections of our own first experience with goldfish. We bought a couple from a departmental store, we took them home in a small bowl, we transferred them to a larger bowl, and there we left them. We kept them in a dark corner of the room, we changed the water frequently and made no attempt to equalize the temperatures of the water, we fed the fish at irregular intervals and with unsuitable food; in fact we did everything that we should not have done and left undone all those things that we should have done. That the fish did not die in a matter of weeks, but actually lived for several years, is a tribute to the hardiness of the species but no credit to us.

To begin with the water, the most important matter so far as fish are concerned.

Except that some water is freshwater, some hard, some soft, and that some water is salt water, to the ordinary man water is just water. To the chemist, water is a combination of hydrogen and oxygen (H_2O) and almost always contains impurities. Some of these impurities are harmless to goldfish, but others are harmful to them, and, because they are, the water in an aquarium or pond is a matter of life and death.

Environment

The best water with which to fill an aquarium or pond is water drawn from a natural pond or stream; but great care must still be exercised, because water running over a black and oily bottom is invariably toxic, and, if the water is drawn from a stagnant pond that is overhung by trees, it may be dangerous; the leaves of some trees, notably laburnum, holly, and rhododendron, are poisonous to fish. The safest course is to draw water only from a pond or stream in which fish are known to be living. Failing this, rain-water drawn from a well-established water-butt or tank should be used. Here again, however, a note of warning must be sounded; for though rain-water, as it is formed in the upper regions of the atmosphere, is the purest that nature supplies, it has a strong affinity for organic impurities, so that rain-water in towns is usually polluted with smoke and noxious gases, and must, therefore, be regarded with suspicion. The importance of water was appreciated three and a half centuries ago; in *The Book of Vermilion Fish* (1596), Chang Ch'ien-tê writes: 'As for the water, to take running water from a river or lake is best, and clear cold well water is next to it. What must not be used is water from the canals in the city.'

It is inadvisable to use water drawn direct from the tap; for, apart from harmful chemicals, nearly always tap-water is alkaline. If force of circumstances compels the aquarist to use water from a tap, the water may either be matured, by allowing it to stand for several days outdoors or it may be boiled, allowed to cool, and then aerated. Water that has been boiled loses its mineral salts. They may be replaced by adding to every gallon of water a level teaspoonful of cooking salt, sea-salt, rock-salt, or one of the proprietory 'water rectifiers'.

Tap-water is frequently chlorinated, but this need not trouble the aquarist; for tests have shown that goldfish are affected only if they are continuously exposed to chlorine in a concentration as strong as two parts in ten million (though half this strength is sufficient to destroy the eggs of fishes) and water is rarely, if ever, chlorinated to this extent. Nevertheless, we advise the removal of as much chlorine as possible. A simple and effective way to de-chlorinate water is to add one grain (by weight) of sodium thio-sulphate (photographic hypo) to every gallon of water. The chemical should be dissolved in the water before the water is poured into the aquarium or pond.

Broadly speaking, freshwater may be either neutral, acid, or alkaline. The neutrality of water, or its degree of acidity or alkalinity, is known as its pH (potential hydrogen) value. Much mystery has been made about the pH value of water, but, in reality, there is nothing very mysterious about it, nor is the subject so complicated as some would have us believe. Tusting Cocking defines the pH value as 'a number used to express the concentration of ionized hydrogen in an aqueous fluid and is thus indicative of the reaction of that fluid, that is, the neutrality or the degree of acidity or alkalinity. According to the theory of electrolytic dissociation all liquids of which water is a constituent contain free, positively charged hydrogen (H+) ions and negatively charged hydroxyl (OH—) ions. When the numbers of these two ions present in a liquid are exactly balanced the liquid is said to be neutral. If there be an excess of hydrogen (H+) ions the liquid is acid, and conversely if the hydroxyl (OH—) ions be in excess, it is alkaline.' Absolute neutrality has a pH value of 7·07 (usually taken as 7·0). The addition of acid increases the H ion concentration, consequently the pH of all acid solutions is less than 7·07. The addition of alkali increases the concentration of the OH ions, and decreases that of the H ions, so that the pH of all alkaline solutions is greater than 7·07. The range of pH values extends about equally on each side of 7·07; for the complete range of pH values forms a graduated scale from about − 0·3 to 14·5.

It is very easy to determine the pH value of the water in an aquarium or pond. B.D.H. '6676' Indicator, or Johnson's Comparator Test Papers, may be used: the pH of the water being indicated by certain colour changes. But though in theory it is easy enough—perhaps too easy—to test water for pH value, in practice complications arise. Water extracts alkali from glass and cement, with a consequent rise in the pH value of the water in a new aquarium or pond; and even in an old aquarium or pond, from which the alkali from the glass and cement has for long been extracted, it has to be taken into consideration that since water at a low temperature is saturated with carbon dioxide—and some of this is lost as the temperature rises—there is a resulting increase in the pH value of the water. Finally, there is always a greater acid content in the morning than at the end of the day after the plants have had the opportunity to absorb the carbon dioxide.

Testing water for pH value, therefore, is rather more trouble than it is worth. Moreover, it is pointless unless the aquarist intends to alter the pH artificially, and this raises further complications. At one time it was thought that goldfish throve best in alkaline water, and lumps of plaster of Paris, or chalk, were placed in aquaria and ponds in order to keep the water alkaline. This has for long been proved a fallacy. The very reverse is the case: goldfish thrive best in water that has a slightly acid reaction, and a pH value of 6·6 or 6·8 is about right. Although the pH value of water may be altered artificially, by the addition of an acid or an alkali, we do not recommend the practice. It has to be done very carefully, because it is unwise to subject a goldfish to a pH change of more than four-tenths on the scale per day, taken in two steps of two-tenths each. And then, however careful the aquarist may be, it is our experience that he produces only a tank full of chemicals. The best that we will say is that most tap-water is alkaline, and it may be improved by straining it through peat. Water that is too acid may be improved by adding a tablespoonful of powdered egg-shell to every 10 gallons of water.

Undue significance must not be attached to the pH value of water, and experienced aquarists do not greatly trouble themselves about it. They take the precaution to fill their aquaria and ponds with safe water, and replace water lost by evaporation with fresh water drawn from the same original source. For the rest, they judge the quality of water more by eye than by any chemical test. Good water should be of a greenish-amber tint, and have a beautiful crystal-clarity that is very different from new clear water drawn from a tap, and yet so difficult to describe. Unhealthy water may be recognized by its faint blueish tinge and oily clarity: such water lacks essential mineral salts and should be changed at once. Writers on aquarium-management are very fond of recording that 'old water is best for goldfish'. This may or may not be true. Water that has been standing for a long time is not necessarily healthy water, and, conversely, the fact that water has not been standing for long does not necessarily mean that it is unhealthy water. If there are few fish in a large aquarium, plenty of plant-life and sufficient light, that aquarium is biologically balanced and the water may be termed 'old' even though it may have been drawn from the tap only a few weeks before; but if the aquarium is overcrowded with fish, insufficiently planted, and receiving too little light, the fish will not thrive, and the water will be unhealthy even though it may have been standing for years. In a word, it is not a case of the water being old or new in length of time, but of its being healthy or unhealthy.

Very often the water will become cloudy soon after the aquarium or pond has been filled. This should not be taken as a sign that the water is unhealthy. In the process of maturing many changes in the appearance of water occur. At the first change the water looks opaque: subsequently it becomes green. The opaqueness is due to chemical change; the greenness to the presence of algae (most freshwater algae are green) to the development of which new water, because it is usually alkaline, is very susceptible. Infusoria and rotifers also bring about a cloudy appearance of the water. These changes do not always take place in an aquarium, but they always occur in a pond; for algae are present in all waters, and the spores are carried by the wind to other waters. So long as these conditions do not go too far they are to be welcomed. The objection to algae is that they are unsightly. There are many ways of controlling them artificially, but we recommend none. Other difficulties apart, artificial control in only a temporary expedient, and the trouble will return after a time. Algae flourish best in water that is hard and alkaline and where there is an excess of light. Nature has her remedy, and, if the aquarium or pond is well stocked with aquatic plants, the trouble will rectify itself in time; the water will become acid, and the plants will grow and reduce the light on which the algae depend for existence. Fish, aquatic plants, bacteria, algae, dissolved salts, and the like, are all essential to a mature aquarium, but it takes some considerable time to establish itself and the water to obtain that crystal-clarity of which we have already spoken. Our advice, therefore, is to leave Nature to clear the water—this she will do in her own way and time—though assistance may be given by removing an excess of sediment, and reducing the amount of food given to the fish.

One particularly obnoxious form of algal growth, known as blue-green algae, sometimes appears in an aquarium, and should be controlled; for it has a pungent and unpleasant odour, develops rapidly, and covers the plants and surface of the water with a slimy growth. The most satisfactory method of control is to dissolve 2 grains (by weight) of copper sulphate in 4 ounces of water,

V. The Veiltail Goldfish is generally considered the most graceful of the fancy breeds. In the best specimens the dorsal fin is high, the caudal fin and anal fin are paired; the pectoral and ventral fins are elongated.

VI. The Moor is a variant of the Veiltail but has protuberant eyes and is all-black in colour (*see* Plate IX). The best specimens are a soft velvety black with no metallic reflections.

VII. The Oranda is a variant of the Veiltail (*see* Plate V) with a dermal overgrowth on the head (bramble-head).

VIII. The Pompon is a breed in which the narial septa, which divide the two nostrils, are abnormally developed into bunches of fleshy lobes (*see* p. 67).

add a teaspoonful of the solution to every gallon[1] of water (first removing the fish and snails) and allow to stand for twenty-four hours. The aquarium may then be emptied, refilled, and the fish and snails returned. Copper sulphate at this concentration (approximately one part in two million) will not harm the higher plants.

In the early spring the clouding of water in a mature pond is quite natural; during the winter months many things have happened to bring about this result. Varying temperatures, the death of minute animal-life, the decaying of plant life, and so on, have all played a part in making the pond unattractive to the eye. Normally there is no need to worry; with better weather and a more genial temperature the water will soon clear. But if the water in a mature pond or aquarium gradually takes on a thick turbid appearance—just as though a little milk had been poured into the water—and if a faint but unpleasant smell is detected, the water should be changed at once. If deaths have not already occurred they may be expected at any moment. It is a common practice among inexperienced aquarists (and some experienced ones) to give fish much more food than is necessary for their immediate wants. Pieces of worm, dead flies, dried foods, and the like, are thrown into the water regardless of the fact that the fish cannot eat every morsel. That which is not eaten decomposes and putrifies the water. The turbidity of the water is due to fungoid growths of a whitish nature, which are the outcome of an exuberance of decomposing nitrogenous organic matter. The condition is popularly called 'sour water'. It may occur at any time of the year, but it is most likely to occur in the summer months when decomposition is hastened by warmth. But no matter at what time of the year the condition arises, there is no alternative except to disinfect the aquarium or pond (see page 123), refill with fresh water, and begin again; a partial change of water is useless.

Great play has been made with the expressions 'balanced aquarium' and 'balanced pond'. Strictly, however, the 'balanced' aquarium or pond is an unattainable ideal. It implies an aquarium or pond in which all the inhabitants are interdependent on each other, as they are in a natural stretch of water, and it takes very little thought to understand that this result cannot be achieved in

---

[1] To determine the number of gallons of water in a rectangular or square container, the following formula may be used: Multiply the length by the width by the depth in feet, and the product by 6¼.

an aquarium or man-made garden-pond. In a loose sense, however, the 'balanced aquarium' and 'balanced pond' are attainable, by not overcrowding the fish, by stocking with plenty of plants, and by arranging for the aquarium or pond to get sufficient light. In this way we are imitating Nature, even if we have to help her by feeding the fish, pruning the plants, and removing from time to time much of the sediment that collects on the bottom.

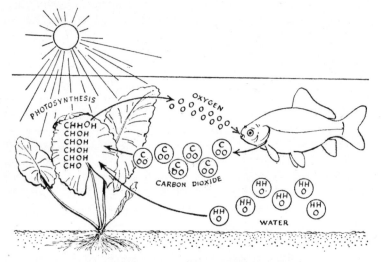

Fig. 24. THE PRINCIPLE OF 'BALANCE'
The respiratory exchange between plants and fishes.
Under the stimulus of light (photosynthesis) carbon dioxide and water are built by the plant into carbohydrate. Unwanted oxygen is liberated into the water to be used by the fish.

The principle of 'balance' is intimately connected with the oxygen requirements of the fish. Expressed in a few words, the representatives of the animal kingdom inhale oxygen and exhale carbon dioxide, and if there were no means of replacing the used oxygen, in the course of time all animal life would die; for no animal can live without oxygen. Nature, therefore, has provided a remedy, and, under the influence of light, the representatives of the vegetable kingdom take in carbon dioxide through their leaves (using carbon to build up their green tissues and fibres) and liberate oxygen. Thus, the oxygen-breathing animals cannot live without the aquatic plants, the aquatic plants cannot flourish without the oxygen-breathing animals, and neither can live nor flourish without light. The process is known as photosynthesis: it is of fundamental importance.

Yet no matter how many plants there may be in an aquarium or pond, they alone will not supply sufficient oxygen to support the animals, and oxygen must be drawn from the air that comes into contact with the surface of the water. An experiment, which need not be repeated, shows that a 2-in. goldfish will live for months in a soup-plate holding less than a pint of water, but the same fish will die in a matter of hours if it is placed in a narrow-necked bottle holding a quart of water. The explanation is that in a bottle the surface of water exposed to the air is so small that the water cannot absorb all the oxygen that a fish requires, but in a soup-plate nearly all the water is in contact with the air.

It is obvious, therefore, that the shape of the aquarium or pond in which goldfish are kept is of great importance to them. A vessel 12 in. long, 8 in. wide, and 24 in. deep holds exactly the same amount of water as a vessel 24 in. long, 8 in. wide, and 12 in. deep, but as an aquarium for goldfish the latter vessel is doubly to be preferred to the former because it exposes to the air twice the surface area of water. It is exactly the same with a pond. A pond built in the shape of a saucer will hold in comfort many more fish than one built in the shape of a cup, even though a pond built in the shape of a cup may hold three or four times the amount of water than one built in the shape of a saucer.

The general rule is to allow 24 square in. of surface-area to every inch of goldfish, excluding the caudal fin. Thus, an aquarium with a surface measurement of 24 in. by 12 in. (a reasonable size for an aquarium) will hold, as an example, six 2-in. fish or four 3-in. fish; and a pond with a surface measurement of 72 in. by 48 in. (6 ft. by 4 ft. is a reasonable size for a formal pond) will hold, for example, thirty-six 4-in. fish. An experienced aquarist can actually keep more fish in a confined space than a novice, because he knows better how to maintain good conditions, but normally the rule should never be broken, and, indeed, it is better to keep well within the limit imposed, to allow for the growth of the fish. Moreover, the rule applies only to an established aquarium or pond, and it is best to begin with only a few fish and gradually increase the number. It is inadvisable to keep goldfish in an aquarium with a surface-area of less than 160 square in., and even this is a minimum, confining the aquarist to keeping no more than two small fish. We have already condemned the round glass bowl as a receptacle in which to keep goldfish: we insist sternly that however well cared for it involves some cruelty because the fish can never get sufficient oxygen.

The depth of the aquarium or pond is of no importance, except that it should never be so shallow nor so deep that the aquatic plants fail to grow properly. An aquarium for goldfish may be anything from 9 to 15 in. deep, in proportion to its superficies. A pond should be about 24 in. deep; for it is unsafe to winter goldfish outdoors in water less than 18 in. deep, and 24 in. gives a margin of safety. For goldfish a pond deeper than 24 in. is not necessary in a temperate climate.

After the water and the oxygen requirements of the fish, the most important consideration is the plants. Aquatic plants have many functions to fulfil. They oxygenate the water, they absorb impurities, they give shade to the fish, they are decorative, and they furnish a spawning-ground and afford cover for fry.

The number of aquatic plants available reaches many thousands. Frances Perry catalogues between 200 and 300 different species and varieties of water-lily alone; and there are thousands of submerged species, floating species and marginal species. We cannot do more, therefore, than list under suitable headings a few of the better-known plants, but we have taken care to mention only those plants that can be obtained from British native waters or from horticulturists who specialize in the cultivation of aquatic plants.

SUBMERGED PLANTS (*cold-water aquarium*)
Acorus gramineus var. *pusillus*—Dwarf Rush.
Cabomba caroliniana—Fanwort.
Ceratophyllum demersum—Hornwort.
Elodea densa.
Eleocharis acicularis—Hair Grass.
Fontinalis species—Willow Moss.
Lagarosiphon major (*Elodea crispa*).
Ludwigia Mullertii.
L. palustris.—Water Purslane.
Myriophyllum verticillatum—Water Milfoil.
Ranunculus species—Water Crowfoot.

Sagittaria species.
Vallisneria spiralis—Tape Grass.
V. spiralis 'torta' variety.
Vallisneria gigantea—Giant Tape Grass and the variety of
  V. spiralis known as 'marmorata' may be planted if the
  aquarium is a large one.

FLOATING PLANTS (*cold-water aquarium*)
  Azolla caroliniana—Fairy Moss.
  Hydrocharis Morsus-ranae—Frog Bit.
  Lemna species—Duckweek.
  Riccia fluitans—Crystalwort.
  Small specimens of *Stratiotes aloides*—Water Soldier—may be
  placed in the aquarium, but it is not an ideal subject for
  aquarium culture.
  Eichhornia crassipes—Water Hyacinth—may be cultivated
  during the summer months if the aquarium is a large
  one.

All the above are suitable for an unheated aquarium. If the temperature of the water never falls much below 65° F., a selection
may be made from the following plants:

SUBMERGED PLANTS (*heated aquarium*)
  Acorus gramineus var. *pusillus*—Dwarf Rush.
  Cabomba caroliniana—Fanwort.
  Ceratophyllum demersum—Hornwort.
  Ceratopteris thalictroides—Underwater Fern.
  Cryptocoryne species—Water Trumpet.
  Elodea densa.
  Eleocharis acicularis—Hair Grass.
  Ludwigia Mullertii.
  Marsilea quadrifolia—Four-leaved Clover.
  Myriophyllum hippuroides—Water Milfoil.
  M. pinnatum.
  Sagittaria species.
  Vallisneria spiralis—Tape Grass.
  V. spiralis 'torta' variety.
  Echinodorus intermedius—Amazon Sword Plant—*Vallisneria
  gigantea*—Giant Tape Grass, and the variety of *V. spiralis*

The Goldfish

known as 'marmorata' may be planted if the aquarium is a large one.

FLOATING PLANTS (*heated aquarium*)
Azolla caroliniana—Fairy Moss.
Ceratopteris pteridiodes—Floating Fern.
Lemna species—Duckweed.
Riccia fluitans—Crystalwort.
Salvinia species.
Eichhornia crassipes—Water Hyacinth—may be cultivated if the aquarium is a large one.

Although most of these plants will flourish well in an average aquarium, it must be borne in mind that the light, the planting medium, the chemical content of the local water, and the like, play a big part in determining which plants shall flourish and which shall not. The novice-aquarist, therefore should not be disappointed if he finds that some plants do not flourish. Some experimentation is necessary for the aquarist to find out which plants will grow best in his aquarium.

It is better to overplant than underplant an aquarium. As a start we recommend one plant for every 4 square in. of bottom-area of the aquarium. This is the irreducible minimum, and some aquarists recommend as many as one plant for every square inch of bottom-area. The rule is only very general, and does not include small clumps of decorative plants like *Fontinalis* and *Eleocharis*. Even the novice-aquarist will appreciate that a few clumps of *Eleocharis*, each containing about thirty plants, are insufficient to manage the organic affairs of a large aquarium. Each clump must be counted as one plant only. There is one slight danger in overplanting an aquarium: during hours of darkness the plants give off carbon dioxide (which asphyxiates fish) instead of oxygen. It follows, therefore, that an excess of plant life in an aquarium can be harmful to fish, even if it does not kill them. On the whole we suggest that the aquarist should begin by stocking the aquarium with a minimum of one plant for every 4 square in. of bottom-area and be prepared to add more plants later if the fish, by constantly rising to the surface of the water, show that there is not enough plant-life to oxygenate the water sufficiently; or if conditions show that there is not enough plant life to keep the water healthy. Equally, the aquarist must be prepared to reduce the number of plants (see page 122), but this is very unlikely if the original planting does not exceed one plant for every 4 square in. of bottom-area, and the aquarium is well lit during the day-time.

The function of floating plants is to provide shade for the fish. They do not need to be planted: they float on the surface of the water and derive their nourishment from the water without taking root.

The function of submerged plants is to oxygenate the water, absorb impurities, and decorate the aquarium. Those that have roots are planted by spreading out the roots and pressing the root into the planting medium. If the plant has a crown it should be given a gentle pull, so as to leave the crown resting on the top of the planting medium; the plant will not flourish if the crown is buried. Plants that are propagated as cuttings should be planted by gently pushing about an inch of the stem (it is a mistake to plant too deeply) into the planting medium. Each plant should be planted separately (not a number tied together in a bunch) to allow the free circulation of water about the roots. If a plant rides to the surface it may be held in place by attaching it to a stone with a short length of bass, or by attaching to it a small strip of lead. But only soft lead should be used for this purpose; in reasonable quantities it is harmless to goldfish, and this is more than can be said for some metals. When the plants have been set in position, the planting medium should be raked over. A small toasting-fork is ideal for this purpose.

Before planting, all plants should be picked over, dead leaves removed, and the plant thoroughly examined for undesirable insects and eggs. It is a wise precaution to disinfect all plants (no matter from what source they have been obtained) for about a quarter of an hour in a solution of slaked lime diluted one part to six parts plain water. Finally, the plants should be well rinsed in running water.

If a layer of peat-moss or peat-mould, or a thin layer of fallen oak or beech leaves, has been placed under the planting medium, nothing further in the way of manure for the plants is necessary, but if this has not been done a small pellet of dried rabbit's or guinea-pig's excreta may be inserted into the planting medium at the root of each plant. Not that we consider this method of fertilizing plants necessary; for it is an established fact that the excrement of the fish fertilizes the plants. For the same reason we see no advantage in placing a layer of loam under the planting medium. Some aquarists approve of it, and it may be all right with some species, but goldfish do a lot of rooting in the planting medium, and if they expose the loam trouble nearly always follows in the confined space of an aquarium.

It need occasion the aquarist no surprise if some of the leaves of the plants die soon after planting. It is quite a usual occurrence and, if the planting has been properly done, and if the aquarium is receiving sufficient light, new leaves will soon appear.

No animal life should be introduced into an aquarium until about two or three weeks after planting, in order to give the plants time to take root. It is a wise precaution, immediately before introducing the goldfish, to give each plant a gentle pull to ensure that it has taken firm root. It sometimes happens that the root of a plant dies, but the leaves continue to derive nourishment from the water, so that the plant is actually dead though it has the outward appearance of being healthy. In a garden a dead plant is merely unsightly, but in the confined space of an aquarium it is a danger to the fish, since it pollutes the water.

As to whether an aquarium should be planted when it is empty, partly filled, or full, this is largely a matter for the convenience of the individual aquarist. For ourselves we prefer to plant when the aquarium is full, or nearly so, because only in this way is it possible to ensure that the desired effect is being obtained. To plant an aquarium that is full it is not necessary to work up to the elbows in water; indeed, by using a stick about 18 in. long with a rounded notch cut in one end (or, better still, two such sticks, one in each hand) it is hardly necessary to wet the hands. The plant is held in the notch of one stick, while the other stick presses the stem, or roots, of the plant into the planting medium which is then raked over. If the planting is done when the aquarium is empty, a piece of wet paper should be laid over that part of the aquarium immediately after it has been planted, to prevent the plants from drying up.

For the pond the most important plant is the water-lily, 'The Queen of the Water-garden'. There is a very wide range of choice, but it is not enough to choose a water-lily merely because the colour of the flower, or the shape of its petals, appeals to the aquarist. It is essential to select only those water-lilies that grow in the same depth of water as that of the aquarist's pond. For a water-lily accustomed to grow in water 3 ft. deep will not grow well in water 2 ft. deep; and, by the same token, a water-lily accustomed to grow in water 2 ft. deep will not grow well in water 3 ft. deep. Furthermore, the aquarist must take into account the surface-area of the pond; for every plant must have room to develop naturally, and be given ample room to spread itself to the best advantage. Nothing looks worse than a pond that is over-crowded with the leaves of water-lilies. As a general rule a water-lily planted in water from 6 to 12 in. deep will cover a surface-area of 1½ to 2 square ft.; in water from 12 to 18 in. deep, a surface-area or 4 square ft.; in water from 18 to 24 in. deep, a surface-area of 5 to 6 square ft.; and in water about 36 in. deep, a surface-area of 8 to 10 square ft. In order to assist the aquarist in making a choice, we have catalogued a number of wild and cultivated water-lilies, according to the best depth of water. The colour in parentheses is that of the flower.

WATER FROM 6 IN. TO 12 IN. DEEP

Nymphaea tetragona (snow-white).
Aurora (copper-yellow, changing to deep orange-salmon, and finally to ruby-red).
Pygmaea Helvola (sulphur-yellow).
Seignoureti (buff-yellow, shaded pink and orange-red).

WATER FROM 12 IN. TO 18 IN. DEEP

Nymphaea odorata (white).
Albatross (white).
Esmeralda (rose-white, heavily mottled and striped deep rose).
Phoebus (yellow, striped red passing to copper-red).
Solfatare (yellow, flushed rose).
Sultan (cherry-red, faintly stained white).
Vesuve (amaranth-red).

WATER FROM 18 IN. TO 24 IN. DEEP

Darwin (red, spotted and stained white).
Fabiola (rich pink).
Formosa (rose pink, passing to deep rose with age).
Galatée (soft rose, spotted and splashed white).
Gloriosa (bright currant-red).

Masaniello (pale rose-pink, passing to deep rose-pink with
age).
Murillo (deep rose-red).
Newton (rose-crimson).
Rose Nymphe (pale pink).
William Doogue (delicate pink, passing to white with age).

WATER FROM 24 IN. TO 36 IN. DEEP
Nuphar lutea (yellow).
N. pumila (yellow).

WATER 36 IN. DEEP
Nymphaea alba (white).
Colossea (flesh, passing to white with age).
Picciola (amaranth-crimson).
Virginalis (snow-white).

Before planting, the dead leaves and broken foliage should be
removed and the roots (not to be confused with the rootstock)
should be trimmed.

The best method of planting a water-lily, as well as the other
deep-growing submerged plants, is direct in the planting medium.
The pond should be drained, the plants weighted with pieces of
lead, or by being tied to stones with bass, and set directly in the
planting medium. This should then be rammed down to prevent
it from rising when the water is added. The Odorata and Tuberosa
groups of water-lilies have long fleshy rhizomes, and these should
be set under about an inch of planting medium with the crown
just exposed. The Marliacea group have large rounded tubers and
fibrous roots, and they should be set vertically with the roots
spread out and the crown above the planting medium. The Lay-
dekeri group, as well as many others that flourish in shallow water,
have a rootstock not unlike the Marliacea, but smaller, and it is
best to set them in a semi-horizontal position with the crown just
exposed.

Apart from water-lilies and their allies, the following plants are
all suitable for planting in the deep part of a pond:

Potamogeton species—Pondweed.
Ranunculus species—Water Crowfoot.
Vallisneria gigantea—Giant Tape Grass.
V. spiralis 'marmorata' variety.

Environment

When the deep part of the pond has been planted the pond is ready to be filled (see page 118). It is unwise to fill the pond immediately, because the shock of 18 in. or more of cold water will not help the plants, already suffering from being transplanted while active. The water should be run in gradually. At first, only sufficient to cover the crowns of the plants, and this should be left for two or three days. A little more water may then be added, and so on, until the pond is full. It may take a few weeks but the extra trouble involved is worth the delay because it makes for better growth of the plants.

When the deep part of the pond has been planted, and the pond has been completely filled with water, the aquarist may turn his attention to planting the surrounding ledge with submerged plants. A selection may be made from the following list:

Callitriche species—Starwort.
Ceratophyllum demersum—Hornwort.
Elodea canadensis—Canadian Water Weed.
Hottonia palustris—Water Violet.
Lagarosiphon major (*Elodea crispa*).
Myriophyllum spicatum—Water Milfoil.
Potamogeton species—Pondweed.
Ranunculus species—Water Crowfoot.
Sagittaria species.
Elodea densa and *Vallisneria spiralis*—Tape Grass, may be
   planted if the pond is in a sheltered position.

To be successful a pond must be well stocked with submerged plants. It is these that do much to aerate the water, and more to keep the water pure. Natural ponds in which fish are living are nearly always packed with submerged plants. Aquarists can hardly do better than imitate nature, but very few do. We recommend that the pond should be planted with a minimum of twenty plants for every square foot of its bottom-area, and the aquarist should be prepared to increase the number of plants if, later, it is found that the plant-life is insufficient to keep the water healthy. If it is pointed out that this is only about half the number of plants that we recommend for stocking an aquarium, the reason is that ponds vary very much more than aquaria, and it is to be remembered that in a pond much is done by the marginal plants to absorb impurities, and by the wind and rain to keep the water re-oxygenated and refreshed. The submerged plants are, of course, planted in exactly the same way as we have described for planting in an aquarium.

The planting of sub-aquatics in the surrounding ledge and bog garden—if one is attached to the pond—follows. The plants should be chosen with some care. It is important that they should bear some relation to the size and nature of the pond and its surroundings. If the pond is a large one, plants of dignity should be chosen, since small plants would appear insignificant. In the same way, if the pond is a small one, it is out of place to plant large showy plants which would serve only to dwarf the pond. As a general rule the planting of sub-aquatics should not be overdone; the least overcrowding will spoil an otherwise good effect, and it is best to plant in drifts, since isolated plants do not look well. Even if the pond is a large one, a better effect is obtained by keeping to a few outstanding species than making some attempt to display a larger number of different species. Grasses, reeds, and rushes always look well; particularly so if they are grown in conjunction with irises. If the pond is a formal one their tall erect growth contrasts well with the large floating pads of the water-lilies, and if the pond is an informal one, they echo what is found in nature. For a start only a few sub-aquatics should be planted (just enough to take off the bareness of the pond) because if the plants do not flourish other species will have to be tried, and if the plants flourish they will have to be thinned out later. Either way, therefore, heavy planting at the start is a pointless waste of time and money. We remain conscious of the fact of the many differences in individual tastes, but would add that irises, marsh marigolds, and some of the more decorative grasses, should find a place around the margins of every pond; and, of course, it is desirable to choose plants with different flowering seasons. Actually there is not much latitude in this respect, since few aquatic plants flower before March or after September, but such latitude as there is should be taken advantage of. For marginal planting we suggest a selection from the following lists.

For SHALLOW WATER

 Alisma Plantago-aquatica (*Plantago*)—Great Water Plantain.
  (Rose flowers. Height 2–3 ft.)
 Cladium Mariscus (*germanicus*)—Twig Rush.
  (Light brown spikelets. Height 5–6 ft.)

Cotula coronopifolia—Brass Button.
  (Golden yellow flowers. Height 9 in.)
Glyceria aquatica—Reed Manna Grass.
  (Greenish spikelets. Height 4–6 ft.)
G. aquatica 'variegata'.
  (Pink, yellow, and green, striped foliage. Height $1\frac{1}{2}$–2 ft.)
Gratiola officinalis—Hedge Hyssop.
  (Bright blue flowers. Height 9 in.)
Iris Pseudacorus—Yellow Water Flag.
  (Golden yellow flowers. June–July. Height 3–5 ft.)
Nesaea verticillata (*Decodon verticillatus*)—Swamp Loose-strife.
  (Purple flowers. Height 3 ft.)
Orontium aquaticum—Golden Club.
  (Yellow flowers. Mid-summer. Height $1\frac{1}{2}$–2 ft.)
Pontederia cordata—Pickerel Weed.
  (Pale blue, spotted green flowers. Summer. Height $1\frac{1}{2}$–2 ft.)
Preslia cervina (*Mentha punctata*).
  (Lavender-blue flowers. Height 15 in.)
Rumex Hydrolapathum—Great Water Dock.
  (Dark green leaves reddening with age. Height 4–6 ft.)
Sagittaria macrophylla.
  (White flowers. Mid-summer. Height 3 ft.)
S. sagittifolia—Common Arrowhead.
  (White flowers. Mid-summer. Height $1\frac{1}{2}$ ft.)
S. sagittifolia 'japonica'.
  (White flowers. Mid-summer. Height $2\frac{1}{2}$ ft.)
Scirpus lacustris—Bulrush.
  (Chocolate-brown umbels. Height 3–8 ft.)
S. Tabernaemontani var. *zebrinus* (*Juncus zebrinus*)—Zebra Rush.
  (White, green, tranversely barred culms. Height 5 ft.)
Scutellaria galericulata—Skull Cap.
  (Pale blue or lavender flowers. Height 15 in.)
Stachys palustris—Woundwort.
  (Pale purple flowers. Early summer. Height 2–4 ft.)
Typha latifolia—Great Reed Mace.
  (Dark chocolate-brown pistillates. Height 6–8 ft.)

For the bog-garden

Anagallis tenella—Bog Pimpernel.
  (Bright pink flowers. Summer. Height 3 in.)

Anemone rivularis.
  (Snow-white flowers. June. Height 2 ft.)
Dodecatheon Meadia—American Cowslip.
  (Light purple flowers. March–April. Height 1–1½ ft.)
Eupatorium cannabinum—Hemp Agrimony.
  (Pale purple or lilac flowers. July-August. Height 3–6 ft.)
Gaultheria procumbens—Partridge Berry.
  (White flowers followed by scarlet berries. Height 6 in.)
Gunnera manicata (*brasiliensis*)—Prickly Rhubarb.
  (Rich green flowers. Height 7–8 ft.)
Hosta undulata (*Funkia lancifolia* var. *undulata*)—Plantain Lily.
  (Pale lavender flowers. August–September. Height 1½ ft.)
Osmunda Claytoniana—Clayton's Flowering Fern.
  (Vivid green fronds. Height 3 ft.)
O. Regalis—Royal Fern.
  (Pale green fronds changing to deep russet in autumn. Height 4–5 ft.)
Physostegia virginiana (*virginica*)—False Dragon Head.
  (Rose-pink flowers. July–September. Height 4 ft.)
Pinguicula grandiflora—Irish Bog Violet.
  (Mauve-violet flowers. Spring. Height 6 in.)
P. vulgaris—Labrador Violet.
  (Pale violet. May–July. Height 6 in.)
Primula Florindae—Giant Cowslip.
  Sulphur-yellow flowers. July–August. Height 3 ft.)
P. sikkimensis—Himalayan Cowslip.
  (Pale yellow flowers. June–July. Height 2 ft.)
Sarracenia flava—Trumpet-leaf.
  (Canary-yellow flowers and yellow-green trumpets. May–June. Height 2 ft.)
Viola blanda—Sweet White Violet.
  (White flowers veined lilac. May. Height 5 in.)
V. canina—Dog Violet.
  (Blue flowers. April. Height 4 in.)
Zantedeschia aethiopica (*Calla aethiopica*)—Arum Lily.
  (White flowers with golden spadices. April-June. Height 2–3 ft.)

FOR SHALLOW WATER AND THE BOG GARDEN
  Acorus Calamus—Sweet Flag.

(Greenish-yellow flowers. June–July. Height 3–4 ft.)
Butomus umbellatus—Flowering Rush.
(Pink or purple flowers. June–August. Height 2–4 ft.)
Calla palustris—Bog Arum.
(White flowers. April–June. Height 9 in.)
Caltha palustris—Marsh Marigold.
C. palustris 'plena'.
(Bright gold flowers. March–June. Height 9–15 in.)
C. polypetala.
(Bright gold flowers. March–June. Height 2–3 ft.)
Carex Pseudo-cyperus.
(Dark green spikelets. Height 2–3 ft.)
C. riparia—Great Pond Sedge.
(Brown spikelets. Height 2 ft.)
Cyperus Eragrostis (vegetus).
(Mahogany umbels. Height 2 ft.)
C. longus—English Galingale.
(Chestnut-brown umbels. Height 2–3 ft.)
Iris laevigata—Water Iris.
(Rich blue flowers. June–September. Height 2 ft.)
I. laevigata 'alba'.
(Snow-white flowers. Height 2 ft.)
I. laevigata 'atropurpurea'.
(Rich violet flowers. July. Height 2½ ft.)
I. Pseudacorus 'alba'.
(White flowers. Height 2½ ft.)
I. Pseudacorus 'Bastardii'.
(Soft primrose-yellow flowers. Height 3 ft.)
I. Pseudacorus 'variegata'.
(Yellow flowers. Height 3 ft.)
Juncus inflexus (glaucus)—Hard Rush.
(Grey-blue foliage. Height 2 ft.)
Lysimachia Nummularia—Creeping Jenny.
(Gold flowers. Early summer. Height 6 in.)
L. Nummularia 'aurea'.
(Gold flowers and leaves. Early summer. Height 4 in.)
Mentha aquatica—Water Mint.
(Lilac to purple flowers. August–September. Height 1–4 ft.)
Menyanthes trifoliata—Bog-bean.
(White flowers flushed pink. May–July. Height 1 ft.)

Mimulus luteus—Water Musk.
  (Golden yellow flowers spotted red. All summer. Height
    1½ ft.)
M. ringens.
  (Soft blue flowers. Height 15 in.)
Myosotis scorpioides (palustris)—Forget-me-not.
  (Sky-blue flowers. May–July. Height 9–12 in.)
Typha minima.
  (Rusty brown pistillates. Height 1½ ft.)

With experienced aquarists, floating aquatic plants are less popular in the pond than in the aquarium. Indeed, if a water-lily is planted, floating plants are neither necessary nor desirable. In a very small pond, however, and if no water-lily or other centre-piece has been planted, a few floating plants may be introduced, to furnish shade for the fish and break the monotony of a bare expanse of water. A selection may be made from the following list:

Hydrocharis Morsus-ranae—Frog Bit.
Stratiotes aloides—Water Soldier.
Utricularia vulgaris—Bladderwort.
Azolla caroliniana—Fairy Moss—and *Lemna* species—Duckweed—should be avoided; for they multiply very rapidly and are apt to become a nuisance. *Lemna minor*, however, is a valuable food for goldfish, and if it is introduced for this purpose, periodically any excess must be raked off, otherwise the fish will live more or less in perpetual darkness.
Riccia fluitans—Crystalwort—is not hardy, but may survive if the pond is in a sheltered position.
Eichornia crassipes—Water Hyacinth—is not hardy, and though it may flourish in the summer months, it must be wintered indoors.

Although an aquarium may be planted at any time of the year, the best time for planting a pond is May and June, though planting may be done in April or July with a reasonable chance that all will go well. Plants with a bulb rootstock, however, such as *Calla*, should be planted in the late autumn.

As in an aquarium, so in a pond, it is a wise precaution to dis-

IX. The Telescope-Eyed Veiltail. Comparison with Plate VI
shows that if this fish was all-black, instead of mottled, it
would be a Moor.

X. A Telescope-Eyed Veiltail in which the eyes are oddly
sited. The phenomenon is not uncommon among fishes.
Such fish are in no way handicapped, but they are not much
esteemed by aquarists.

XI. The Pearl Scale. Each scale is topped with a nacreous excrescence that gives the fish an armoured appearance. The breed is a rare one except in the Chinese province of Kwangtung where it is quite common (see p. 71).

infect all plants before planting them, no matter from what source they are obtained; and the plants should be given two or three weeks to become established before introducing any animal life into the pond. If it is practical to do so, during this period the pond should be shaded. Until the plants have taken firm root an excess of heat will wither the leaves and kill the plants. Here again, however, and as in the case of an aquarium, there is no cause for alarm if the original leaves of the plants die soon after planting; if the plants have been properly set, and if the conditions are right, new leaves will soon sprout.

We have been at pains to explain the right water to use, the oxygen-requirements of goldfish, and the plants and proper method of planting aquaria and ponds. For these matters are very important and answer the question which most of our non-aquarist friends ask when they see for the first time our numerous aquaria: 'But how on earth do you change all this water?' The answer is that we do not, because if an aquarium is properly set up in the first place the water in it need never—we mean the Gilbertian hardly ever—be changed. At the present time we have an aquarium which has been set up for many years, and beyond the addition of small quantities of water, to make good losses by evaporation, the water has never been changed, and is as sweet and clear as when the aquarium was first filled. We see no reason why it should not remain in this condition indefinitely, and, indeed, Innes records that in the aquarium at Battery Park, New York, there is a small aquarium that had not at the time of writing been disturbed for over thirty years.[1]

This ideal state of affairs is not exceptional. It can be achieved by anyone who takes a little trouble to set up the aquarium properly in the first place. But the job must be properly done from the very start, because if it is not the aquarium will prove a failure and tinkering at it will not help. Preparing the aquarium to receive the goldfish, therefore, is a very important matter. Yet we do not intend to say very much about it. The subject has been discussed *ad nauseam* in a large number of books, and the titles of many of them will be found in our bibliography. There are three, perhaps four, main considerations in setting up an aquarium. They are, cleanliness, light, heat and the choice of a suitable planting medium. We have something to say about them in a broad and

---

[1] William T. Innes, op. cit., p. 70.

general way, and without going into the minutiae of setting up aquaria.

To goldfish cleanliness is even more important than godliness. Before anything is placed in the aquarium, therefore, it should be thoroughly washed and disinfected in a pale solution of potash permanganate. This is not being finicky. We know that all sorts of rubbish is thrown into ponds and the fish still thrive, but we also know that a large pond in the open air is very different from the confined space of the home-aquarium; and, in any event, even if the fish come to no harm, no one particularly wants a smelly aquarium in his house. Dust and tobacco smoke, not to mention the cat, are harmful to fish, so that the aquarium should always be kept covered with a sheet of glass, raised about a quarter of an inch to allow the free circulation of air. It should also be kept away from a gas fire; apart from the fact that proximity to a fire is not conducive to an equable temperature (about which we shall have more to say later) the fumes of coal gas are harmful to goldfish. In fact a lot of things are harmful to them, and goldfish should never be introduced into a new aquarium until it has been soaked for several days in many changes of water to rid it of any impurities. Nor should an aquarium be set up in a newly-painted room, because the fumes of fresh paint, varnish, shellac, turpentine, indeed anything that contains wood spirit, will affect goldfish in from thirty-six to forty-eight hours.

The importance of proper lighting cannot be over-estimated, but too much light is almost as bad as too little light. It is wrong to place an aquarium in a south window (a very usual place among novice-aquarists) or anywhere where the midday sun will fall on it. If the aquarium is to be lighted by daylight, then the best position is about 1 to 2 ft. from a window that faces north, east, or west, in that order. In this position the back of the aquarium (and possibly the sides) may have be shaded during the summer months by distempering or pasting a thin sheet of paper over the glass. Algae multiply in strong daylight. Our preference is to keep an aquarium well away from a window, and to light it by artificial light. In this way we can control the light and are independent of the vagaries of English weather: we can also obtain more artistic effects, since daylight is too diffused to produce deep shadows; and we are not worried by a rampant growth of algae, because those algae that do grow under artificial light are usually of the mossy type that cling to the rocks and look quite attractive. The amount of artificial light necessary to keep an aquarium in good condition can be determined by multiplying the length of the aquarium in inches by three and a quarter. The result will give the wattage of the electric lamp needed, for ten hours daily, provided the lamp is in a reflector shade raised not more than 6 in. above the surface of the water. But at best the formula is only approximate, because some plants need more light than others. The light may be reduced if the aquarium receives some daylight, and the depth of the water has a slight effect on the amount of light needed to support the aquarium at its best. Some experimentation is necessary, therefore, to find the exact amount of light necessary to keep the fish and plants healthy, but any adjustment necessary should be made in the wattage of the lamp, rather than by reducing or increasing the length of time the aquarium is lighted. Ten hours daily is about the right time. If it is lighted for too long the plants grow long and stringy and look unsightly. Less than ten hours daily is not to be advised, because water has a limited capacity for storing oxygen, so that slow oxygenation over a long period is better than rapid oxygenation over a short period.

If the aquarium is to be heated—as it should be, certainly in the winter, if fancy goldfish are kept—it is inadvisable to place it near the fire. It is a false economy in the long run, because goldfish need an equable temperature, and trouble will certainly follow if the temperature rises to about 75° F. in the evening (which it may do after the fire has been alight all day) and drops to about 50 degrees at dawn. There are many ways of heating an aquarium. The most satisfactory is to use an electric immersion-heater. Most dealers stock reliable heaters with and without thermostatic control, and in a number of different voltages and wattages. Another method which is quite satisfactory, is to raise the aquarium some 6 in. above its stand and place a small lamp, or run a gas jet, underneath, taking the precaution, of course, to place an asbestos sheet between the flame and the bottom of the aquarium. If the aquarium is raised on a strong wooden box, lined with felt, electric lamps inside the box will keep the water warm. If three or four lamps of different wattage are used, the temperature of the water can be controlled to a nicety. The ingenuity of the aquarist will suggest many other ways of heating an aquarium, but whatever method suggests itself, two points call for special notice: one is fairly obvious (and because it is might be overlooked), the obvious one is that an eye should be kept on the temperature of the water to prevent the fish from being parboiled. The less obvious one is that powerful heating apparatus is not necessary. It is not so much a matter of heating the water but of preventing it from getting too cold. This is not splitting hairs. It will be found that if the aquarium is filled with water at a certain temperature, it takes very little heat, even if the aquarium is a large one and the weather very cold, to keep the water more or less at that temperature. We recommend a slight reduction of the temperature at night-time, as this approximates more closely to natural conditions.

The planting medium is important because it plays a large part in determining the acidity and alkalinity of the water. Red builder's sand nearly always causes trouble, and silver sand is so fine that it packs closely and prevents the roots of the plants from spreading. Coarse grit and small pebbles are not to be advised; particles of food can lodge under them and foul the water, they get sucked up and block the siphon when the aquarium is being cleaned, and a small goldfish has been known to choke to death on a pebble, though the accident is a rare one. We prefer a fine grit, such as will pass through a 1/16-in. sieve, or a coarse white sand with grains about the size of a pin's head. It is best to slope the sand from about 3 in. at the back of the aquarium to about 1 in. at the front. This displays the plants to the best advantage, and the sediment tends to come to the front, from where it can more easily be siphoned out. Rocks should also be chosen with care. For the most natural effects waterworn sandstone is hard to beat, but tufa and pumice-stone are good. For artistic effects, slate, Thames flints, Somerset, York, or Westmorland stone, Mendip spa, and granite, are all suitable. Limestone and marble should be avoided: they turn water hard and alkaline, and marble has the further drawback that it coats the leaves of the plants with a fine white deposit. We have nothing to say about models of divers, mermaids, treasure-chests, sunken galleons, and other bric-à-brac, except that they should remain in Ye Olde Curiositie Shoppe where they belong. Even shells and pieces of coral look incongruous, though, with a little artistry, irregular lumps of coloured glass can often be fitted into the underwater picture.

Environment

The best way to fill an aquarium with water is to place a sheet of thick paper on the bottom of the aquarium, stand a jam jar on it, and run the water into the jar with a slender siphon, the more slender the better.

For those who like filtration, and we agree that filtration greatly helps to keep the water clear, so that fancy goldfish are seen at their best, there are plenty of good filters sold by dealers. Artificial aeration, too, is a great help. It benefits the fish in very hot weather and enables the aquarist to keep more than the 1-in.-of-fish-to-every-24-square-in.-of-surface-area rule permits. We recommend an electrically-operated aerator pump. There are many other ways of aerating an aquarium, ranging from a drip on the water to rigging up a fountain in the middle of the aquarium, but we have yet to learn of a better way than an electric pump. There are many different makes on the market: the most expensive is the cheapest. It usually is.

As to preparing a pond for goldfish, only a few words are necessary on the most suitable planting medium, making the concrete safe for the fish, and protecting the fish from fish-eating birds and cats.

In our experience the best planting medium for a pond is a good turfy loam, preferably the top spit off pasture land, to which some ordinary bone-meal has been added. It has been found that the best mixture is a 32-pot[1] of ground bone meal to a barrow-load of loam. Horse manure and pig manure are useless for the cultivation of aquatic plants, but old cow manure is excellent. The cow manure should be at least three or four years old, and it should be mixed in the proportion of one part of manure to six parts of turfy loam. The turf should be cut in the autumn, stacked layer by layer with the manure, and protected from the sun and rain. The stack should be turned during the winter at intervals of six weeks. Leading horticulturists consider this to be the perfect planting medium for water-lilies. For the surrounding ledge, in which the marginal plants are grown, pure loam is sufficient and there is no need to mix it with cow manure or bone meal. The planting medium should be laid on the bottom of the pond and surrounding ledge to a depth of about 8 in. and covered with a 2-in. layer of well-washed coarse sand. But as the amount of sand necessary for even a small pond is considerable it saves a lot of time and trouble to use one

[1] A pot approximately 6¼ in. in diameter and 6 in. deep.

of the proprietary composts instead, because they are already cleansed.

New concrete is very dangerous to fish because cement contains a quantity of free lime. Goldfish, therefore, must not be introduced into a pond until the free lime has been removed. The best way to do this is to fill the pond with water, leave it for a week, and then thoroughly scour the pond with a stiff scrubbing-brush. The pond is then emptied and refilled, and the operation repeated at least half a dozen times at weekly intervals. Other methods, which are less laborious, are to apply one of the proprietary dressings expressly made to prevent the release of free lime from cement, or to paint the pond with a bituminous paint. The objections to these methods, however, are that the dressing and paint do not remove the free lime, but merely seal the surface so that the lime cannot be absorbed by the water, and though the method is very effective for a time, trouble will arise if the dressing or paint deteriorate or if they are not properly applied in the first place. Three or four applications of sodium silicate (water-glass) dissolved in four times the amount of water, may be used as a dressing. The dressings should be applied with a soft brush and allowed to soak well into the cement. Finally, the free lime may be removed by the use of chemicals. The pond is filled with water, and, after a day or two, acid is added until a test of the water for pH (see page 94) shows that the water is neutral. The process must be repeated daily, until a test taken before the addition of acid shows that the water is no longer absorbing free lime from the cement. The pond is then emptied and refilled with fresh water.[1]

Filling a pond with water follows the same lines as filling an aquarium, only, of course, on a larger scale. A sheet of brown paper is placed on the bottom of the pond, a bucket stood on it, and the water is run into the bucket very slowly.

As for protecting goldfish from fish-eating birds and cats, very little can be done about this. The only way to give the fish adequate protection is to cover the pond with fine wire meshing. Unfortunately this is unsightly. In districts where birds are notoriously active in raiding ponds, some protection can be given to the fish by criss-crossing strong black twine across the pond. In cities

[1] The practice of first stocking the pond with fish taken from the wild, to serve as guinea-pigs, is not to be advised. The risk of introducing parasites with the fish is very great.

and towns, where the danger from cats is likely to be greatest, particularly at night, a small pond may be covered during the hours of darkness with wire meshing in a wooden frame to facilitate handling. Owls have been known to take goldfish in ponds, and in country districts snakes sometimes find their way there, especially in the hot weather, and kill the fish. On the whole, however, the aquarist is almost certain to lose a number of fish as the result of depredations by fish-eating birds and cats, and we can only suggest not stocking a pond, designed primarily for ornamental purposes, with the more expensive breeds of goldfish.

We must touch upon the important matter of maintaining aquaria and ponds. The fact that all goes well with the goldfish and plants is no guarantee that all will continue to go well with them, and that there is nothing more for the aquarist to do once he has set up his aquarium or pond. On the contrary, sooner or later his services will be needed to restore the balance of life; without some attention, no aquarium or garden-pond can remain in a healthy condition indefinitely.

Perhaps a fish, or a mollusc will die, and the body must be removed before it decomposes and pollutes the water. Or perhaps a fish will show signs of being ill, and needs to be isolated; a sick fish is not only a nuisance in an established aquarium or pond, it is a danger to healthy fish.

Consider the aquarium.

Apart from the removal of sick fish and corpses, periodically the aquarist will find that it is necessary to remove dead plants and decaying leaves. Dead plants should be pulled out and replaced with fresh ones. Dead leaves should be cut off, as close as possible to the main stems, with long scissors. Plants that are flourishing must be pruned from time to time; they must not be allowed to grow so luxuriantly that they hamper the fish and spoil the look of the aquarium. When pruning it is best to remove the older portion of the plant and give the new shoots a chance to grow.

Rocks that have to be moved, or have become displaced, may be shifted with the help of long wooden forceps.

Periodically it will be necessary to remove the algae growing on the glass of the aquarium. A safety-razor blade at the end of a stick is a useful tool for the purpose. Some of the algae will remain in the water, making it green and dirty. It should be allowed to settle and then removed with a sediment remover (known to

Chinese aquarists 350 years ago!) or siphon. Only the front glass needs to be cleaned regularly; for, within reason, algae on the back and side glasses are beneficial, since they are good oxygenators, afford the fish a valuable addition to their diet, and shield the fish and plants from an excess of light entering the aquarium at an unnatural angle. Rocks that have become overgrown with the hard, mossy, types of algae are very ornamental and much coveted by experienced aquarists; but the hairy, or filamentous types should be removed. Very patient aquarists have been known to wipe the algae off the leaves of aquatic plants, but we would not care to do it ourselves or suggest that our readers should do so. There are limits.

Although the aquarium may be covered with glass, a certain amount of dust is bound to settle on the surface of the water, particularly during the summer months. Dust, as we have said, is bad for fish and should be removed. The best way to do this is to lay a sheet of clean blotting paper on the surface of the water and allow the water to soak through before removing the paper. The process should be repeated until all the dust has been removed.

A considerable amount of sediment collects on the bottom of an aquarium. A small amount will do no harm, and, in fact, is necessary to supply the plants with manure. But an excess of sediment should be removed, and it is time to do so when it swirls about as the fish swim to and fro. Generally speaking it is as well to siphon out the sediment once a week. If filtration is installed, the water, drawn off together with the sediment, may be returned through the filter. If there is no filter in the aquarium the water should be passed through a filter made by placing three or four iron nails over the hole in a clean flower-pot, placing over them a layer of charcoal, and finally a layer of clean silver sand.

Sometimes a patch of the planting medium turns black and develops a cobweb-like appearance. Usually it is due to putrefying food, and is, therefore, most likely to be seen in the corner where feeding takes place. The affected planting medium should be removed with a sediment remover and replaced by clean run down a length of tubing.

Periodically the aquarium will have to be topped up, to make good losses by evaporation. In this event the fresh water should be at the same temperature as the water in the aquarium, and drawn from the original source.

Environment

Goldfish are extremely sensitive to anything unusual. A couple of large stones brought quickly together under water can stun them, and has been known to kill them. It is important, therefore, to do nothing that may alarm them. The bare hands should never be used to catch a fish; it frightens them, and there is great risk that the scales or fins will be damaged. A fine-meshed net should always be used, but if handling a fish cannot be avoided the hands should be wet. The common practice of tipping the fish out of the net (sometimes from quite a height) is a minor form of cruelty.

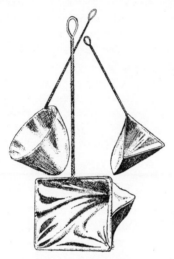

Fig. 25. AQUARIUM NETS

The round net is for catching fish in circular cans. The triangular net is for catching small things in awkward corners. The rectangular net is the most useful type for general purposes: the mouth should be at least 6 in. across.

The net should be submerged and the fish allowed to swim out of its own accord. Tapping the glass to attract the fish is not necessary, and in many cases only drives the fish to hide among the plants; it is better to agitate the surface of the water gently. If the aquarium is lit by artificial light this should not be turned on suddenly; nor should artificial aeration be set in motion so suddenly that a dormant fish is unexpectedly carried to the surface by the flow of air. If the room in which the aquarium is kept is occupied until a late hour (midnight or past) it is kindest to screen the aquarium from a bright light; for goldfish like a few hours' rest, even if the aquarist does not. In all these, and similar matters, a little thought will show the right lines to follow.

A careful watch should be kept for any sign of lack of oxygen in the water. It is a sure sign when all the fish are seen gasping at the surface. Hungry fish sometimes rise to the surface to beg for food, but they can easily be distinguished from fish that need oxygen, because they rise to the surface only on the approach of a human being, whereas fish in need of oxygen remain permanently at the surface of the water and go down only when frightened, and then only for a few moments. If the aquarium has been going well for some time and the fish are seen at the surface on a dull and heavy day, when the barometer is low, there is no need for alarm; the action of the fish is due to the weather and they will return to normal when the weather changes. Once the aquarist is sure that the fish are in need of oxygen, he must take immediate steps to remedy the conditions in the aquarium. There is not a moment to waste. If artificial aeration is available it should be set in motion. If no artificial aeration is available, a partial change of water should be made. But this will relieve the fish only for a time, and a permanent cure must be sought. If the water is not polluted (if it is, a complete change of water is necessary) the plants should be examined. Dead plants should be removed and replaced by new ones, decaying leaves should be cut off, more plants should be added, and the light increased to ensure that the plants will flourish. If, after all this, the fish, after a time, again begin to skim the surface and gasp for air, the only remedy is to reduce the number of fish.

It is important to note that goldfish in an aquarium that is well stocked with plants, will sometimes be seen gasping for air first thing every morning, but not at other times of the day. This often puzzles novice-aquarists, but the explanation is simple. Oxygenating plants give off oxygen only under the influence of light, and when there is no light they give off carbon dioxide which is asphyxial. If the aquarium is not overstocked with fish, a reduction of the number of plants should be considered; in the confined space of an aquarium it is important to have only sufficient plants to maintain the balance between animal and vegetable life. The notion that an aquarium cannot be stocked with too many plants is a fallacy, since at night-time an excess of plants will prove dangerous, especially if the aquarium is a small or medium-sized one with no margin between the limit imposed by the size of the fish and the surface-area of the water. An alternative remedy is to aerate the water last thing at night. Indeed, to be on the safe side, many experienced aquarists aerate the water all night, even though they maintain a blanced aquarium. We ourselves do so; for though it is possible for the fish to suffer from a lack of oxygen, within reason no harm can come of an excess of oxygen, and if the flow of air is reduced to a steady stream of very small bubbles it does not disturb the rest of the fish. If the aquarist has to leave his aquarium unattended for several days, it is always safer if the water is artificially aerated during his absence.

When it is necessary to disinfect an aquarium (or pond), the fish and molluscs should be removed, and 3 grains (by weight) of permanganate of potash to every gallon[1] of water should be dissolved in the water. After about three hours the sterilizing solution may be drawn off, the aquarium (or pond) refilled, and the fish and molluscs returned. In extreme cases, such as when parasites are present, it is better to remove the fish and molluscs, then take down the aquarium, disinfect it with a proprietary germicide, and after thoroughly washing it, set it up anew with fresh plants and planting medium. The fish and molluscs may be given a sterilizing bath, as prescribed on page 140, before returning them.

Although we have detailed a number of routine jobs in the maintenance of an aquarium, the work is not quite so laborious as a reading of it may imply. The less an aquarium is fussed with the better, and, as a general rule, if it has been properly set up in the first place it requires very little further attention. An aquarium of goldfish is very ornamental and cannot fail to improve the appearance of any room, but, of course, it must be well-cared for. It does not mean that a great deal of time has to be spent every day in looking after the fish and plants. A few minutes every day, to feed the fish, to remove uneaten food, to see that all the fish are in good health, and that all the moluscs are alive, is ample. Once a week the aquarist will have to spend half an hour, perhaps a little longer, overhauling the plants, removing excess sediment, cleaning the

[1] To determine the number of gallons of water in a pond, the following formulae may be used: *Rectangular or square pond*, see footnote page 97; *Circular pond*, multiply the radius in feet by 3 1/7, by the depth in feet, and the product by 6¼; *Oval pond*, multiply the product of the axes in feet, by .7854, by the depth in feet, and the product by 6¼.

filter if one is installed, and cleaning the front glass, and even this last job may not be necessary as often as once a week. All this takes no longer than it does to clean a bird-cage, and certainly far less time than it takes to groom a dog; but it is important to note that such attention as is necessary must be given regularly, because once you neglect an aquarium the whole thing becomes a nuisance rather than the attraction that it is with a little care.

The maintenance of a pond follows much the same lines as the maintenance of an aquarium, with some modifications. A pond, as it is more like a stretch of natural water than an aquarium, needs less attention as a rule, but some other considerations have to be taken into account.

To keep up the appearance of a pond, the plants must be pruned and dead plants removed and replaced by new ones periodically. A small oxygenating plant may be planted in the surrounding ledge in the same way as we recommended in an aquarium (see page 104). A large plant, that takes root in the deep water of the pond is best weighted with lead and sunk into position. Plants that break loose may be replanted in the same way. The older leaves of a plant will, of course, die soon after replanting, but new shoots should start to come through after about a week or ten days. If they do not, and if a plant withers and dies soon after planting, it is usually due to the fact that the plant has been subjected to too strong a light before it has become firmly rooted. The remedy is to shade the pond for a few days. If the leaves of the plants turn yellow the planting medium should be suspected. A small quantity of the planting medium should be lifted out, and changed if it smells sour. If the planting medium is healthy, however, the cause may be that it is of too fine a grain, so that the roots of the plants have difficulty in spreading. And if this is not the cause, it may be that the plants have been too deeply planted.

The leaves of water-lilies and other large-leaved plants, are sometimes attacked by the Water-lily Beetle (*Galerucella nymphaea*). It is dark brown in colour and about the size of a ladybird. Another pest is the reddish-black Water-lily Aphis (*Rhopalosiphum nymphaea*). Both these pests will be eaten by goldfish, so the best control is to drive them into the water with the jet from a high-pressure hose. The hosing should be repeated several days in succession to make sure that no insects escape. The Brown China

Environment

Mark Moth (*Hydrocampa nymphaeata*) lays its eggs under, or near the edge of the leaves of water-lilies and other aquatic plants. The eggs hatch out into cream coloured caterpillars which feed freely on the foliage. The best method of control is to weight the plants so that the leaves are held under water for about two days. The caterpillars then drown or get eaten by the fish. The False Leaf-mining Midge (*Cricotopus ornatus*) is very rare, but sometimes turns up in an ornamental pond. Its presence can be detected by the fact that it eats serpentine lines over the surfaces of the leaves of aquatic plants. The affected part should be cut away and burnt, and if the insect has taken a firm hold the plant should be uprooted and destroyed. Nicotine spray and Bordeaux mixture, which some writers recommend, are poisonous to goldfish and should not be used to control pests on aquatic plants. Nor should the insecticide D.D.T. be used. Tests have shown that in quantity D.D.T. is toxic to goldfish and that even as little as eight grains of D.D.T. in one thousand gallons of water may cause them serious illness.

Water-voles and water-shrews rarely find their way to orna-mental ponds. If they do, trapping and shooting are the only ways to get rid of them. And they should be got rid of; for they do considerable damage to aquatic plants.

For removing an excess of algae from the walls of a concrete pond a wire brush attached to a long stick is very useful. But, within reason, algae do more good than harm. The form of alga known as blanket weed or flannel weed, however, should be removed; also the equally objectionable algal growth that develops into masses that look like tangled bunches of sage-green hair. These growths do much to spoil the appearance of the pond, and, if not kept in check, will eventually stifle the aquatic plants. There is no satisfactory way of ridding a pond of these objection-able growths, because they are caused by an excess of light, so the only real solution is to move the pond to a shadier position, or at least shade it by erecting a screen. Various chemicals have been suggested, but in our experience any chemical strong enough to kill algal growths that have taken firm hold will harm the aquatic plants. In any case, the use of chemicals does not remove the cause—an excess of light. If it is impractical to move the pond or erect a screen, the only way of controlling blanket weed and its ally is to keep them down as much as possible by raking them off the surface of the water as soon as they appear. After all, it is mainly a matter of keeping up the appearance of the pond, and the method has the advantage that it involves no danger to the fish (as would chemicals if wrongly used) and it is less laborious than periodically emptying the pond and scouring it (a method of controlling blanket weed that is recommended by some aquarists). Blanket weed should be examined immediately after removal from a pond, because small fish sometimes get entangled in the filaments.

Without emptying it is difficult to remove the excess of sediment that collects on the bottom of the pond. Much can be done with a soup-ladle attached to a pole, or a straight-edged landing-net of very fine mesh. But in extreme cases the only way is to empty the pond and clean it out. Unless disease is present there is no need to scrub the concrete; in fact it is better not to do so, then the fresh water will mature quicker. Actually, unless the pond is in perfect condition, a clean out should be undertaken annually; for a very considerable amount of sediment collects in the course of a year. In itself the sediment is not dangerous, and we know a number of ponds that have remained uncleaned for years with no ill effects to the fish, but in every case the ponds are large ones that contain sufficient water not to be upset by small amounts of pollution that would soon poison a smaller body of water. A reasonable quantity of sediment at the bottom of a pond does more good than harm. The fish can get down into it in the winter and keep much warmer; but an excess of sediment can be, and often is, dangerous to the fish, because when the weather suddenly changes the bottom water is affected by the changing pressure and the sediment generates carbon dioxide—which asphyxiates—and hydrogen sulphide—which poisons them. A good test is to lift out some of the planting medium and smell it. If the pond is healthy the planting medium will have a riverine smell, but if the planting medium smells rank and is black it is time to clean out the pond. If it is found necessary to give the pond a complete turn out, it is as well to do the job thoroughly. Everything should be taken out of the pond, the walls and bottom scrubbed with a strong solution of potash permanganate, and the pond set up anew with a fresh planting medium, and plants that have been trimmed of dead and dying leaves.

In the summer, dust and scum settle on the surface of the

water. A jet from a high-pressure hose will clean the water, and has the added advantage that it refreshes the goldfish and helps to make good losses by evaporation. In dry weather a pond loses a remarkable amount of water by evaporation.

A sharp look out should be kept for any signs of lack of oxygen in the water. The symptoms are the same as in an aquarium (see page 122) and so are the remedies. Although it is very rare for a pond to be deficient in oxygen, nevertheless, the higher the temperature the less the oxygen in the water, so that during hot dry spells oxygen may be reduced to a level insufficient to support the fish.

In the autumn the fallen leaves of trees and shrubs should be raked off the water. They look unsightly, and an excess of decaying vegetation may prove fatal to the fish. At this time of the year many aquarists cover small ponds with wire netting. It is a good idea, provided the leaves are removed periodically to ensure that light reaches the pond.

As winter approaches some aquarists reduce the oxygenating plants to a minimum. Goldfish in hibernation require very little oxygen, and during the long nights and short days of the winter months an excess of oxygenating plants in a pond can be harmful. We have never found it necessary to remove healthy plants from a pond. In an established pond the plants die down of their own accord and sprout anew in the spring. In any case, if the aquarist decides to remove any healthy plants from the pond, he would do well not to remove the sagittarias; their roots do much to keep the planting medium wholesome.

Though there is little to fear from the normal English winter, some steps should be taken to protect the fish as much as possible from the dangers of freezing. Provided the deepest part of the pond is at least 18 in. (24 in. to be on the safe side) and the ice is broken daily, the fish should survive the winter outdoors. It is unwise to break the ice at haphazard, because the broken pieces only solidify and form a greater thickness of ice; and, moreover, cracking the ice with a crow-bar or hammer is likely to kill the fish by concussion. The better method is to drill a few holes in the ice. These, each at least 1 in. in diameter, will be enough to allow noxious gases to escape and admit all the air that is necessary. Snow should be swept off the ice. The likelihood of 'winter-kill', as it is called, is greatest when snow on top of the ice prevents light penetrating and when there is dead and decaying vegetation in the pond. If there is rooted vegetation, and the ice is kept clear, the water will be sufficiently oxygenated to support the fish. Tennis-balls, a rubber tyre, pieces of cork, indeed anything that is resilient and floats, may be placed in the pond to provide elasticity and take the strain off the walls of the pond. If the pond is a small one (holding no more than about 300 gallons of water) and if it is near an electric supply point, much can be done to prevent the water from freezing by placing an electric immersion-heater of 120 watts in the water. For a larger pond several immersion-heaters may be used. It is worth it if the goldfish are expensive specimens.

Finally, then, apart from an annual clean, which is best under-taken in April or early May, a pond requires very little attention from the aquarist, always provided that the pond was properly constructed and prepared in the first place. The main routine jobs are: a daily inspection to feed the fish and make sure that they are healthy and that otherwise all goes well with the pond; a weekly overhaul of the plants, an examination of the planting medium, and, if necessary, the removal of blanket weed and fallen leaves from the water. In the cold months, when the fish are hibernating and oxygenating plants are reduced to a minimum, the pond requires very little attention. An inspection every morning and evening to cut holes in the ice and sweep off snow if necessary, is about all that is required. Again, as in the case of an aquarium, we should stress the importance of carrying out these routine jobs. Far too many aquarists are under the impression that gold-fish will look after themselves, with no more than an occasional bit of food, if that. This is a fallacy. The goldfish is remarkably hardy, but in a garden-pond can no more look after itself than can a budgerigar in an aviary. Goldfish, in fact, need to be cared for just as much as any other animal kept in captivity; and aquatic plants, if they are to flourish and so keep the water sweet, need to be tended just as much as carnations. It may be that goldfish and aquatic plants require less attention than budgerigars and carnations, but they do require some attention, and always more than the majority of inexperienced aquarists give them.

We need add only a few words about scavengers.

The Freshwater Shrimp (*Gammarus* species) and the Water-hog Louse (*Asellus* species) are excellent scavengers, but no good for

XII. The Celestial. A breed that is characterized by eyes that gaze upwards, and no dorsal fin.

XIII. Celestial Goldfish are seen at their best in a garden pond. In this country we would recommend wintering them indoors.

XIV. The Water Bubble Eye. The eyeballs are situated near the top of the head, below is a gelatinous substance in the form of a bubble. The breed is well-known to the Chinese and is highly prized in the province of Kwantung. Elsewhere it is very rare (*see* p. 70).

XV. A male goldfish showing nuptial tubercles (the so-called 'pearl organs') on the gill plates and pectoral fins (*see* p. 196).

our purpose because goldfish eat them avidly. Frog-tadpoles are spoken of, but we have never found much use for them, because when small the goldfish eat them and when large they leave the water. Besides, tadpoles soon learn to neglect decaying food and algae in preference for fresh fish-food, and we cannot blame them.

On the whole, therefore, the only suitable scavengers for the goldfish aquarium and pond are molluscs (snails and mussels) and even these are far from being all that has been claimed for them. Some snails (e.g. *Limnaea stagnalis*) are greedy devourers of aquatic plants, and a handful of them in an aquarium will strip it bare of leaves in the proverbial no time; you cannot stop them adding to the sediment; and no one has yet had the wit to train them to remove the algae from the front glass by going up and down it like a lawn-mower. Still, a few snails, for those who like to see them, are useful in an aquarium or pond, since they help to keep down the rapid growth of algae in hot weather, and are quite useful in breaking down uneaten fish-food into comparatively harmless sediment.

We recommend Ram's-horn Snails (*Planorbis* species). They exist mainly on decaying matter and algae, do little, if any, damage to aquatic plants, and are not unattractive in appearance. With one exception[1]—which need not greatly concern us—they are pulmo-branchiate and rise to the surface of the water to breathe, so that, within reason, they will not disturb the balance of the aquarium. The best species, because they are the most handsome, are the White Ram's-horn (*Planorbis albus*) and the Red Ram's-horn (*Planorbis corneus* var. *rubrus*.) The former is by no means rare in British freshwaters. The latter is very rare in Britain; it is a native to central Europe, probably Germany, but can be bought from most dealers for a matter of a few pence. Both these snails are suitable for an aquarium (cold or heated) and pond. So also is the Great Japanese Snail (*Viviparus malleatus*) a handsome animal with a greenish-brown shell that grows to about the size of a golf-ball. For the heated aquarium only we may add the Paper Snail or Australian Red Snail (*Bullinus pyramidata*) with a pinkish to pinkish-gold shell and a bright pink to vivid red body; and the Malayan Live-bearing Snail (*Thiara tuberculata*) with a greenish-olive to light brown trumpet-shaped shell. Aquarists will recognize the latter under its older generic name of *Melania*.

---

[1] Actually *Planorbis crista* (Nautilus Ram's-horn), the smallest of the genus.

Acid water eats into the shells of snails and causes them to become pitted and scarred with greyish-white marks. Their condition in an established aquarium or pond may, in fact, be taken as a rough guide to the pH value of the water; the more and deeper the pitting and scarring, the more acid is the water. Ram's-horn snails, particularly the red variant, appear to be more susceptible to this trouble than other species, and they do not live for long in water that is too acid. Frequent removal of the sediment that collects about the crowns of the aquatic plants and behind rocks, helps to prolong their lives. Keeping the water alkaline will prolong their lives still further, but as goldfish favour slightly acid water it is better to let the snails go and replace them when necessary.

Snails are very partial to lettuce, so if they become a nuisance in a pond, they may be collected by dropping a lettuce leaf in the water and removing it when it is covered with snails.

We doubt the wisdom of introducing mussels into an aquarium; although they move infrequently, when they do they plough up the plants. They soon die, because they live on micro-organisms and no aquarium can supply these in sufficient quantities for their needs.

In a pond mussels are of some use, because they help to purify the water, and, indeed, a number of large mussels in a pond will clear it of green water. But mussels should be introduced only with certain precautions, otherwise more harm than good will result. They should be confined within a ring of stones, to prevent them from ploughing up the plants when they move, and from time to time they should be given a light tap with a stick, to determine if they are alive or dead and their rapidly decomposing bodies putrefying the water. The mussel-larva (glochidium) attaches itself to a fish and causes a gall to form. This is not likely to harm a large and healthy goldfish (though it does it no good) but small or weakly fish are likely to suffer. The aquarist, therefore, should keep a sharp look-out for any fish that has mussel-larvae attached to it and the fish should be netted out of the water and given the same treatment as we recommended for ridding it of argulids (see page 187).

The largest and best known mussel found in British freshwaters is the Swan Mussel (*Anodonta cygna*). It grows to a length of about six inches and has a greenish-brown shell. The Duck

Mussel (*Anodonta anatina*) is smaller and its shell is yellowish-brown. It is not quite so widely distributed as the swan mussel, and it has not yet been found in Ireland. Probably the handsomest species is the Zebra Mussel (*Dreissensia polymorphia*). It is dull brown in colour with wavy cross bands of a darker colour. It is widely distributed, although it is not native to British freshwaters and appears to have been introduced here about the beginning of the nineteenth century.

Chapter V

SELECTING AND TRANSPORTING

Oh, how hard it is to find
The one just suited to our mind!
Campbell, Song (published in *The New Monthly*, 1823)

In chapter II we have described the many breeds of fancy goldfish. There is a large number from which to select. In practice, however, the number of breeds is limited; not only are several of them unobtainable in this country, but some of the more grotesque are suitable only for the specialist, and a rich one at that, since the fish are expensive to buy and hard to keep alive when bought.

There are three ways in which goldfish may be kept: in individual aquaria, in a communal aquarium, and in a pond.

If accommodation is available, it is our opinion that the most attractive way of keeping goldfish is in individual aquaria; that is to say, by setting up several small, or medium-sized aquaria and keeping a different breed of goldfish in each. We have in mind an aquarist who has disposed about his home five medium-sized aquaria, Shubunkins in one, Lionheads in another, Fantails in another, Veiltails in another, and Moors in another; and one has only to see this arrangement to reach the conclusion that this method is superior to the more usual one of having one large communal aquarium with many breeds competing against each other for first notice. It is true that several small, or medium-sized aquaria involve more trouble in maintenance, and a bigger initial cost than one large communal aquarium, but, these considerations apart, the two methods cannot be compared. The large communal aquarium is altogether too reminiscent of a window-display in a pet-shop, or a public aquarium, where, of necessity, the aim is to exhibit as many different specimens as possible in a limited space.

Not every aquarist, however, can spare the necessary time and space to maintain several aquaria in his home. The majority have to be content with a communal aquarium, and, when it comes to stocking it we suggest that a selection be made from the following breeds:

Shubunkin.

Fantails, scaled and calico.

Telescopes, scaled and calico.

Moor.

It is advisable to find room for at least one Moor in every communal aquarium. By so doing the slightest sign of bad condition is easily observed; a greyish film seen on the head or body of a Moor (which would probably pass unnoticed on any other breed) is a warning that the water needs changing.

The Common Goldfish and the Comet, may, of course, be given room in an aquarium, but actually they are best reserved for the pond, since neither is sufficiently attractive in general appearance to justify being kept in an aquarium, when so many other more attractive breeds are available.

Veiltails are unsuited to a communal aquarium; they should be given one on their own; for, though they are not delicate fish, neither are they hardy, and they cannot stand rough treatment. Moreover, their particular beauty demands that they should be kept in an aquarium by themselves if they are to be seen and appreciated at their best.

Lionheads, Orandas and Celestials are also unsuited to life in a communal aquarium. They are delicate fish that call for certain attentions. Lionheads and Orandas are handicapped by the wart-like excrescences on their heads. They make the gill-covers inflexible; breathing becomes difficult, so the fish should be kept in water that is artificially aerated. In our experience the Oranda is less susceptible to sudden changes of temperature than the Lionhead; but the Lionhead is further handicapped by the lack of a dorsal fin, and the Celestial is handicapped by upturned eyes and no dorsal fin, and is particularly hard to keep alive. From this the plain, and rather obvious fact emerges: the further the divergence of a fish from its ancestral form, the more difficult is it to keep alive, because every departure from normal throws a further handicap on the fish. In any case, the characteristic features of the Lionhead, Oranda, and Celestial are so striking that they are entirely out of place in a communal aquarium.

When it comes to stocking a pond with goldfish, the aquarist is limited to selecting only from the following breeds:

Common Goldfish.

Shubunkin.

Comet.

For, as we have said in Chapter II, none of the other breeds, with the possible exception of the Moor, is sufficiently hardy to endure a protracted low temperature, or the sudden changes of temperature inevitable outdoors. It is the same with the other fancy breeds. During the summer months some aquarists keep these fish in ponds. We find it pointless to do so; for, apart from the fact that with the possible exception of the Celestial (see Plate XIII) the fish cannot be seen at their best, the fins are very liable to be damaged.

Having said this much, we must now leave it to the individual aquarist to decide for himself which breeds he will keep, and how. For the guidance of the novice, however, the following communities are suggested for balanced aquaria of different sizes. These communities will not overcrowd the aquarium of the specified length and width if small fish (not bigger than 3-inch) are chosen: indeed, the fish will have plenty of room in which to develop.

Aquarium 48 in. by 15 in.

2 Calico Fantails (1 with telescope eyes).

2 Scaled Fantails (1 with telescope eyes).

2 Shubunkins.

2 Moors.

Aquarium 36 in. by 15 in.

1 Shubunkin.

2 Calico Fantails (1 with telescope eyes).

1 Scaled Fantail.

2 Moors.

Aquarium 24 in. by 12 in.

2 Scaled Fantails.

2 Moors.

   or:

2 Shubunkins.

1 Scaled telescope-eyed Fantail.

1 Moor.

Selecting and Transporting

Aquarium 18 in. by 12 in.
1 Calico telescope-eyed Fantail.
2 Moors.

The changes may be rung with the calico Comet and the various types of Nymphs, though these breeds are likely to be hard to come by nowadays, since they are no longer recognized as show-fish.

Goldfish are available from a number of sources, ranging from the specialist breeder and the large and expensive deparmental store to the small and inexpensive pet-shop. In fairness to the small pet-shop, we should add that fish sold by the more expensive shops are not necessarily better than those sold by the less expensive shops. Indeed, sometimes the reverse is the case, since the bigger the shop the more usually (though not necessarily) is it concerned only with making a profit. On more than one occasion we have bought excellent fish from small pet-shops in back streets, and we have seen very inferior fish offered at high prices in large stores. The plain fact is, of course, that goldfish offered for sale—no matter where—are usually a mixed lot, and, from whatever source the aquarist chooses to buy, he must make his selection with care.

Probably the best way to buy goldfish is direct from a reputable breeder. This, however, is a counsel of perfection not always possible to follow; but we must sound the warning that there is probably no surer way of being fobbed off with inferior fish than to buy in response to the advertisement of an unknown breeder or dealer and without first seeing the fish. It is frequently done, despite the admirable legal injunction, *caveat emptor*, warning the inexperienced against buying pigs in pokes. If it can be avoided, it is better not to buy goldfish (particularly fancy fish) without first inspecting them. It is true that the fish can be sent by passenger train, the aquarist can arrange to meet the train, and every reputable breeder and dealer will take reasonable precautions to ensure the safe arrival of the fish; but, even so, it is inadvisable to buy fish in this way, because, no matter how high the reputation and honesty of the seller, he cannot be expected to pick out the most desirable specimens, nor can he tell what coloured fish would be most appreciated by the aquarist. A visit to the premises of the breeder or dealer is greatly to be preferred and strongly to be advised. If this course is impossible the aquarist should send as detailed a description as possible of the fish he seeks. Even when dealing with a seller of the highest integrity, the aquarist must be prepared, unless the seller guarantees live delivery, to stand the loss if casualties occur while the fish are in transit.

A healthy goldfish is active, clear-eyed, has a burnished appearance, and if it has one, carries the dorsal fin permanently erect. The aquarist, therefore, may reject immediately any fish that is inactive and dull of appearance. He may also reject at once any fish that lacks a scale, has a split or torn fin, or shows signs of disease. Apart from the shape of the body, finnage, and coloration, which we have mentioned in Chapter II, the aquarist should choose active fish and fish whose fins stand up well from the body, and whose eyes are round and bright and of equal size (eyes of different sizes is a common phenomenon).

Arthur Derham writes: 'Huge tail development is best avoided in young fish; it is mostly those who "drop out" early who have this exaggerated caudal appendage.' The advice is sound. A small fish with good fin (particularly caudal fin) development looks very attractive, and it is a great temptation to buy such a fish, but the temptation should be resisted, since fish that have developed precociously are almost invariably doomed to an early death. Indeed, on two occasions recently we have bought such fish against our better judgment, or rather with the hope that we might be able to raise them to maturity, but miracles rarely occur and both fish died within a few months. In point of fact, to buy young fish is always speculative, and usually, if the aquarist seeks standard types, it is better to buy fish that have reached maturity, even though they are, of necessity, more expensive. The aquarist should avoid buying fish that are known to have been forced on in running water. Light-coloured fish should also be avoided. Experienced aquarists do not consider them desirable: indeed, as long ago as 1596, Chang Ch'ien-tê wrote: 'Among bowl-fish the pure white are absolutely useless' (*The Book of Vermilion Fish*).

If a fish with a divided caudal fin is being bought, the aquarist would be well advised to buy a fish whose caudal and anal fins are entirely separated. Web-tails and tripod tails, and joined anal fins are not considered of any great value, though, of course, they may be bought if nothing more than a household pet, yet something a bit better than the common goldfish is desired.

Beyond these few remarks little advice can be given about selection. What constitutes a good fish can be learnt only by experience, and, as always, experience must be bought and paid for. However, the aquarist would be well-advised to rely upon his own judgment, supplemented with the advice that we have been able to offer. To ask the seller to pick out a fish, or to pay heed to his salesmanship, may result in getting a good specimen; but, more likely, it will not. We cast no reflection on breeders and dealers in general, the majority of whom are honest. They are, after all, in business to make a living, but the aquarist who flaunts his ignorance of what constitutes a good fish has only himself to blame if he receives an inferior fish for his money. Besides, not every breeder and dealer is honest. It was not so long ago that we played the ignoramus in a shop. We were offered some young fish of very poor quality. To our casual remark that they did not seem very attractive specimens, attention was directed to two particularly fine fish. It was pointed out to us that these were the parents, and the offspring would develop into just as good fish. Even if the two fish were the parents it was sheer nonsense, dishonest nonsense. An even worse example occurred in 1926, just after the first fish show held in England. A dealer offered a good, but not exceptional Fantail at a very high price. To the query: 'Why so much?', the dealer replied that it was the fish that had recently won the gold medal. It was very unfortunate for him that he made this reply to the donor of the medal. If, therefore, the inexperienced aquarist seeks first-class fish, and cannot trust his own judgment, let him enlist the help of an experienced aquarist, upon whose judgment he can rely, to select the best fish for the money that he is prepared to pay.

The price of goldfish is subject to wide fluctuations, according to the source from which the fish are bought, the locality in which they are bought, whether the fish are imported or British-bred, and many other factors, such as age and size. As a general rule, however, unless the aquarist has had considerable experience of the care of goldfish, he would be well advised not to pay a high price. Even the experienced man occasionally suffers some losses when he buys fish, so that, for ornamental purposes, inexpensive ones should be bought. Then, if deaths occur they will involve no great financial loss. Half a dozen Veiltails in a large aquarium look very attractive, but to start off in this way, after paying some fantastic price for the fish, is a dangerous practice, except for the rich. We have known it done with a disastrous result. When this book was first published, in 1948, we noted that goldfish were being sold by London dealers for anything from 12s. 6d. upwards; for goldfish, like all else, are subject to the law of supply and demand, and during the war years 1939–45 there was a scarcity of homebred fish and no imports. Today, of course, prices are considerably lower, and good fish can be bought for from half a crown upwards. We shall, let us hope, never return to the days when goldfish were plentiful in chain-stores and markets for 3d. apiece. By contrary, half a century ago a Moor Goldfish, owned by Otto Gneiding of New Jersey, was valued at 5,000 dollars. During the war of 1914–18 it patriotically changed colour to red, white and blue, and its name from 'Old Black Joe' to 'Miss Liberty' and toured the U.S.A. to promote the sales of Liberty Bonds. It lived for more than twenty years.

Francis Buckland once took home some goldfish, wrapped in damp moss and a cloth, in a carpet-bag. There are better ways of transporting fish. For a short distance a newly-acquired fish may be carried in almost any container that holds water. Vessels made of glass, china, porcelain, enamel and tin are safe for fish, and for a small fish a jam jar (the 2-lb. size) or a tin can is quite good enough for the purpose. Although during the second World War a battalion of American soldiers brought their goldfish mascot ('Oscar') to England in a whisky bottle filled with water (and subsequently kept it in a water-filled steel-helmet) this is another method of transporting fish that is not to be commended! For long distances, or for a large fish, or if several fish have to be carried, a travelling-can is to be advised. A good type of travelling-can is shown in the accompanying illustration. The handy-man will find no difficulty in making such a can. Tinplate is the most satisfactory metal; it is light and does not harm fish. The one drawback is that it rusts very easily, and, though rust within reason has never yet harmed a fish, a tin travelling-can (we write from experience) is liable to spring a leak at an awkward moment. The travelling-can, therefore, should always be thoroughly dried after use, and it should be stored in a dry place. To prolong its life the inside may be given a thin coating of a bituminous paint. As a final precaution, when transporting fish the aquarist is advised to carry a tube of cold solder to effect a temporary repair

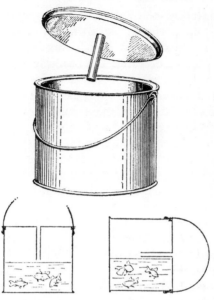

Fig. 26. AN 'UNSPILLABLE' TRAVELLING-CAN

A metal tube, reaching half-way to the bottom of the can
serves as an air inlet. If the can is less than half full of water,
and the lid fits, it cannot spill in any position. The sectional
diagrams (below) show the can upright and on its side.

if necessary. Most metals are harmful to fish, and vessels made of
copper, brass, and bronze are particularly to be avoided, for they
are poisonous. Zinc or a galvanized container should not be used;
for these, at all events when new, are harmful, though they may be
rendered safe if the inside of the vessel is given several thin coats of
a bituminous paint. Iron is reasonably safe (though it is harmful to
snails) but is unnecessarily heavy for the purpose. Wood, unless
matured, is harmful, and though it is well known that the Chinese
hawk small goldfish round the streets in shallow wooden tubs
(about 18 in. in diameter and 6 in. deep) slung from a pole carried
over the shoulder, it may not be so well known that new tubs
are always painted white inside and the top edge red: and the
paint is not renewed, because it has no need to be, when it has
worn off.

On reaching their destination fish that have travelled a long
distance should be refreshed by applying artificial aeration to the

water in the travelling-can. Indeed, if fish have to travel very long distances the water should be artificially aerated during the journey, and a tablespoonful of salt (not table-salt) should be added to every gallon of water. The best way to aerate the water, however, is to pass a length of rubber tubing, with a diffuser at the end, through one of the holes in the lid of the can, and pump air with a bicycle pump or, more conveniently, with a small bellows which can be operated by foot.

A newly-acquired fish should be taken home in some of the water in which it has been living, and then two or three partial changes of water, over a period of about a fortnight, will acclimatize it to that in which eventually it is to be kept. During this period the fish should be closely watched for any signs of disease. A fortnight in quarantine will usually be sufficient to show whether it is safe to introduce a newcomer into the aquarium or pond. During the isolation period the fish should be fed sparingly at first, and the feeding gradually increased. Fish kept by dealers for sale have usually been very sparingly fed, and a heavy meal after a long fast is as bad for fish as it is for all animals.

Before introducing a new fish into an established aquarium or pond, careful aquarists give it disinfecting baths twice a week during the quarantine period. Six crystals of permanganate of potash (or seven or eight drops of Condy's fluid) are dissolved in a pint of water. The solution is then poured into a suitable vessel, and the fish is allowed to swim in the solution for about ten minutes. If, however, the fish shows signs of distress, by behaving in an unusual manner, it should be removed immediately and placed in a weaker solution. Molluscs may be given the same treatment, and if they have been taken from natural waters two or three disinfecting baths at 3-day intervals are an essential preliminary to their being introduced into an aquarium or pond. An immersion for about one minute at a time is sufficient for a mollusc. The disinfecting bath postulates that the fish has the outward appearance of being in health. If a fish shows signs of disease it should, of course, be given the treatment prescribed in Chapter VII for its particular ailment.

Fish are notoriously curious, and a new fish introduced into an aquarium or pond in which others are living is, at first, likely to be chevied about. Nothing much can be done about this, though it is a wise precaution to keep all fish in the same aquarium or pond as much as possible the same size. It is best to introduce a new fish into strange surroundings soon after feeding time; fish are not all that coldblooded, and a good meal fosters geniality as much among fish as it does among men!

The Dutch naturalist, Job Baster, in November 1758, received twelve goldfish from England, and placed them in ponds in his garden. He writes: 'With the exception of four, which I found dead and floating after a few days, I never saw them again. I have heard that this calamity has happened to others who placed these fish in their fish-ponds. In my opinion it is caused by the fact that the fish, poured out from the jar into the water, are struck with fear, swim to the bottom too quickly, and there they stick smothered too deeply so that they are unable to get out of the mud and are suffocated. Hence I thought it better afterwards to hold the container, in which the fish are, tied on the end of a rope, and let it down into the water so that they can swim out quite naturally.' Baster did the right thing, though he did not know the reason for it. Today we know that fish that have been living in an aquarium should never be introduced into a pond until all danger of frosts has passed. They must be given time to become acclimatized to possible sudden changes of temperature, and if they are not they are liable to succumb. Baster's method of floating the can in the water, until the two temperatures equalize, and the fish swim out of their own accord, is now the recognized method of introducing fish into a pond.

In the decade before the outbreak of the second World War, the importation of goldfish into England was carried on in a big way. The precise figures are not available, and estimates are unreliable, but there need exist no doubt that, before the second World War, large numbers of goldfish (mainly the fancy breeds) were exported annually from China and Japan. An issue of *Asahi* (Tokio, 1931), states that at Koriyama alone from twelve to thirteen million goldfish were set free every year in rearing ponds. Oriental breeders—at all events the Chinese—have never shown much interest in the common goldfish, and most of these, that up to 1940 were sold in chain-stores and pet-shops for the proverbial two a penny came from Italy and America. The figures are more reliable; we have it on the word of a London dealer that he imported as many as twenty thousand goldfish from Italy in one month.

The Goldfish

At one time imported fish had to travel long distances by comparatively slow train and even slower boat (from China!) in large containers. The result was inevitable; despite aeration and other precautions, hundreds of fish died or were killed by being dashed against the sides of the cans in rough weather. Those that survived the journey were in a weakened condition and many of them died soon after arrival, unable to withstand the change of water, climatic conditions, and the like. Experienced dealers who imported fish considered themselves lucky if a can of fish reached them from abroad with a loss of not more than ninety per cent.

Today we have altered all that. The fast-moving aeroplane, sealed plastic bags, and shots of oxygen, make the importation of fish a much simpler and more reliable business, and a considerably more comfortable one for the fish. Nonetheless, if there is any choice in the matter we would recommend our readers to buy British-bred fish rather than imported ones. There are several reasons for this, and patriotism is not among them. British-bred fish are always more expensive than imported ones, but the extra cost is worth while. Nor can the aquarist be certain of imported fish; there are ways of drugging inferior fish to make them appear healthy.

Chapter VI

FOODS AND FEEDING

New dishes beget new appetites.

RAY, *A Compleat Collection of English Proverbs*

The feeding of fry is reserved for mention in the chapter on breeding (Chapter VIII). We are concerned in this chapter only with adult fish; and we may begin by pointing out that goldfish, whether kept in an aquarium or a pond, have to be fed. The belief that adult fish can subsist by 'finding things in the water' is founded on a fallacy. It is true that, in some shops, gold-fish for sale are given very little, if any, food, but the reason for this is a commercial one. Hungry fish are more active than well-fed fish, and uneaten particles of food cloud the water. By giving the fish very little food, just sufficient to prevent starvation, they are displayed at their best, and if the activity of the fish and the clarity of the water impress the inexperienced buyer, it is, never-theless, a minor form of cruelty which we cannot condemn too strongly. A goldfish, like any other animal, needs to be properly and regularly fed.

Goldfish are omnivorous, or nearly so; like human beings they will eat almost anything. Indeed, to catalogue all the foods that may be given to goldfish would require a volume to itself, but may be divided into two main categories: live foods and dried foods. It is our intention to name the more important foods in each group with a short note on each.

LIVE FOODS. Live food is generally regarded as the best for fish, because it is more in keeping with nature and their taste. From an almost endless list, the more important live foods, nourishing and not difficult to obtain, are crustaceans, insect-larvae and worms. Those mentioned are sub-headed for convenience under the generic and trivial names of the most common species in each group.

CRUSTACEANS

DAPHNIA PULEX (Water Flea) is a small crustacean, no relation
to the domestic parasite. It obtains its trivial name only on account
of its habit of moving about actively with a very jerky motion. As
a food for goldfish it is very valuable; for its main source of food is
algae, and from them it obtains oil. 'It is to this oil', Laurence
Wells writes, 'that the herring owes its oiliness and the cod its
valuable liver. It will be realized then, that the value of *Daphnia* as
fish food is no fad, it is an unassailable fact'.[1] At the same time, we
find it necessary to add that daphnids are very laxative and, therefore, should not be fed to fish in excessive quantities.

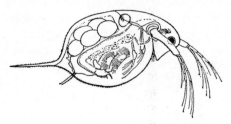

Fig. 27. WATER FLEA (*Daphnia*)
(Greatly enlarged)

Daphnids may either be bought from a dealer or collected by
the aquarist himself. They are to be found in the shallow verges of
stagnant ponds, particularly those ponds in the neighbourhood
of farms. Daphnids are most active when the sun is low, both in
the evening and morning, and are often to be found in such
quantities as to give the water a reddish-brown tinge. A sweep
with a fine-meshed net will capture them in large quantities, but
not too many should be taken at a time; for, if they are, the weight
of those at the top of the container will kill those underneath. It is
important not to give a catch of daphnids direct to the fish; many
undesirable insects may be included in the catch. A pure culture
must first be obtained.

To obtain a pure culture, a stock pond should be started. A rain-
water butt, or a tank, is placed in a well-lighted corner of the
garden and filled with water to a depth of about 18 in. Refuse

[1] A. Laurence Wells, *Live Foods for Aquarium Fishes* (London, 1938).

from the aquarium or pond is put into it, and also some cow-manure, approximately one tablespoonful of manure to every gallon of water. This should be allowed to stand for two or three weeks before stocking with daphnids. A catch may then be turned into a bowl, and desirable specimens transferred to the stock pond with a pipette. From time to time dying plants, the leaves of lettuce, and the like, may be added, as they assist in the formation of the food on which daphnids exist. Snails may also be kept in the stock pond; for daphnids flourish better when snails are present. When daphnids are required for the fish they may be obtained by skimming the surface of the stock pond (taking care not to disturb the bottom) with a fine-meshed net. They should then be rinsed in running water and given to the fish. Careful aquarists even place the daphnids in a white enamel bowl, or similar container, and make an inspection for dirt and undesirable insects that may have been taken with the net. In point of fact, one cannot be too careful; for when we consider the many kinds of decomposition that take place in water in which daphnids flourish best, and the amount of dirt that will fall into a pond kept in the open, it seems to be only by great good luck that gold-fish fed on daphnids do not contract contagious diseases more often. The best temperature for breeding *Daphnia* is said to be about 70° F.

The stock pond will last for a considerable time. Although the male *Daphnia* is rare, and to be seen only at certain seasons, the female needs to be fertilized only once. Remarkably, not only does the one fertilization suffice for all successive broods, but also serves for the next two or three generations.

A stock pond of this nature will enable the aquarist to have a supply of daphnids for about nine months in the year. A small supply can be maintained throughout the winter if a stock pond is set up in a greenhouse, but it should be placed near a window, because light is as important as warmth.

Another method of cultivating *Daphnia* (suitable for the aquarist who has no garden) is to obtain a number of enamel pie-dishes, or similar containers, and fill them with aged water. Into each dish a few daphnids, and a teaspoonful of green water and water containing infusoria[1] are introduced. A bruised lettuce leaf

---

[1] Strictly, infusoria is a large group of microscopic animals provisionally regarded as the highest subdivision of the Protozoa. Here and elsewhere, however, we use

or banana skin may be placed in each dish with advantage. Every day a teaspoonful of green water and water containing infusoria should be added to the dishes. If the daphnids are given sufficient food they will multiply rapidly. Methods of cultivating infusoria are given on page 206, but we are not sure that cultivating infusoria is really necessary. We have bred daphnids in jam jars and fed them solely with the sediment removed from an established aquarium. To feed the fish, all that is necessary is to pour the contents of a dish into the aquarium, though it is better to strain the water from the dish through a muslin bag and empty the contents of the bag into the aquarium, so that the cloudy water from the dish will not foul the aquarium. The dish may then be restocked, and, indeed, if it is refilled promptly, it is almost certain that the few daphnids, always left clinging to the sides of the dish, will restart the culture. Daphnids consume a remarkable amount of oxygen for their size. There must, therefore, be no overcrowding, if there is the culture will soon be gone. To provide artificial aeration may come as a surprise to many, but it certainly helps to keep the culture alive until the aquarist has struck the balance between the rate of multiplication and the number that he needs to feed to his fish.

CYCLOPS VULGARIS is a live food for goldfish that some authorities consider better than *Daphnia*, while others will have none of it. In our view it is quite satisfactory.

Cyclops will be found in much the same places as *Daphnia*, and, indeed, a catch of daphnids will nearly always include many *Cyclops*. They can be cultivated and fed to fish in the same way.

Cyclops is easily recognized, and well named; for it is characteristic that it has a single median eye near the upper surface of its head. A further prominent feature is a pair of large pear-shaped egg sacs attached to the enlarged portion of the body (cephalothorax) of the female.

The belief that *Cyclops* turns parasite to fish has for long been exploded, and as food for goldfish it may be introduced into aquaria and ponds with confidence. The belief appears to have been founded on the fact that the allied *Ergasilus* and *Thersitina* are semi-parasitic to fish.

the word 'infusoria' to cover all forms of minute animal and vegetable life which goldfish-breeders cultivate for feeding to fry, etc.

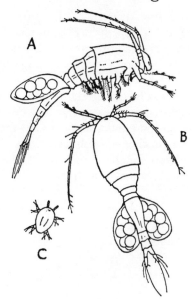

Fig. 28. *Cyclops*
(A) Side view; (B) Upper view; (C) Nauplius
(larva)   (Greatly enlarged)

CYPRIS FUSCA is similar in appearance to *Daphnia*, but smaller. It is found in much the same places as *Daphnia* and *Cyclops*. It can be captured, cultivated, and fed to goldfish in the same way.

Many aquarists consider that *Cypris* is an excellent food for fish (indeed of little less value than *Daphnia*) but we are not convinced that this is so, because its carapace is hard and horny. It is, however, a useful food to offer as a change of diet, and it is in no sense harmful, except to snails as it works its way under their shells and irritates them.

GAMMARUS PULEX (Freshwater Shrimp) is a very common crustacean, and an excellent food for fish. Like *Daphnia* and *Cyclops* it moves with jerky motions. But there the similarity ends; for it is very much larger and bears a marked likeness to the common shrimp.

It can be reared in a stock pond as already recommended (it feeds on decaying matter, animal and vegetable), but this is not necessary, except perhaps for town-dwellers, as it can be found in abundance in almost every stream and ditch. It is fairly large (it grows to a length of three-quarters of an inch), and can be netted out when required as food for fish. It is, in fact, better to take it from natural waters when required than to breed it, as it does not live long unless kept in running water or a large pond. It will not thrive in very soft water.

It is to be found usually among the roots and on the stalks of marginal aquatic plants, and, as it can live out of water for a considerable time, so long as its body is kept moist, it will frequently be found in bunches of fresh watercress. The best way to transport it is in damp aquatic plants; for if placed in a can of water the jolting is likely to kill it.

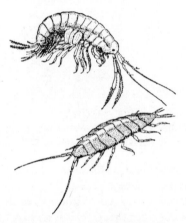

Fig. 29. FRESHWATER SHRIMP (*Gammarus*)
WATER-HOG LOUSE (*Asellus*)

ASELLUS AQUATICUS (Water-hog Louse, Hog Slater, or Freshwater Louse) is exceedingly common in most ponds, where it will be found creeping on the bottom and on the leaves of submerged aquatic plants. It is fairly large, and grows to a length of about half an inch, so may be netted out when required as food for fish, if the aquarist does not wish to go to the trouble of rearing it, which he can do in a stock pond. It feeds mainly on decaying vegetable matter.

The *Asellus* is a cousin of ONISCUS ASELLUS (Wood Louse) and related species, which are to be found usually under stones, and by stripping off the bark of a dead tree. Wood lice may be cultivated by placing a few under stones or logs, where the soil is slightly damp, and feeding them on sliced potato.

Both *Asellus* and *Oniscus* are excellent food for goldfish, on account of their high calcium content.

Artemia salina (Brine Shrimp) has to be cultivated by the British aquarist. It is not found wild in the British Isles.[1]

It is not difficult to cultivate *Artemia*. One ounce of sea-salt is dissolved in a quart of water, and the brine allowed to stand for twenty-four hours. A pinch of the eggs (which, of course, must be bought from a dealer) is then dropped in the brine, and the young hatch out two or three days later, the length of time depending on the temperature at which the brine has been kept. The nauplius of *Artemia* is very small. It will extract sufficient nourishment from the brine to maintain it for three or four days: thereafter, it must be fed with infusoria (see page 206), or a very fine dried food, such as sifted dried shrimp.

According to Wells,[2] the eggs of *Artemia* will hatch in two days, if kept at a temperature of 70°F., and in three days if kept in room-temperature (50 to 60°), but some experimentation may be necessary to obtain the most satisfactory temperature (60 to 70° is said to be the best temperature) and strength of the brine.

Before brine shrimps are fed to fish they should be thoroughly rinsed in fresh water to rid them of brine.

INSECT-LARVAE

Goldfish are notoriously partial to the larvae of insects, and, along with many other species, e.g., the Anabantids, they are used in many parts of the world as larvicidal fish.

Insect-larvae are a valuable live food for goldfish, and he who feeds his fish on them is not only satisfying his fish, but doing mankind a good service.

The following are the most common and easily obtained insect-larvae in Britain.

The Larva of Culex pipiens. *Culex pipiens* is known to most people as the Common Gnat. The female gnat lays her eggs on the surface of water. The egg is cylindrical in form, but tapers off at the end, and is provided with a cap at the other end. Each

[1] The Great Salt Lake of America is one of the main sources of supply.
[2] A. Laurence Wells, op. cit., p. 144.

egg is covered with a sticky substance that dries on exposure to air, and the whole cluster of eggs (numbering from two hundred to three hundred) is built into a little raft that floats on the surface of the water, with the pointed ends of the eggs upwards. These egg-rafts are an excellent food for goldfish, though they are so small (less than a quarter of an inch in length) that there is something to be said for waiting until the eggs hatch and the larvae have reached an appreciable size.

The larva of the gnat is easily recognized. When at rest it suspends itself, head downwards, from the surface of the water. In this position the breathing apparatus is exposed to the atmosphere, while the head searches for minute particles of food. A quick sweep with a fine-meshed net will capture the larvae in quantities. The catch should be examined, undesirables rejected, and finally rinsed in running water and given to the fish.

The larva undergoes several moults during its growth. The last one reveals it in the form of a pupa. The pupa is also a good food for goldfish, and it may be captured and given to the fish in the same way. The pupa is easily recognized; for the head with the antennae, mouth-organs, legs and wings, of the future imago, are altogether in a large rounded mass, from which the comparatively narrow abdomen extends. The pupa rests on the surface of the water, but, when disturbed, sinks to the bottom with a sort of head over heels falling motion.

The egg-rafts, the larvae, and the pupae of gnats are not hard to obtain. In the summer months they can be found in most stagnant waters. Indeed, the aquarist, if he has a rain-water butt in his garden, need go no further to capture them in large quantities. Aquarists who live in towns, and who have no gardens, have been known to place tubs and buckets of water on roofs, or outside back doors, and even to place low-powered lights over the water to attract the female gnat to lay her eggs. Others make a point of visiting the country once a week, where they collect egg-rafts, larvae and pupae, which they keep in jars of clean water until required. The jars should be kept in a cool place, to retard development, and covered with a piece of muslin held in place with a rubber band and drawn up into a bag to form a trap for any gnats that develop.

THE LARVA OF CHIRONOMUS PLUMOSUS. *Chironomus plumosus* is popularly known as the Midge, and the larva as the Blood-

worm. The bloodworm is a good food for fish, it is easily recognized as a worm-like creature, bright scarlet in colour, about
three-quarters of an inch to one inch in length when full-grown,
moving about the water by vigorously looping its body first on
one side and then on the other in figure of eight motions.

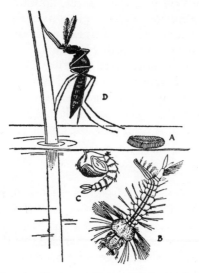

Fig. 30. COMMON GNAT (*Culex pipiens*)
(A) Egg-raft; (B) Larva; (C) Pupa; (D) Adult.
(Enlarged)

Like the larvae of gnats, bloodworms can be captured in the
summer in most stagnant ponds (especially those surrounded by
trees) and rainwater butts. The best way to take them from a pond
is to stir the bottom of a likely pond vigorously and allow the
sediment to settle. If bloodworms are present they will be seen
wriggling in the water and may be captured with the sweep of a
fine-meshed net. If kept damp, and in a cool place, they will live
for an appreciable time out of water. Bloodworms and glassworms
(page 152) are furnished with a pair of powerful mandibles, and,
according to some authorities, there is the risk that they will eat
their way out of fish that bolt their food. We have never known it
to happen, and if it has, the accident must be so rare that it may be
ignored.

The egg of *Chironomus* may also be fed to goldfish. It appears as a transparent sausage-shaped capsule containing what looks like a coiled spring.

THE LARVA OF CHAOBORUS PLUMICORNIS. *Chaoborus plum- icornis* is popularly known as the Plumed Gnat, and the larva as the Phantom-larva, the Glassworm, or Phantomworm. The phantom-larva is very similar in size and appearance to the blood-worm, but is transparent as its popular names imply. As a food for goldfish it is excellent, and many aquarists rank it as the best of all live foods. It has the further advantage of being available during the winter months, when most live foods are scarce.

It is rarer than the larva of the gnat and midge, but, when found, is usually present in large numbers. It may be captured with a sweep of a fine-meshed net, and then looks like a mass of jelly. It is pre-dacious and feeds on small insects and crustaceans.

WORMS

LUMBRICUS TERRESTIS (Earthworm) has been described as God's gift to the aquarist. There is some truth in this, for the earthworm is easy to obtain at all seasons of the year and no fish has been known to refuse it. It is recognized that there is no better food for bringing a fish into breeding condition, and it acts as a mild laxative, an important consideration when fish are kept in the confined space of an aquarium or pond.

Pink worms should be chosen, also the red worms that are to be found on lawns. Worms that frequent manure heaps and heavily manured soil should be avoided. We will not say that they are poisonous, but the fish refuse them and they are left to putrify and foul the water. The worms may be recognized by the red rings on their bodies, and the fact that they exude an unpleastant yellow secretion. We have been told that keeping these worms for a few days in damp moss makes them palatable to fish, but we have no experience of this. Worms up to about 2 in. in length are best. Bigger ones are inclined to be tough. Small worms may be given whole, but large worms should be cut into suitable lengths. A discarded safety-razor blade in a holder makes an ideal tool for the job. The operation is, we admit, a most unpleasant one, and those who are squeamish may first kill a worm by dropping it into boil-ing water. Worms should be washed clean of mud before they are cut up, and afterwards they may be given a quick rinse in running water, but the final rinsing should not be overdone, as the inside (blood and decomposing vegetable matter) is an excellent food for fish, readily eaten by them, and too much rinsing only wastes it. Our own method is to place the chopped worms in a 1-lb. jam jar of water, stir, and pour off the liquid.

A mixture of mustard and water, or $\frac{1}{2}$ oz. of permanganate of potash in 2 gallons of water, will bring earthworms to the surface. An alternative method is to place some rotten pieces of sacking in an odd corner of the garden and throw over them all the old tea-leaves from the pot. If this is left for a time and kept covered with fresh grouts, some worms will always be available, even in the driest of weather. Earthworms may be kept through the winter (when the ground is too hard to dig) in boxes of damp, but not wet, earth. They should be kept in a cool place, and may be fed on mashed potato, preferably unsalted, and leaves.

TUBIFEX TUBIFEX (Mudworm or Riverworm) is one of the oligochaete worms. It thrives in running, preferably tidal, water, which contains much organic matter. Given the right conditions the worms will colonize rapidly and cover large areas; but they make tubes for themselves in the mud, into which they retire at the slightest tremor. The only way to find the worms, therefore, is to stand on the bank and remain perfectly still until they come out of their tubes, and their bodies can be seen waving to and fro in the water, when they can be collected with a ladle. The catch should be placed in a lidless wooden box, and if kept in a cool place, and the surface of the mud kept moist, it will last for some considerable time. When the worms are required to feed to the fish, a quantity of mud should be placed in a shallow pan of water and stirred. The worms will gather together in pink writhing balls and may be picked out with a forceps. Alternatively, the worms may be separated from the mud by placing a quantity of the mud in a tea-infuser, closing the lid, and swishing it to and fro in a bucket of water.

As will be seen, collecting and cleaning *Tubifex* is a troublesome and messy job, and dealers sell it free of mud. *Tubifex* cannot be cultivated, but once obtained they will live for quite a long time out of water, if their bodies are kept moist. They can be sent long distances by post, if packed in damp moss or grass. They may also be kept in running water or in water that is changed frequently; stagnant water, or water that is warm, kills them.

Tubifex are sufficiently small to give whole to fish, but they should not be dropped into the aquarium or pond. If any are missed by the fish they will promptly burrow into the planting medium, colonize, and become a nuisance. The worms should be placed in a feeding-basket, sold by most dealers for a few pence. This, semi-spherical in shape and perforated, is made of celluloid and floats on the surface of the water. As the worms wriggle through the perforations the fish jerk them out one by one.

There is no reason to believe that *Tubifex* turns parasite to fish. They are, in fact, a good live food, with the further advantage that they are obtainable in winter when most other live foods are scarce.

ENCHYTRAEUS ALBIDUS (Whiteworm) is very popular among experienced aquarists. But this, we think, is only because it is easy to cultivate and there is no need to grub in dirty ponds; for it is a filling, rather than a nourishing food, and, therefore, not to be recommended as staple diet, though it has its value as a change.

Enchytraeus is creamy yellow in colour, grows to a length of about three-quarters of an inch, and is usually to be found under dustbins, and the like. It may be given whole to big fish, but should be pulped for small fish.

To cultivate enchytrae (as they are commonly, but erroneously, called) a lidless wooden box, about 18 in. long, 12 in. wide, and 6 in. deep, is half filled with humus, or loose loam, and care should be taken to see that no ants or beetles are introduced into the soil. It is, in fact, a good idea to sieve the soil and bake it in an oven. Several shallow hollows are made in the soil, and these are filled with food for the worms. The food may consist of almost anything in the way of household scraps reduced to a soft pulp. Laurence Wells recommends 'a "mash" of boiled potatoes, bread, oatmeal, or even dog-biscuits'.[1] Austin Watson recommends 'a mess of sour bread and milk', also 'a little cold boiled cauliflower, stalk or leaves . . . lightly moistened'.[2] Other aquarists have other recipes. Our own is a mash of boiled potatoes, cheese-rind and bread or biscuit, moistened with a little milk and cod-liver oil. The better the worms are fed the better it is for the fish, because the food is passed to them through the worms in only a slightly

[1] A. Laurence Wells, op. cit., p. 144.
[2] F. Austin Watson, *Aquarium and Pond Management for Beginners* (London, 1933), and *Fishponds and Home Aquariums* (London, 1936).

altered form. The worms are placed on top of the food and covered with a sprinkling of humus. The humus should be kept damp, but not so damp that a lump of it will smear the hand. To retain the dampness, the box should be covered with a sheet of glass in contact with the humus. It is best to keep the box in a dark and airy place, at a temperature of about 55° F., and out of the reach of mice. The temperature is of importance, for at 75 degrees the worms die, and at 35 degrees they will not breed. When the worms are required to feed to the fish they should be taken from each hollow in turn, but not from any one hollow more often than once a week. Before feeding to the fish the worms must be separated from the humus, and the simplest way to do this is to place a quantity of the humus in a saucerful of water. The worms will collect on the surface of the water, from where they may be scooped up and given a rinse in running water before feeding them to the fish in a feeding-basket. The box should be inspected occasionally, to ensure that the humus is damp and to replace any food that has turned rancid. It is best to allow the box to stand for a month before taking the first supply of worms.

Small crustaceans, insect-larvae, and worms, are the main live foods, but, since the goldfish is virtually omnivorous, there are many other live foods that may be offered as a change of diet.

Black-fly, *Green-fly*, and *House-fly*, may be given with confidence provided, of course, they have not been in contact with toxic sprays. The last may be used freshly killed, though it is better to give the fly alive, first cutting off its wings with a sharp scissors (the operation does not hurt the fly) to prevent it flying out of the water. Flies are easiest caught in a wire-mesh trap baited with boiled ox-liver.

The *Larva of the Flesh-fly* (better known as the Bluebottle-fly), popularly known as the Gentle, may also be given. Gentles may be cultivated in the summer months by allowing a piece of meat or fish to go bad. Flies lay their eggs on it, resulting in a few days in a horrible smell and a large number of gentles. Gentles may be kept for a considerable time in pickle bottles buried in the ground.

The *Larva of the Mealworm Beetle*, popularly known as the Mealworm is a suitable food for large goldfish. Mealworms may be bought from dealers, and if a regular supply is desired a number should be placed in a large tin filled with bran and bread. In time the worms will pupate into beetles, and the beetles, in turn, will produce more worms.

The *Eggs of Ants* (actually they are not the eggs of ants but the pupae of ants) may be given if they are taken direct from the nest. The 'Ants' Eggs' sold in packets are useless. They are merely the dried and empty pupae cases of the ants and contain no nutriment.

The *Spawn of Water-snails*, which will be found adhering to the leaves of aquatic plants, is a satisfactory food for goldfish, as is also the *Spawn of Frogs*. The spawn of toads is not to be recommended, and, though the egg of the frog is very similar to the egg of the toad, they may be distinguished by the fact that whereas the eggs of the frog cling together in jelly-like masses, the eggs of the toad cling together in a long chain, sometimes a yard or more in length.

Snails, aquatic or terrestrial, may be removed from their shells and fed to the fish. Small snails may be given whole, but large ones must first be pulped. *Mussels*, freshwater and salt-water, and *Slugs* may also be fed to goldfish in the same way. Snails, mussels and slugs may first be killed by dropping them into boiling water. Death is instantaneous.

Large fish will eat the *Small Tadpoles of Frogs*, though the larger tadpoles are distasteful to fish, as are also the tadpoles, large or small, of toads, which some say may be poisonous. The tadpole of the toad is darker in colour than that of the frog. The tadpole of the newt may be recognized by the fact that its external gills are longer and more plume-like than those of the tadpole of the frog and toad. We have had no experience of it as food for fish.

From all that we have written it will be seen that live food for goldfish is more plentiful in the spring and summer than in the autumn and winter. This is the natural order of things, but, even in the winter, the aquarist has plenty of substitutes for live foods, which he may give his fish as a change of diet.

Scraped raw meat, tinned cat and dog foods and finely chopped raw liver (the last must first be well washed and given sparingly, or the blood will foul the water) are satisfactory foods for goldfish. So also are scrambled egg, finely chopped fish (boiled or raw), finely-chopped crab, lobster, and the like, which may be either tinned or fresh. To quote Margery Elwin: 'There is a number of items in the kitchen which, in small quantities, appeal to the finny taste, for instance, chopped shrimp and scallop, fish paste, and scraped boiled fish or raw liver, the latter being a great tonic to fishes who have learned to eat it.' Betts writes: 'Little scraps from the dinner table are always acceptable, provided they are free from sauces, vinegar, and the like.'[1] He is careful to add, and we would stress this point, that such foods should be given only as a change of diet and when live foods are hard to obtain. For, when all is said, daphnids and earthworms are the best foods for goldfish, and the aquarist will not go far wrong if he regards these as the staple foods, ringing the changes as much as possible on the others.

It is advisable to give goldfish an occasional feed of green food. A lack of green food is detrimental to their health. The best, because it is the most natural, is *Lemna*, and nearly all goldfish will eat it avidly. When this is not available good substitutes are the boiled and finely-chopped leaf of spinach, cabbage, and Brussels sprouts, also the leaf of a lettuce, which may be given boiled or raw and finely-chopped. In a well-established aquarium or pond the fish will always find some green food among the aquatic plants, but a feed of *Lemna*, or green vegetable from the kitchen, about once a fortnight is to be recommended. If *Lemna* is taken from native waters it should be thoroughly cleansed before giving it to the fish (see page 103). Failure to take this precaution may result in trematodes (flukes), and other undesirable parasites, being introduced into the aquarium or pond.

DRIED FOODS. Although it may be true that goldfish can live on a diet of dried foods, it is inadvisable to rely exclusively on them. There are many reasons for this. Firstly, some of the dried foods sold in packets are nothing more than crushed dog-biscuit, which, in most cases, does not appear to be relished by the fish, and contains little, if any, nourishment. Secondly, even the dried foods sold by reputable firms —who cannot afford to make mistakes—contain a quantity of starchy matter, and a too starchy diet is as bad for fish as it is for human beings. Thirdly, dried food swells in contact with water, and if the food swells inside the stomach of the fish it leads to indigestion, constipation, and derangement of the air-bladder, and though this can be avoided to some extent, by soaking the food, or better still by scalding it, before giving it to the fish, they do not seem to like it so much as when given dry. Fourthly, it is difficult to estimate the quantity

[1] Leonard C. Betts, *The Goldfish* (London, 1939).

to give, and any uneaten dried food quickly decomposes and fouls the water. Fifthly, fish, like most animals, enjoy a varied diet, and to feed them exclusively on dried food is a minor form of cruelty.

All this is not to say, however, that dried food should never be given to fish. On the contrary, in the autumn, just before the weather becomes cold, a little dried food may be given to goldfish that live in ponds. It supplies them with bulk to help them through the winter. Fancy goldfish, that live in an aquarium, may also be given dried food occasionally—'to encourage that quaint corpulency which is so much a part of their attraction',[1] to use Austin Watson's expressive phrase.

As for the dried foods that may be given, the list is almost as inexhaustible as that of live foods. Apart from that sold in packets, brown bread-crumbs, crushed biscuits of good quality, and oatmeal dry or as porridge, are all satisfactory. The proprietary health-food, known as Bemax is not only nourishing but helps to bring out the colours of the fish. Dried *Daphnia* is sold by dealers, and though it is a filling food it is not particularly nourishing, and is not to be compared with live *Daphnia*. Dried shrimps may also be given: common shrimps are dried in a slow oven, and, when crisp, crushed to a suitable size. Crushed vermicelli, bran and white bread-crumbs have been recommended by some authorities, but the value of these is not very great, though we admit the impossibility of convincing aquarists who feed their goldfish on these foods that the fish live only because they are very hardy, and are able to survive despite the food.

Some aquarists prefer to make their own dried fish-foods (prepared foods), and many, including some of the large commercial breeders have recipes that they will not divulge, but which their experience has proved will help to induce a rich coloration, promote strong skeletal growth, and, in the Fantail and Veiltail breeds, produce the desired spherical body. In this connection, C. B. Hall writes: 'The artificial feeding of fish, after many years of experimenting, has now become a science. An extra growth, sometimes five-fold, has been the result of artificial feeding, but to attain this growth, and keep healthy, the fish must have at least 25 per cent of natural food.' German research-workers go even further; for, with their customary thoroughness, the Germans

---

[1] F. Austin Watson, *Fishponds and Home Aquariums* (London, 1936).

have investigated the artificial feeding of fish with all the help that modern science has to offer, and this has enabled them to make the claim that fish which are not entirely carnivorous (as are gold-fish) do not develop fully on a diet limited to live food. At first sight the implication is that Nature does not know her own business, since, it would seem that in their natural state the Cyprinidae, which are not wholly carnivorous, must exist wholly on live food. This, however, is not so, since in natural waters fish have access to various aquatic plants, the roots of higher plants, and other matter, all of which are denied to them in an aquarium or man-made pond. Also the Japanese, who with some 250 years of piscicultural experience behind them cannot be ignored, are firm believers in the artificial feeding of goldfish; and foods composed of various cereals, dried insects (including the larvae of silk-worms) and honey are regularly fed to goldfish by Japanese breeders. The well-known Japanese 'wafer' foods are made with rice-flour and eggs. In most European and American hatcheries the fish are fed on a cooked mixture of cereal, meat, shrimp, milk and cod-liver oil. Usually it is given wet. Innes gives several good recipes for dried foods. In one he recommends one-quarter of a tumblerful of powdered cod, three-quarters of a tumblerful of powdered shrimp, 3 teaspoonsful of wholewheat flour, 1 teaspoonful of Epsom salts, 3 teaspoonsful of baking-powder, and 3 teaspoonsful of powdered (precipitated) chalk. These ingredients are well mixed and then kneaded into a dough with 2 raw eggs and water. After baking in an oven the food is allowed to cool, cut into thin slices, thoroughly dried, and crushed into suitable sizes.[1]

Although there is, therefore, a body of authoritative opinion in favour of the artificial feeding of goldfish, many authorities, whose opinions are to be respected, frown on too much cereal food for fish. The goldfish in the excellent aquarium in the Zoological Gardens of London, for example, are fed on raw horse-heart, raw liver chopped very fine, chopped earthworms and biscuit-meal; but biscuit-meal is given only occasionally because of its fattening properties. In a letter to the present writers, the Curator of the aquarium writes: 'Fatty degeneration causes swim-bladder trouble.' Many other authorities raise much the same objection to cereal foods, and there is no doubt in our minds that artificial

[1] William T. Innes, op. cit., p. 61.

feeding can be overdone, and that an excess of starchy food is harmful to fish. A balance must be struck.

In truth, when fish are fed artificially, it is very important that the ingredients should be chosen not only for their nutrient value and palatability but also for the purpose for which they are intended. Fantails and Veiltails need a food with a fairly high starch content, in order to develop their globular-shaped bodies, but the starch content must not be so high that it will bloat them or give them acute indigestion. Active fish, like Comets, require a food containing plenty of energy-giving and strong skeletal-forming elements, such as liver, powdered fish bones, and the like. A good dried food should contain many ingredients, animal and vegetable, and many commercial dried foods are made up from a dozen or more different ingredients. Mineral salts, carbohydrates, and proteins (in that order) are essential, but fats may be excluded. Cooking should not be overdone, as too much cooking destroys essential vitamins; and when crushing and grading food, the crushing should not be so thorough that the food is reduced to powder which only sinks to the bottom of the aquarium or pond and is left to foul the water.

An excellent recipe for general use is to mix together one pint of finely-minced raw bullock's or horse's heart, one-third of a pint of finely-minced cockles or mussels, one-third of a pint of finely-chopped lettuce or spinach leaves, and one-third of a pint of wholemeal bread baked in an oven until crisp and crushed to a fine flour. The ingredients are well mixed. The addition of two teaspoonsful of precipitated chalk is invaluable for promoting sturdy growth by virtue of its lime content. Two coffee-spoonsful of Epsom salts are added to supply a laxative element. The mixture is kneaded into a soft dough with the addition of honey, and baked in an oven until the top is a rich brown. When cold the mixture is crushed and graded to suit the requirements of the fish.

An original recipe, invented by the present writers, which is suitable for all breeds of goldfish is, one large potato cooked in its skin, one teaspoonful of precipitated chalk, one cupful of soyabean flour, half a cupful of finely-chopped spinach or lettuce leaf and two cupfuls of oatmeal. These ingredients are well mixed together and then kneaded into a dough with half a cupful of diluted meat-extract and a little milk. The dough is cooked in an oven, allowed to cool, and finally crushed and graded.

Foods and Feeding

Dried foods should be kept in closed tins, glass jars with screw-tops or similar containers; otherwise flies and other insects will get into the food, breed there, and so render the food useless. Indeed, if a quantity of food has been made, it is best to crush and grade only sufficient for a week's feeding. Coarse pieces are less likely to be attacked by insects and their larvae than food that has been crushed. In the same way, it is better to dry foods in a slow oven, rather than in the sun, in order to prevent flies and other insects from depositing their eggs in the food.

We have considered, at some length, the various foods that may be given to goldfish, and must now turn our attention to the method of feeding.

FEEDING. Fish that live in an indoor aquarium remain active all the year round, and, therefore, they should be fed regularly at least once daily, twice daily if they will take the food readily. Fish that live in a pond are kept under conditions that prevail in nature, and, since goldfish hibernate, and do not eat in very cold weather (being unable to digest their food if they do), they must be well fed in the summer, so that they can build up a reserve of energy in the form of body fat to see them through the hibernating period. As a general rule, therefore, goldfish kept in a pond should be fed twice daily during the summer months. When the weather is warm goldfish will feed almost continuously, and though there is usually some live food available in an established pond (gnats and midges lay their eggs in the water, *Daphnia* and *Cyclops* develop, and earthworms, attracted by the moisture, fall in) it is never likely to be in sufficient quantity to satisfy the appetites of healthy goldfish and build them up for their winter fast. In the autumn the feeding should be reduced gradually, first from twice a day to once a day, then to every other day, then to twice a week, then to once a week; finally, when the weather becomes really cold, the fish will hibernate, and feeding may be discontinued until the following spring.

When feeding is recommenced it should be increased gradually: first, once a week, then twice a week, then every other day, then once a day and, finally, with the arrival of the hot weather, the fish should be fed twice daily. In point of fact, the aquarist cannot go far wrong if he bears in mind that the higher the temperature of the water the more food is required by the fish, and the lower the temperature the less food, because among so-called cold-blooded animals the digestive organs and the consumption of food bear a distinct relationship to the temperature. Meanwhile, the aquarist should not be tempted to feed the fish if a warm spell in winter brings them temporarily out of hibernation. This only encourages the fish to remain active throughout the winter, with the result that with the arrival of spring all their energy is spent and they will be too enfeebled to ward off disease. Fish that are allowed to hibernate undisturbed are always more healthy in the spring than those fish that have remained active throughout the winter.

Fish should be fed at regular times, and the temptation to feed them when they make gestures to be fed in between times must be resisted. Otherwise particles of food will be rejected and left to foul the water. As for the time of day at which fish should be fed, the investigations of W. S. Hoar, who studied fish-life at the request of the Canadian Department of Fisheries, have shown that fish do most of their eating in the day-time and seldom eat before 5 a.m. and after 10 p.m. This confirms our own observations, that it is best to feed goldfish first thing in the morning and give the second feed (if there is one) some hours before sunset, in order that the food may be digested before the fish settle down for the night's rest. Moreover, if the aquarium is not lit by artificial light, feeding late in the evening will result in many pieces of food being missed by the fish and left to foul the water.

As we have said, all dried foods should be soaked, or, better still, scalded, before being given to the fish. This is simplest done by sprinkling the food into a saucerful of boiling water. It may then be poured into a muslin net and held under a running tap, to get rid of the finer particles. The use of a feeding-ring (which can be bought for a few pence at most pet-shops) is recommended. The feeding-ring (usually it is square!) is made of blown glass or celluloid, and floats on the surface of the water. Food placed in the ring always falls in one spot, where the fish know where to find it, and the removal of uneaten particles of food is simplified. If food is thrown haphazard into the aquarium or pond it spreads to the sides, where the fish are not always able to find it and removal of uneaten particles of food is made more difficult. A temporary feeding-ring may be made by cutting a hole, about 2 or 3 in. square, in a thin piece of cork. To further simplify the removal of uneaten particles of food, some aquarists make use of a reservoir. Many dealers sell reservoirs, but one can be made quite easily because it is only a matter of cementing stones round the edges of a thin and flat piece of stone or slate about 6 in. square.

The reservoir is placed on the bottom of the aquarium immediately under the feeding-ring. The food falls on to the flat surface where it is confined by the surrounding stones. The fish can easily find the food, and it is a simple matter to remove uneaten particles with a sediment remover or dip-tube.

The quantity of food to be given must be left to experience; for, of course, large fish need more food than small, and the appetites of fish of the same size vary. Moreover, the appetite of an individual fish varies from day to day. The general rule is never to give more food than the fish will eat in about ten minutes rapid feeding; but it is better to give the fish a small quantity of food, and follow with another small quantity, and so on, until the fish no longer take the food readily. This involves a little more trouble, but it is worth while in the end. In this connection we agree with Francis Buckland, who writes: 'It must be remembered that the more you feed your fish in ponds the quicker they will grow and the larger they will become,' but we cannot agree with his recommendation to hang a dead cat, or rabbit, fur and all, in a tree over a pond, in order to keep the fish supplied with gentles.[1]

It has been said that most goldfish die through over-eating. Taken literally, this is not true. A goldfish, like most animals excepting man, usually knows when it has had enough, but trouble is certainly brought about by too much food being given to fish, since any uneaten food invariably decays and fouls the water. All excess food, therefore, must be removed the moment that the fish have finished eating. Uneaten pieces of worm, and the like, can be removed from an aquarium with a dip-tube or with a sediment remover; but fine dried foods, and the like, can be removed only by means of a siphon. It is very difficult, if not impossible to remove uneaten particles of food from a pond, so that the aquarist is advised always to underfeed, rather than overfeed, fish that are kept there. In a healthy pond there is no fear that the fish will starve; for, as stated, there is always some food available in that place.

The size of food given to fish during the different stages of their growth is an important consideration. If the food is too small the

[1] Francis Buckland, *The Natural History of British Fishes* (London, 1881).

larger fish will not trouble to eat it, and if the food is too large the smaller fish cannot eat it, or may choke to death trying to do so. German authorities have drawn attention to the fact that 1-in. fish should be given food about the size of a pin's head, fish between 1 in. and 2 in. long should be given food slightly larger than a pin's head, and 3-in. and larger fish should be given food about the size of a lentil. This generalization applies to live foods as well as to dried foods. Large larvae of gnats, for example, have been known to choke to death small fish.

It is preferable for the aquarist never to allow anyone else to feed his fish, since the person left in charge (even if he is experienced) will inevitably lack knowledge of the precise quantity of food to give. If fish must be left without food for a short period they will come to no harm. We have often left the fish in our aquarium for a fortnight without food, and they have been none the worse on our return. It would, in fact, be quite safe to leave goldfish for a month or more without food; in an established aquarium goldfish can live for a very long time without additional feeding, because they can obtain nourishment by nibbling the aquatic plants; and their habit of taking up a mouthful of the planting medium, churning it in their mouths to extract the edible particles, and finally rejecting the unedible, is remarkable. Not that we recommend half-starving fish, and if the aquarium has to be left for more than two or three weeks it is kinder to make some arrangement for the fish to be fed. The most satisfactory way is to place the necessary food in suitable containers (making allowance for the fact that no one will be present to remove any uneaten particles of food) and label the containers with the dates on which the contents should be given to the fish. The person who is left in charge cannot then go wrong. All he has to do is empty the contents of the containers into the aquarium on the days shown on the labels.

We would stress the fact that goldfish are best kept healthy with live food and a varied diet. In the spring and summer there is never any shortage of live food for fish, and, indeed, the aquarist is faced with an embarrassing number of alternatives. In the autumn and winter it is not quite so easy to find a variety of food, but a little experimentation will indicate the right lines to follow. If this means that the aquarist will have to go to some small trouble to keep his fish supplied with a variety of nourishing food, we can but remind him, along with Laurence Wells, that any aquarist worth his salt will go to a certain amount of trouble to keep his fish, not only in good health, but in the best condition possible.[1]

Finally, in order to guide the novice-aquarist, we end this chapter with two specimen 15-day menus:

15-DAY MENU: SPRING AND SUMMER

1. *Daphnia* and/or *Cyclops* and/or *Cypris*.
2. *Enchytraeus*.
3. Earthworms.
4. Wood-lice.
5. *Daphnia* and/or *Cyclops* and/or *Cypris*.
6. Gnat-larvae and/or Gnat pupae.
7. Bloodworms.
8. Earthworms.
9. Prepared food (commercial or recipe on pages 159, 160).
10. *Tubifex*.
11. *Daphnia* and/or *Cyclops* and/or *Cypris*.
12. *Asellus*.
13. Earthworms.
14. *Gammarus*.
15. *Lemna* or green vegetable from the kitchen.

If a second feed is given it should be something different, selection being made from, phantom-larvae, flies, gentles, ants'-eggs (from the nest), snail-spawn, frog-spawn, mussels, slugs, small frog-tadpoles, etc.

15-DAY MENU: AUTUMN AND WINTER

1. Earthworms.
2. Scraped meat and/or chopped liver.
3. *Tubifex*.
4. Prepared food (commercial or recipe on pages 159, 160).
5. Earthworms.
6. Chopped fish.
7. *Enchytraeus*.
8. *Tubifex*.
9. Prepared food (commercial or recipe on pages 159, 160).

[1] A. Laurence Wells, op. cit., p. 144.

10. Earthworms.
11. Scraped meat and/or chopped liver.
12. *Enchytraeus.*
13. Earthworms.
14. Prepared food (commercial or recipe on pages 159, 160).
15. Green vegetable from the kitchen.

If a second feed is given (goldfish kept in aquaria may be fed twice a day if the temperature of the water is above 50 degrees) it should be something different. Selection being made from scrambled egg, biscuit, dried *Daphnia*, dried shrimp, etc., and also (if available) from phantom-larvae, snails, mussels, slugs, etc.

Chapter VII

DISEASES, PARASITES AND ENEMIES

Diseases of their own accord,
But cures come difficult and hard.
BUTLER, *The Weakness and Misery of Man*

Goldfish that are well kept and properly fed will remain surprisingly free from diseases, enemies and parasites. Yet, it must be added, however carefully an aquarium or pond is managed, sooner or later, trouble in some form or another is almost certain to occur. It is as well to be thoroughly conversant with the numerous treatments (not necessarily cures!) for the various diseases and enemies that attack fish, for the parasites that may infest them, and for the accidents to which they are liable.

THE MEDICINE CHEST

Before we pass on to these matters, it would perhaps be advisable if we listed the most important medicaments and implements that the aquarist should keep handy for the treatment of ailing fish, for first-aid, and for painless destruction in extreme cases.

Medicaments

Chromate of Mercury (2½ per cent solution). Epsom Salts. Formalin (40 per cent solution). Friar's Balsam. Glycerine. Halibut Oil. Paraffin Oil. Permanganate of Potash. Peroxide of Hydrogen. Sea-salt or Cooking salt or Rock-salt. Iodine crystals (2 gms. dissolved in 10 fluid ounces of hot water). Vaseline.

Implements

One or two fine-meshed landing nets. Cotton wool. Apparatus for giving artificial aeration. Thermometer. Apparatus for raising the temperature of the water. Two or three pieces of flannel, each about six inches square. 1-gallon tank (8 in. by 6 in. by 6 in.). Large shallow pan and two or three small shallow pans (porcelain or enamel for preference). Two or three fountain pen fillers. Small forceps with pointed ends and one with flat ends. Small surgical knife or razor. Block of hard wood (about 10 in. by 5 in.). Liquid measure. Dry measure. Hypodermic syringe with a very fine needle. Bone knitting needles of different sizes. One or two small camel's-hair brushes.

The lists are not such awe-inspiring ones as they may seem at first glance. With the exception of the salt, Epsom salts, and perhaps permanganate of potash, only small quantities of the medicaments are necessary, and some may never be needed. As for the implements, none is expensive, and, in any case, most houses can supply much that is needed. For example: a ½-pint tumbler can serve as a liquid measure; spoons[1] can, at a pinch, serve as alternatives to a dry measure; and saucers, soup-plates, or vegetable dishes, can always be used instead of shallow pans. It is always best, however, to keep such implements and receptacles as may be needed especially for the treatment of sick fish. It has long been known that the sight of a goldfish being given treatment in a casserole from the kitchen brings out the worst in an otherwise amiable wife.

The medicine chest should always be kept near the aquarium, or handy to the pond, and, after treating a sick fish, all the implements and receptacles that have been used should be disinfected. This is a necessary precaution to protect healthy fish from becoming infected; for many of the diseases that attack fish are contagious. The medicine chest should be kept locked, especially if there are children about the house. Some of the medicines are poisonous, and a surgical knife or a razor, or even a hypodermic syringe, is a dangerous weapon in the hands of a mischievous child.

DIAGNOSIS

As we have pointed out in a previous chapter (Chapter V) a healthy goldfish is active, clear-eyed, has a burnished appearance and carries the dorsal fin erect: its faeces are short, and drop from the vent soon after appearance. If, therefore, a fish is sluggish, or if the dorsal fin drops, or if the faeces are long and white and hang from the vent, or are stringy and interspersed with air bubbles, it is a sign that the fish is in poor health. Normally the faeces are

[1] Approximately, a level teaspoon holds ⅛ oz., a dessertspoon ¼ oz., and a tablespoon ½ oz.

dark in colour, but the colour depends largely upon the feeding, and cannot be taken as a guide to the health of the fish.

The trouble may not be serious, and it can often be corrected by dropping some Epsom salts in front of the fish at feeding time. This method of dosing, however, suffers from the drawback that, although the immediate result may be beneficial, it cannot be continued indefinitely because the salts are not destroyed; they will accumulate in the aquarium or pond and increase the salinity of the water, and this is not desirable. A better method, therefore, is to give the fish a dose of halibut oil. This may be done either by soaking a pill of bread in a drop of halibut oil, or by injecting hypodermically a small earthworm with a drop of oil, and dropping the pill or worm in front of the fish at feeding time. If the fish refuses to take its medicine in this way, Ida Mellen recommends purging it by a 2-minute immersion in castor oil, and then removing it to a bowl of water, until the oil has risen from the body, before returning it to the aquarium or pond. We have no experience of this and it sounds remarkably drastic.

If, a few days after a thorough purging, the fish shows no sign of being better, it is clear that something serious is the matter, and a more thorough diagnosis must be made. Inexperienced aquarists, therefore, should consult the following table, in which we have catalogued the symptoms of the chief diseases that attack goldfish, and the parasites that may infest them. Once the complaint has been diagnosed, its cause and treatment may be looked for in the pages that follow. To simplify reference, the diseases, parasites, and the like, are arranged in five main groups: Accidents and Large Enemies, Bacterial Diseases, Fungoid Diseases, Organic Diseases, and Parasitic Diseases.

The aquarist should take particular note of the cause of the complaint; more than half the battle in treating an ailing fish lies in remedying the conditions that brought on the complaint. Moreover, this does much to protect the other fish.

Finally, before attempting to treat an ailing fish the section on treatment (page 171) should be thoroughly mastered.

Loss of scale or eye. Wounds and bruises. Split fin. Fish left for too long out of water. Fish attacked by a large insect—*Accidents* (page 174) also *Large Enemies* (page 175).

Ulcers on body. Gills livid. Eyes coated and glazed—*Achlya* (page 182).

Fish knocks itself against fixed objects. A transparent-green insect-like creature, about the size and shape of a small ladybird, is attached to fish—*Argulus* (page 187).

Yellow areas with dark blue centres on caudal fin and gills. Later, on body—*Bacillus columnaris* (page 180).

Body bloated. Loss of appetite and activity. Later, inflamed areas on body—*Bacterial Disease* (page 180).

Membranes of gills inflamed. Later, gills swollen. Skin dull, and milk-white patches on body. Loss of appetite and moping—*Branchiitis* (page 182).

White film in centre of eye. Later, film covering whole eye—*Cataract* (page 183).

Loss of appetite and fish lies on side. Slimy, blue-white mucus on body. Later, loss of scales—*Chilodoniasis* (page 188).

Irregular opaque spots on body. Later, spots unite and spread along body like a burn. Scales along this streak appear rough, opaque, and inflamed—*Costiasis* (page 188).

Sluggishness. Veins in caudal and other fins distended and blood-red in colour. Later, fins split and rot—*Cyclochaeta* (page 188).

Fish struggles to rise to surface, and sinks like a stone. Fish lies on bottom—floats head downwards—swims with undulating motions—turns over on back, and cannot regain normal attitude—*Derangement of the Air-Bladder* (page 183).

Body bloated, and scales stand out from body—*Dropsy* (page 184).

Inflamed areas on sides. White froth, or foam mass, on body—*Epitheliosis* (page 180).

Bubbles round eye. Eye protrudes—*Exophthalmia* (page 184).

Fish dashes about wildly and knocks body on fixed objects. Fins twitch. Rate of breathing accelerated. Fish constantly rises to surface—*Gyrodactyliasis* (page 190).

Loss of appetite and sluggishness. White spots, each about the size of a pin's head, on fins and body—*Ichthyophthiriasis* (page 190).

Sluggishness. Air bubbles in faeces. Belly swollen—*Indigestion* (page 185).

Thread-like worm attached to fish—*Lernaea* (page 191).

Dark grey fuzzy patches on body. Later, patches turn black, peel, and leave raw spots—*Melanosis* (page 185).

Exhaustion and debility. Fish hides on approach of a human being—*Nervous Shock* (page 185).

Sides and belly turn red. Sluggishness. Fish rises to surface and lies on its side. Belly violently inflamed and ulcerated—*Red Pest* (page 180).

Greyish-white fuzzy scum on body—*Saprolegnia* (page 182).

Female fish in breeding pond has distended body. Loss of appetite—*Spawn Binding* (page 186).

Loss of appetite. Listlessness. Body loses lustre. Fish lies on bottom—*Sporozoan Disease* (page 191).

Fish remains stationary, wabbling its body from side to side in slow clumsy motions—*Trembling* (page 186).

Loss of appetite and sluggishness. Fish hollow-chested and sunken-eyed—*Tuberculosis* (page 180).

White tumours on body or fins. Bulges on body—*Tumours* (page 186).

TREATMENT

When treating a sick fish the following points should be observed.

1. Do not resort to giving a medical-bath on the slightest provocation. In many cases prompt treatment is essential, but it is dangerous to resort to chemicals merely because the fish is listless. The fish should be isolated, purged, observed closely for a day or two; and only if no improvement is then shown should a medical-bath be given.

2. A medical-bath should be prepared each time that it is required, and if a fish has to be kept in it for a prolonged period it is desirable to transfer the fish to a fresh bath daily.

3. It is always preferable therefore, to place the fish first in a weak solution and gradually increase the dose to the full strength which should on no account be exceeded.

4. When transferring a fish from an aquarium or pond to a medical-bath, and vice versa, and when transferring the fish from one medical-bath to another, great care should be taken to ensure that the temperatures are equal. It is best to test the waters with the same thermometer.

5. When salt is recommended as a treatment, it is best to use sea-salt. Cooking salt or rock-salt are suitable alternatives. But table-salt should not be used (though in an emergency it might be

better than nothing) as it may contain chemicals that are harmful to fish. Actually the ideal is sea-water, and if this can be obtained it should be diluted with five parts of fresh-water, increasing to one part sea-water in three parts fresh.

6. If a fish shows signs of distress (for individual fish differ as much as human beings in response to treatment) when placed in a medical-bath, it should be removed immediately, and placed in a weaker solution. Any unusual behaviour on the part of the fish may be taken as a sign of distress.

7. Medical attention should be given at sunset. This allows the fish all night to recover from the shock of netting and being given the unusual treatment.

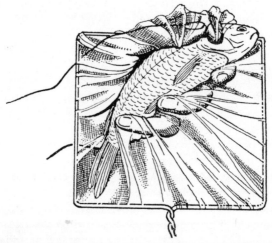

Fig. 31. A Good Way to hold a Fish for Treatment
Note that the gills and tail are held gently but firmly by the fingers while still remaining in the net. Only the part to be treated is exposed.

8. The fish should be handled as little as possible. The aquarist need not fear for himself (since there is no disease that can be passed from fish to man, and, with the possible exception of the tapeworm *Diphyllobothrium latum*, no parasite that infests fish infests man) but the handling of a sick fish may result in haemorrhage of the gills and instant death. Moreover, since the eyes of a fish have no lids they are easily liable to infection from the touch of a hand. If handling a fish is necessary, the hands should be wet,

preferably by being dipped in a pale pink solution of permanganate of potash. If the fish has to be treated out of water for any length of time its head should always be covered with a wet cloth, to protect the eyes and keep the gills moist.

9. Ailing fish should be kept in isolation until they are cured, and a close watch for disease should be kept on the fish that have been in contact with it. Even if a fish is not suffering from a contagious disease, it is as well for the comfort of the fish to keep it away from healthy and active fish. The isolation tank should be kept in a quiet place and away from too strong a light. It must be kept scupulously clean, with no plants. The water should be shallow. It is advisable to aerate the water artificially. The best temperature for the water is 68° F., and any change of temperature should be made very gradually. Green water is ideal; for this acts as a tonic to fish, and in some cases it alone is sufficient to effect a cure.

10. If a fish fails to respond to treatment after a reasonable length of time, it is a kindness to destroy it painlessly (see page 193) rather than let it linger on.

11. If it is necessary to disinfect an aquarium or pond, we give preference to permanganate of potash or Condy's fluid, and the method of disinfecting is explained on page 123. Ammonia, copper sulphate, formalin, chlorinated lime and other chemicals are recommended by some aquarists. They must be used with particular caution.

12. If a dead fish is to be sent by post for a post mortem examination,[1] it should be wrapped in a clean wet cloth without squeezing, then wrapped in greaseproof paper, and finally packed round with cotton wool in a tin box. The parcel should be posted as soon as possible after the death of the fish, and it should be accompanied with a statement giving as much information as possible with regard to the condition under which the fish was kept, the condition of the other fish in the aquarium or pond, and, in particular, the behaviour of the fish immediately before its death.

Instructions for preserving dead specimens are given on page 193.

---

[1] The present writers do not accept dead specimens for post-mortem examination, but they will be pleased to furnish aquarists with the name and address of a qualified ichthyotomist.

ACCIDENTS AND LARGE ENEMIES

ACCIDENTS. Since any break in the skin of a fish offers a locus for the germs of disease to enter the body, no wound, such as a lost scale or split fin, should ever be neglected. The fish should be netted out of the water, and the wound touched with a camel's-hair brush dipped in a mild disinfectant. For this purpose any of the following will be found satisfactory.

Three crystals of permanganate of potash dissolved in $\frac{1}{2}$ pint of water.

A $2\frac{1}{2}$ per cent solution of chromate of mercury.

A 10 per cent solution of neo-silvol.

One-eighth of an ounce of salt dissolved in a $\frac{1}{4}$ pint of water.

Four drops of Condy's fluid in $\frac{1}{2}$ pint of water.

Aquarium-fish should be treated twice daily until the wound has healed. For pond-fish it is enough to clean the wound with one of the above disinfectants and then smear it with vaseline or Friar's balsam.

Severe bruises are very dangerous to fish. Ida Mellen has very properly pointed out that the rough treatment that would break the bones of a mammal, will break no bones in a fish, but will send bruises so deep into the tissues and muscles that there is no chance of recovery. In serious cases of bruising, the fish may lie quietly on the bottom, or it may float weakly on the surface. She records having cured light cases of bruising by immersing the affected fish in paraffin oil (for 1 to 3 minutes, according to what the fish would endure), and a week later giving the fish a bath in a solution of aluminium sulphate—$1\frac{1}{4}$ oz. dissolved in a gallon of water. We ourselves have cured mild cases of bruising by giving the fish the salt bath as prescribed for *Saprolegnia* (page 182).

Goldfish with telescope eyes sometimes lose these, either by being knocked against a hard object, or by being sucked out by another fish. Minnows are notorious offenders in this respect. The offender should be looked for and removed. The loss of an eye does not appear to inconvenience a fish to any great extent, and, therefore, it need not be destroyed.

As we have seen, in Chapter I, goldfish can live for a considerable time out of water. Fish, which by accident have been allowed to remain for a long time out of water, may sometimes be revived by administering one or two drops of brandy with a fountain-pen filler. For the benefit of doubters, our information is that it is the shock of the spirit, more than anything, that rouses the fish.

LARGE ENEMIES. Goldfish that live in aquaria are more or less protected from their natural enemies. Those that live in ponds are not so fortunately placed, and the chief enemies from which they need protection are:

The Larvae of Dragon-flies (Fig. 32).

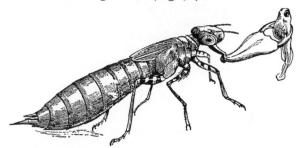

Fig. 32. LARVA OF DRAGON-FLY
(Enlarged)

The Diving Beetles and their Larvae (Fig. 33). The best-known British species is the Great Diving Beetle (*Dytiscus marginalis*). Diving beetles and their larvae are very dangerous, and a small fish attacked by one of the larger beetles will be killed in a matter of seconds.

The Larvae of the Whirligig Beetle (Fig. 34).

The Larvae of the Great Silver Beetle (Fig. 34).

Hydras. The Green Hydra (*Hydra viridissimus*), the Yellow-Brown Hydra (*Hydra vulgaris*), and the Grey Hydra (*Hydra oligactis*) are the three species native to British freshwaters. Hydras are dangerous only to fish up to about ¼ in. in length, but if seen in an aquarium or pond they are better removed (Fig. 35).

Leeches, of which the Medicinal Leech (*Hirudo medicinalis*) and the Horse Leech (*Haemopsis sanguisuga*) are the most generally known; but there are eleven species in British freshwaters, some very small and some almost transparent (Fig. 36).

Water-Boatmen. Of the four British species the best known is *Notonecta glauca*. It is a very predacious insect and fearlessly attacks fish (Fig. 37).

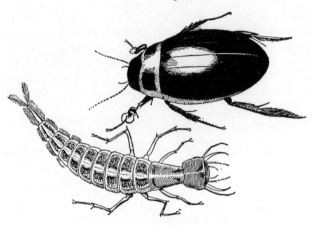

Fig. 33. GREAT DIVING BEETLE (*Dytiscus marginalis*)
AND LARVA
(Enlarged)   (See page 175)

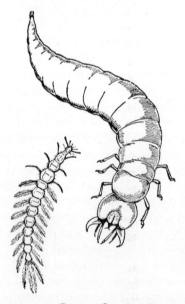

Fig. 34. LARVA OF GREAT SILVER BEETLE (right)
LARVA OF WHIRLIGIG BEETLE (left)
(Enlarged)   (See page 175)

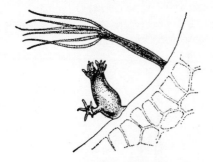

Fig. 35. *Hydra*
Above: Fully extended. *Below:* Contracted with bud.
(Much enlarged)   (see page 175)

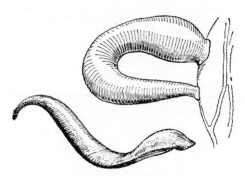

Fig. 36. Leeches   (see page 175)

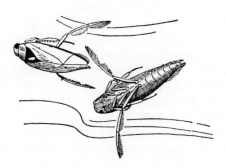

Fig. 37. Water-boatman
(*Notonecta glauca*)   (see page 175)

The Water Scorpion (*Nepa cinera*) (Fig. 38).
The Water Stick Insect (*Ranatra linearis*) sometimes called the
Long Water Scorpion (Fig. 38).

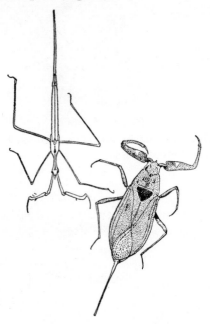

Fig. 38. WATER STICK INSECT
(*Ranatra linearis*)

WATER SCORPION
(*Nepa cinerea*)

With the exception of *Hydra* (which is a freshwater polyp that
attaches itself to aquatic plants or the sides of an aquarium or
pond, and captures its prey by means of tentacles), all these enemies may be removed by hand. They can be recognized by comparison with the illustrations.

Innes records that a large specimen of the great diving beetle
was once placed in an aquarium for observation. It so quickly
attacked a goldfish that the scales fell in a small shower, and the
fish died before it could be rescued.[1] Fortunately not all the insects
mentioned above are so dangerous, and some that we have men-

[1] William T. Innes, op. cit., p. 61

Diseases, Parasites and Enemies

tioned above will probably not attack large fish. But if any insect is seen attached to a fish, the fish should be netted out of the water and the insect killed by squashing it with the fingers or a forceps. A live insect should never be pulled off a fish, because this will harm the fish. A dab of paraffin oil or turpentine will usually cause most insects to loosen their hold, but there is little time for this refinement if a fish is attacked by some of the larger insects, which are sufficiently large to be killed between finger and thumb. The fish should have its wound dressed with any of the disinfectants mentioned on page 174.

Small white leeches that have attached themselves to fish may be controlled by the salt-bath treatment prescribed for *Saprolegnia* (page 182).

Hydras in an aquarium or small pond may be controlled by adding 1 teaspoonful of ammonia to every 4 gallons of water. The fish and molluscs should first be removed. After 2 hours the aquarium or pond should be emptied and refilled with fresh water before returning the fish and molluscs. Usually, it is necessary to repeat the ammonia treatment two or three times. At this concentration it will not harm the aquatic plants. Hydras in an aquarium (but hardly in a pond) may also be controlled by removing the fish and snails, raising the temperature of the water to 100° F., and keeping it at this temperature for 1 hour. The fish and snails may be returned when the water has cooled to room temperature.

Goldfish, of course, have many more enemies than those mentioned above, and the rule to observe is to remove from an aquarium or pond any animal or insect the habits of which are unknown to the aquarist. In fact, any insect should be removed from an aquarium or pond as a matter of principle. In the above list we have not included the Whirligig Beetle (*Gyrinus natator*) and the Great Silver Beetle (*Hydrous piceus*), but only their larvae, because we believe that the adult insects (imagines) are strictly vegetarian, although some authorities say that they will attack small fish. Frogs and toads are best kept out of ponds. During the breeding season a male frog or toad may strangle a fish by clasping it around the gills. Snails destroy the eggs of fish, and, therefore, they should be rigorously excluded from breeding ponds. Although there is no record of the Common Frog (*Rana temporaria*) feeding under water, we have it on the authority of Malcolm Smith of the British Museum (Natural History) that the Edible

Frog (*Rana esculenta*), which is more aquatic in its habits, probably does.

BACTERIAL DISEASES

Polluted water is virtually the first cause of all bacterial diseases. It follows, therefore, that after an outbreak of a bacterial disease the first step is to disinfect the aquarium or pond very thoroughly.

The second step is to correct the conditions that polluted the water. This may mean increasing the number of submerged plants, or the light; reducing the amount of food given to the fish at each feeding, or the number of fish; and so on.

The general treatment of a fish attacked by a bacterial disease is to improve the conditions under which it has been living, and to build it up by offering it plenty of live foods and meaty foods.

The particular treatments are as follows:

BACILLUS COLUMNARIS. Immerse for 20 minutes in a 1-in-30,000 solution of copper sulphate. Transfer to running water. Repeat 3 or 4 days later.

BACTERIAL DISEASE. Immerse daily in a gallon of water in which $2\frac{1}{2}$ oz. of Epsom salts have been dissolved. Leave in the bath for as long as the fish will endure it; ranging from perhaps an hour on the first day to 6 hours on the third and fourth days.

EPITHELIOSIS, or Skin Disease. Immerse for from 1 to 3 minutes (according to what the fish will endure) in a bath made by dissolving $1\frac{1}{4}$ oz. of aluminium sulphate in a gallon of water.

RED PEST (*Bacterium cyprinicida*), or Pond Disease. Transfer to clean swift-flowing water. Raising the temperature of the water may be beneficial. It is known that the bacilli are most active when the temperature is between 50° and 68° F., that their activity ceases at 98·6 degrees, and that they are killed at a temperature of 122 degrees maintained for 10 minutes.

TUBERCULOSIS, or Consumption. There is no proven treatment, but immersing in milk for 15 minutes and rinsing in a $2\frac{1}{2}$ per cent salt solution every other day, is said to do good.

FUNGOID DISEASES

The origin of all fungoid diseases is the same: the spores are present in all still waters. A healthy fish is immune from fungoid diseases because its body is covered by a protective mucus that is constantly being renewed from glands situated in the epidermis. But when a fish is in low health the supply of mucus is interrupted and the spores enter the body of the fish. It follows, therefore, that fungoid diseases are not so much diseases in themselves, as a sign that the fish is run down. Indeed, pond-fish are very liable to be attacked by fungoid diseases in the early spring (because they are weakened after their winter fast) and in the summer (because they are weakened after spawning).

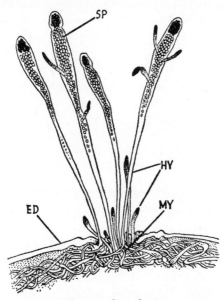

Fig. 39. *Saprolegnia*
(ed) Epidermis of fish; (hy) Hyphae; (my) Mycelial threads in dermis; (sp) Sporangium containing zoospores which are later liberated into the water. (Highly magnified)
(See page 182)

After an outbreak of a fungoid disease it is not strictly necessary to disinfect the aquarium or pond, since a fungoid disease is largely a matter of the health of the individual fish. If, however, more than one fish is affected, or if the outbreak occurs in a small aquarium, disinfecting is a wise precaution. It must be remembered that fungoid diseases are contagious to the extent that conditions which affect one fish are likely to affect other fish in the same water.

The general treatment of a fungoid disease is to improve the fishes' health by omitting dried foods, and offering live foods, meaty foods and vegetable foods.

The particular treatments are as follows:

ACHLYA. Same as for *Saprolegnia* (below).

SAPROLEGNIA, White Fungus or Cotton Wool Disease. Immerse in salt bath (1 oz. of salt in 1 gallon of water). After 24 hours transfer to a stronger bath (2 oz. of salt in 1 gallon of water). After a further 24 hours transfer to a still stronger bath (3 oz. of salt in 1 gallon of water). Retain at this strength, renewing the bath daily, until the fish regains normal. The salt content may then be reduced daily.

American aquarists speak well of zinc-free malachite green. The fish is immersed for 30 seconds in a 1–in–15,000 solution.

ORGANIC DISEASES

Since organic diseases spring from a variety of causes, no general statement can be made. But the causes of the diseases, if known (for in many cases we are still in the dark, and probably will be until medical men know better what to do for man) are here mentioned, together with the individual treatments.

BRANCHIITIS, popularly known as Inflammation of the Gills, is a form of asphyxia, brought on when fish are deprived of oxygen. In an effort to obtain sufficient oxygen the gills become inflamed by being overworked. The ailment occurs among fish that are kept in overcrowded aquaria and ponds; but more frequently among fish that have travelled long distances packed in cans.

Treatment consists in transferring the affected fish to a large shallow pan with water not more than 3 inches deep, giving artificial aeration, and feeding with vegetable foods, such as *Lemna*, or boiled and finely minced green vegetables from the kitchen.

If the ailment is taken in its early stages, about a fortnight of this treatment is usually sufficient to effect a cure. But if the ailment is neglected the gills are liable to become congested, and then any hope of curing the fish becomes remote. Drastic treatment is necessary. The fish should be transferred to a tank containing 1 gallon of water, and 3½ oz. of salt are dissolved in the water. As soon as the fish turns over on its side it should be transferred to fresh water, and kept under a slowly dripping tap for 24 hours. Repeat daily.

CATARACT so-called is very common among goldfish that have telescope eyes. Treatment must be given at once; if the ailment is not checked in its early stages, the fish will eventually be blinded.

The following three treatments have all been found satisfactory. They should be given twice daily until the film has been entirely removed.

Dry the eye, and paint it with a tincture of 1 part iodine to 9 parts glycerine.

Bathe the eye with a solution of $\frac{1}{8}$ oz. of boracic acid in a $\frac{1}{4}$ pint of tepid water.

Apply 2 drops of 1 per cent solution of protargol direct to the eye.

DERANGEMENT OF THE AIR-BLADDER is more usually, but less exactly, known as Swim-bladder Trouble. The complaint is very common among those fancy goldfish with round fat bodies; as we have seen in Chapter I, changes in the relative proportions of the body are accompanied by similar changes in the relation between the two lobes of the air-bladder. Contributory causes are incorrect feeding, or failure to treat a fish suffering from indigestion. The overloaded intestines press against the already distended air-bladder and so prevent it still further from functioning properly. A further contributory cause is keeping the fish for too long at a low temperature. But this is only in the natural order of events, since digestive derangement often accompanies the impaired vitality due to a low body-temperature.

Treatment calls for time and patience. Moreover, once a fish has developed the complaint it always remains susceptible to it at any time. It follows that if the fish is of no value (financial or sentimental) it may as well be destroyed. But a valuable fish can have its life prolonged by the following treatment. Purge: transfer the fish to very shallow water (just enough to cover the dorsal fin), add sufficient salt to make the water taste salty (or tinge the water with a small quantity of permanganate of potash), raise the temperature to 68° F., and give artificial aeration. Renew the bath as required. Fast for one week, and then give relaxing food (such as live *Daphnia* and earthworms), green foods and scraped raw meat. Continue the treatment until the fish regains normal and for some time afterwards.

The following treatments have also proved successful.

Gillis cured a fish suffering from a deranged air-bladder after winter hibernation, by attaching a bent pin to the dorsal fin and tying this to a piece of floating wood.[1]

O'Brien cured a fish with a distended air-bladder by squeezing and massaging it till the air was expelled.[2]

For fish that float and have swollen bodies, Lanier uses a solution of equal parts of Epsom salts and salt: altogether $2\frac{1}{2}$ oz. dissolved in a gallon of water. The fish is immersed for 4 hours, or longer if it will endure it.[3]

There is, however, no known cure for those cases when the fish swims in undulating motions and sinks to the bottom like a stone.

DROPSY is an accumulation of serous fluid in the tissue spaces and cavities of the body. Its cause in fish is not exactly known, and, as yet, there is no cure for it. An unattended dropsical fish dies after about four months.

If the disease is not too far advanced, temporary relief may be given by transferring the fish to shallow water and adding from 6 to 10 drops (according to what the fish will endure) of digitalis, drop by drop, stirring gently.

A better treatment, however, consists in drawing off the fluid with a hypodermic syringe. The body of the fish is pierced between the scales, at a point just below the anterior part of the dorsal fin. If very bloated the response will be immediate: the fluid will flow into the syringe and give the fish relief for about six weeks. Care must be taken not to transfix the fish. In the case of a small fish the needle should enter the body to a depth of not more than about $\frac{1}{8}$ in. In the case of a large fish (6-in. fish or larger) penetration should not exceed $\frac{1}{4}$ in.

EXOPHTHALMIA is popularly known as Pop Eye. It is caused sometimes by a too sudden change in the temperature or in the pH value of the water; sometimes by an excess of artificial aeration. In some rare cases it appears to be a pathogenic variation of *Pseudomonas punctata* in the vitreous humor of the eye.

Treatment consists in transferring the fish to nitrogenous water, raising the temperature to about 5° F. above that to which the

[1] See F. V. Gillis's report in *The Aquarist* (Winter, 1946).

[2] Reported to Ida Mellen. At the time (1928), W. T. O'Brien was Director of the Boston (U.S.A.) Aquarium.

[3] Ida M. Mellen and Robert T. Lanier, *1,001 Questions answered about your Aquarium* (London, 1936).

fish has been accustomed, and feeding live foods and green foods. By 'nitrogenous water' we mean water in which there is much decaying vegetable matter and sediment. This may be prepared artificially, by adding 5 drops of ammonia to every 4 gallons of water. Care must be taken to transfer the fish to half strength then to full strength. After an immersion of 3 hours (or longer if the fish will endure it) it should be transferred to half strength and then to normal.

If the aquarist has a steady hand, and confidence in his skill, he may effect a cure by pricking the bubbles in the eye with a fine needle.

If there is reason to believe that the cause is *Pseudomonas punctata* the disease may be regarded as contagious, and the aquarium or pond should be thoroughly disinfected.

INDIGESTION is caused by neglecting to treat constipation, which, in turn, is usually due to faulty feeding, such as an excess of dried foods. In itself indigestion is not serious, but it must on no account be neglected; if it is, it may lead to more serious complaints —notably derangement of the air-bladder.

The most satisfactory treatment is to purge the fish, fast it for a week, and then feed with moist foods, such as boiled oatmeal, junket and custard. If the fish has been kept in a confined space, or a crowded aquarium or pond, it should be given more swimming room.

MELANOSIS, or Black Fungus, is similar in appearance to *Saprolegnia*, but not in itself associated with it. The cause is unknown, and we have no experience of it. Ida Mellen records that the condition arises as a disorder of pigmentation, due to general debility and blood disorder.

The most satisfactory treatment is as prescribed for *Saprolegnia* (page 182) with the addition of occasionally painting the affected parts with a 50 per cent solution of peroxide of hydrogen.

An alternative, but more drastic treatment is to paint the affected parts with iodine.

NERVOUS SHOCK. Any sudden disturbance (see page 121) is likely to derange the nervous system of a fish. But nervous shock is more common among females than males. Its usual cause is a too hard a drive during the spawning act, or a drive when the fish is not ready to spawn. Complete rest is essential. The fish should be transferred to a tank in some quiet spot, away from the light.

The tank should be approached as little as possible, and then only quietly. A $\frac{1}{4}$ oz. of Epsom salts should be added to every gallon of water. Fast the fish for 48 hours, and then offer chopped earthworms. Maintain these conditions, the feeding being improved, until the fish quietens down.

SPAWN BINDING is due to an accumulation of gas from the decaying ova. The treatment is to strip the fish by smearing vaseline on a bone knitting needle (of a size in proportion to the fish) and inserting it into the vent, taking great care to keep the instrument parallel with the body of the fish. The eggs may then be pressed out by gently working the wet fingers from the pectoral fins towards the caudal fin. The fish should resume feeding. If it does not, the operation should be repeated to remove the remaining eggs.

TREMBLING, popularly known as Shimmies or Shakers, is usually caused by keeping the fish at too low a temperature. But sometimes the cause is due to neglecting indigestion, or by keeping the fish in water with a high mineral content.[1] The treatment is to raise the temperature of the water; or treat for indigestion (page 185) if this is the cause; or change the water if this is at fault.

TUMOURS. White tumours may be removed from the body of a fish with a small surgical knife or razor. After removal, the wound should be smeared with vaseline or painted with friar's balsam.

Similar tumours on the fins may sometimes be removed by wiping the affected fin with a saturated solution of salt ($\frac{1}{8}$ oz. of salt in a $\frac{1}{4}$ pint of water).

Bulges on the body of a fish denote the presence of internal tumours. Nothing much can be done about this. An internal operation demands the hand of the surgeon, and, in any event, few such operations prove successful. Normally the fish should be isolated as a precautionary measure, and painlessly destroyed if it stops feeding for any length of time, but if an internal operation is attempted the fish should be anaesthetized. It should be immersed for about 5 minutes in 100 cubic centimetres of water in which 2 grains of ethyl carbamate (urethane) have been dissolved.

---

[1] The mineral content of water can be determined only by a qualified analytical chemist. As a rule a pint of water is sufficient to carry out an analysis, and the water should be accompanied with a record of the date the sample was taken, whether from a pond or aquarium, full particulars of stocking, planting, and feeding, and the reason for the analysis.

Diseases, Parasites and Enemies

The fish can be revived by transferring it to fresh water for about 10 minutes.

PARASITIC DISEASES

If a fish is infested with parasites the aquarium or pond should be very thoroughly disinfected. Close observation should be kept on the other fish that have been in contact. Once parasites are known to be present in an aquarium or pond, sooner or later all the other fish may be infested.

The particular controls are as follows:

ARGULUS (Fish Louse). Despite its popular name, *Argulus* is not a louse but a free-swimming crustacean that attaches itself to a fish and feeds on its blood. It is usually stated that *Argulus foliaceus* makes the goldfish its host. Recent evidence, however, leads to the conclusion that *Argulus trilineatus* is parasitic to goldfish and *Argulus foliaceus* to the carp, but at the present writing, the facts have not been established.[1]

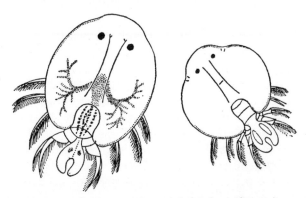

Fig. 40. GOLDFISH LOUSE (*Argulus trilineatus*)
Female.   Male.
(Much enlarged)

Control consists in touching the argulid with a drop of paraffin oil or turpentine, and removing it with a small forceps. The spots on the body of the fish, from which the argulids have been removed should then be smeared with vaseline, or painted with friar's balsam.

[1] See Doctor J. P. Harding's report in *The Aquarist* (June 1946).

When ridding an aquarium or pond of argulids, particular care should be taken to examine the aquatic plants. Argulids are usually introduced with plants taken from the wild (or bought from doubtful dealers) and improperly cleansed in the first place. The introduction of minnows, which eat argulids, is a great help.

CHILODONIASIS, or Slime Disease, is caused by a protozoan parasite, *Chilodon cyprini*, which eventually attacks the gills of the fish and kills it.

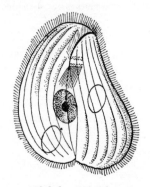

Fig. 41. *Chilodon* (Highly magnified)

Satisfactory controls include giving the fish one or two immersions (20 minutes each) in a $2\frac{1}{2}$ per cent salt solution, or a 1-minute immersion in a 1-in-2,000 copper sulphate solution.

COSTIASIS is caused by a protozoan parasite, *Costia necatrix*, that lives in the mucus on the body of the fish.

Control is difficult, but good results have been obtained with the formalin-bath, as prescribed for Gyrodactyliasis (page 190) or by immersion for 15 minutes in a $2\frac{1}{2}$ per cent salt solution, and repeating every other day.

CYCLOCHAETA is a parasite that attacks fish in low health, such as those suffering from a lack of oxygen, from a sudden drop in the temperature of the water or a protracted low temperature, from a lack of green food in the diet, or, indeed, from anything that lowers their vitality.

It is important, however, not to confuse two issues.

Congestion of the fins (marked by the veins of the fins being distended and blood-red in colour) is frequently followed by the fins splitting and rotting, and is the inevitable result of the activity of the parasite *Cyclochaeta*. The caudal fin appears to be most usually attacked (though the other fins are not immune[1] and the activity of *Cyclochaeta* appears always to be more intense in the caudal fin than elsewhere. In this event the disease is popularly known as Tail Rot. If taken in good time the disease is curable, but a heavy infection may prove fatal.

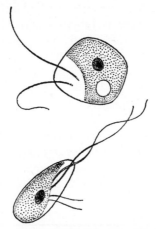

Fig. 42. *Costia* (Highly magnified)

On the other hand, marked congestion of the fins can, and does, occur without the association of *Cyclochaeta*, and the cause appears to spring from a constitutional weakness brought on as a result of incorrect feeding, bad conditions, and the like. In this event the disease is popularly known as Fin Congestion.

In the present state of ichthyopathology it is difficult to say more. Opinion is divided whether congestion of the fins is conducive to the activity of *Cyclochaeta*. There is a case to be made for both theories. The weight of opinion favours the former, but it is a debatable point.

We recommend the following treatments.

If the fins are congested, but not split, immerse the fish in a salt-bath (1 oz. of salt to 1 gallon of water). Continue for 3 or 4 days, during which the fish should be fasted. When feeding recommences, relaxing foods such as live *Daphnia* and earthworms, scraped raw meat and green foods should be given.

If the fins are split, immerse the fish for about 5 minutes in a solution of 6 crystals of permanganate of potash (or 7 or 8 drops of Condy's fluid) in a pint of water, and repeat twice daily. An alternative treatment is to dip the affected fin twice daily in a 50 per cent solution of peroxide of hydrogen.

In extreme cases the rotted part of the fin may be removed with a surgical knife or razor. The stump of the fin should be painted with friar's balsam, or smeared with vaseline, and the fish returned to water. This operation, however, should not be performed if the rotted part of the fin is very close to the body. Instead, the fin may be dipped in undiluted Condy's fluid or paraffin oil.

GYRODACTYLIASIS, or Gill Fluke, is caused by a parasite, *Gyrodactylus elegans*, or the allied *Dactylogyrus*, which attaches itself sometimes to soft spots on the body of the fish, but more usually to the gills, causing hypersecretion of mucus frequently fatal to the fish.

The following controls have all been found successful.

Immerse the fish in 1 quart of water and add 5 drops of formalin, stirring gently, adding up to 10 more drops of formalin at intervals of 1 minute. An immersion should not last longer than 10 minutes, and be repeated on the two following days.

Immerse the fish for from 40 to 60 seconds in 1 part glacial acetic acid to 500 parts of water, and repeat a week later.

Immerse the fish for 2 minutes in a solution of 10 drops of ammonia to 1 quart of water, and repeat 4 or 5 days later, immersing for five minutes. Add the ammonia drop by drop, stirring gently.

ICHTHYOPHTHIRIASIS, White Spot, or Ick, is caused by a protozoan parasite, *Ichthyophthirius multifiliis*, which burrows into the skin of the fish and feeds on its blood. The irritation of the embedded parasite causes the epidermal cells to proliferate and form the characteristic white spots.

The following control has been found successful. Transfer the fish to a clean tank of water, add up to 16 drops of a $2\frac{1}{2}$ per cent solution of chromate of mercury per gallon of water, and slowly raise the temperature to 85° F.: retain at this temperature. Renew the bath every 8 hours, taking particular care to ensure that the tank is sterilized before renewing the bath. During treatment it may be necessary to supply artificial aeration. Quinine hydrochloride (3 grains to every gallon of water) or methylene blue (2 drops of a 5 per cent solution to every gallon of water) may be used as alternatives to chromate of mercury.

An alternative control is to wipe the fish from head to tail with a piece of cotton wool soaked in paraffin oil, and immerse the fish in paraffin for 5 seconds.

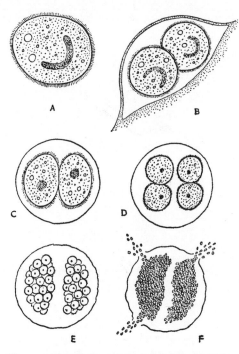

Fig. 43. THE LIFE-CYCLE OF *Ichthyophthirius*

(A) The parasite; (B) Section through blister on fish, showing two individuals; (C, D, E) Reproduction by division within the cyst; (F) The cyst breaking to liberate thousands of small parasites into the water. (Highly magnified).

LERNAEA (Anchor Worm), despite its popular name, is not a true worm but, like *Argulus*, a free-swimming crustacean that attaches itself to a fish and feeds on its blood.

The following are the most satisfactory controls.

Immerse the fish for from ¼ to ½ hour in a 1-in-10,000 solution of permanganate of potash, or from 10 to 15 minutes in a 1-in-4,000 solution of formalin.

Treat the fish as prescribed for *Argulus* (page 187).

SPOROZOAN DISEASE. The cause of this disease is unknown,

but appears to be due to a sporozoan (protozoan parasite) that, like *Cyclochaeta*, attacks fish whose vitality has been lowered.

Control consists in immersing the fish for 1½ minutes in paraffin oil and then transferring it for 2 weeks to a tank with fresh and salt water flowing in (specific gravity 1·013).[1]

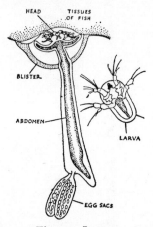

Fig. 44. *Lernaea*

The blister, or furuncle, of skin of fish is sectioned to show head appendages and 'anchor' of the parasite. (Highly enlarged, the larva more so than the adult.)
(See page 191)

To conclude, from all that we have written, it will be seen that the chief source of disease among goldfish is uncleanliness and incorrect feeding. Prevention is always better than cure, and we cannot stress too strongly, nor too often, the need for the aquarist to keep his aquarium or pond clean, to keep a sharp look out for ailing fish and isolate them immediately, to remove unhealthy and dead plants and replace them with fresh ones, to remove the dead bodies of fish and molluscs, to feed the fish regularly with suitable food, to vary the diet as much as possible and to give always some laxative food.

And yet it must be added that, however careful we are, fish that

[1] The specific gravity or density of a substance is the ratio which the weight of its volume bears to the weight of an equal volume of a standard substance. In the case of a liquid (or solid) the standard substance is distilled water at 39.2 degrees Fahrenheit. The specific gravity of a liquid is found by dividing the weight of the liquid by the weight of an equal volume of water. Due regard must be paid to the temperature.

are known to be young and, from all appearance, in good health sometimes die for no apparent reason, and a post mortem reveals nothing. We still have much to learn about the diseases that attack fish and the parasites that infest them. To some extent ichthyopathology is in its infancy. Up to the beginning of the present century, even up to about twenty-five or thirty years ago, fish that fell ill almost invariably died for lack of treatment and complete ignorance of the cause of the disease. The Germans, with their customary diligence, began investigating the causes and treatments of disease in fish. In the field of ichthyopathology much work has been done since the turn of the century. Research work, and the discovery of new specifics, has enabled us to reject the salt-treatment (known to the Chinese at least as early as the eighteenth century—as the panacea for all the ills that attack fish, and to cure diseases once thought incurable. But much work remains to be done, and as yet the way to cure some of the diseases and control some of the parasites that can, and unfortunately do, ravage the inhabitants of aquaria and ponds, eludes the ichthyopathologist. The discovery of penicillin and antibiotics opens up a whole new field of research.

PAINLESS DESTRUCTION. The most expeditious and painless way of destroying a fish is by pithing. A sharp pointed blade is either run through the brain of the fish, or is used to sever the spinal column where it joins the head. This method needs some knowledge of anatomy, and for those who lack this knowledge, or are not sure of themselves, we suggest the following procedure. Remove the fish from the water, grasp it by the tail (using a piece of dry flannel to prevent slipping) and knock the head of the fish sharply on a hard surface. Provided the blow is sufficiently hard death is instantaneous.

Those who prefer more scientific methods, who are squeamish, or if a fish is too small to be grasped by the tail, may drop it in a 5 per cent solution of formalin.

PRESERVING GOLDFISH. To preserve a goldfish, white industrial methylated spirit (not to be confused with the purple diluted spirit sold for fuel) may be used, and, indeed, is recommended by the British Museum (Natural History). It is about 90 per cent pure alcohol. It is reasonably cheap, but, unfortunately, it cannot be bought without an excise permit. An alternative preservative fluid is formalin. Absolute alcohol is unreasonably expensive.

Actually there is no ideal preservative fluid; in alcohol (methylated spirit) the colours fade, and in formalin the specimen becomes very brittle. But alcohol (methylated spirit) and formalin are considered the two best fluids, and of these the former is the better for general purposes.

If the fish has been killed in formalin, this should be washed out with distilled water about an hour after death, and the specimen set in the desired position.

The first essential of good preservation is to ensure that the fluid reaches the stomach and intestines, to coagulate the digestive ferments. This is simplest done by injecting alcohol (65 per cent) or formalin (5 per cent) into the alimentary canal, through the mouth and vent, and through an incision in the body cavity. If the specimen is a large one, more than one injection may be necessary. If injecting is not possible, owing to lack of apparatus, the same result may be achieved by making a deep incision in the abdomen between the pectoral fins, another in front of the vent, and, if the specimen is a large one, perhaps one along the middle line of the body.

The specimen is then completely immersed in a weak preservative bath (50 per cent alcohol, or 2 to 3 per cent formalin) for a period of 1 or 2 days. The higher the temperature the less time should the specimen remain in the bath. The specimen is then transferred to a stronger bath (65 per cent alcohol, or 4 to 5 per cent formalin) for a period of from 7 to 14 days.

Small specimens, if they appear sound (firm and not soft or flexible) may then be considered fully preserved. Larger specimens (or specimens which are discharging blood and mucus) must be placed in a third bath (same strength) and the process repeated as often as may be necessary. Actually the treatment should be continued until an alcoholometer shows that there is no fall in the alcoholic content; but, failing an alcoholometer, the test is when the spirit ceases to become discoloured and no sediment is deposited in the bath.

Weak formalin, or badly contaminated spirit, should be thrown away, but most of the weak spirit can be used again, if it is passed through a filter of powdered charcoal, and brought up to full strength (65 per cent) by the addition of stronger alcohol.

Finally, a rough and ready method of preserving a goldfish is to place it on a layer of salt on a plate, spread the fins in as natural a way as possible, and secure them, and then sprinkle salt on top. If this is now placed in a dry room for about two days, it will be found, when the salt is brushed off, that although the specimen is much shrunken, the general body form and colours will be sufficiently well maintained for elementary study.

Chapter VIII

BREEDING

Referant proavorum sæpe figuras.
LUCRETIUS, *De Rerum Natura*, Book IV

To most people the act of reproduction is associated with the pairing of a male and female of a species, followed by an actual union between the two. In goldfish, however, and indeed in most fishes, not only are the relations of the sexes during the breeding season promiscuous, but no actual copulation takes place between the male (buck) and female (roe). The reproductive organs consist of ovaries (hard roe) in the females, and testes or milt (soft roe) in the males. The ovaries, which lie just behind and below the air-bladder are yellowish in colour and granular in texture. The testes occupy much the same position in the body of the male as do the ovaries in the body of the female, but they are paler in colour, and have a creamy rather than a granular texture, at all events to the unaided eye. The ovaries and the testes are elongated in shape, paired and intimately associated with the kidneys. 'As the breeding season approaches', Norman writes, 'the ovaries become much enlarged, fill a considerable part of the body cavity, and the separate eggs are plainly visible.' It is at this season, therefore, that the sex of a goldfish may be most readily determined. The body of the female becomes swollen, denoting the presence of ova. At the same time the male develops tubercles, each about the size of a pin's head, denoting the presence of testes. The tubercles (sometimes called 'pearl organs') are usually confined to the gill-covers, but they may extend to the skin of the back, and to the pectoral fins (Plate XV). They disappear as soon as spawning has been completed, and it would seem that in some males they never develop. On several occasions we have bred Shubunkins with a male that never developed tubercles on any part of its body, and it could be distinguished from the female only by its slimmer outline. Other breeders have recorded the same fact. Hodge and Derham write: 'During four breeding seasons, only on one occasion has the writer used a male showing these so-called sexual characteristics.' The tubercles have been known to develop on a female fish, so that, on the whole, probably the best way to determine the sex of a goldfish is to watch their behaviour closely; after all is said fish can be depended on to betray their own sex.

Fundamentally the act of reproduction is the same in all verte-brate animals. It consists in the male fertilizing the ova of the female. But, whereas in most of the higher vertebrates the male fertilizes the ova while they are still in the body of the female, in the goldfish, as in nearly all fishes, the ova are first ejected by the female fish and then they are fertilized by the male. The eggs pass from the ovaries to the exterior by way of a canal (the oviduct) which, in the case of the female goldfish, it shares with the excre-tory duct. In the male goldfish a narrow duct leads from each testis to the genital aperture. Briefly expressed, in goldfish the ova and sperms are merely shed into the water, where fertilization takes place. Normally the sperms can live for only one or two minutes in the water, but Mulertt records that in 1856 a Russian pisciculturist found that if the sperms are taken from the male fish and placed in a bottle and kept at the right temperature, they may be preserved for as long as six days. We have no experience of this and cannot say if it is feasible or not. If it is it would greatly help the work of the pisciculturist in crossing different species. Our information is that feeding the sperms would be as important as keeping them at the right temperature.

The act of reproduction is very simple. The germ-cells, or gametes, are primarily fragments of protoplasm containing nuclei that develop into ova in the ovary and spermatozoa in the testes. When the germ-cells are ripe the fish betray great exuberance. The colours of the fish improve, and even the most sluggish of fish become extremely active. Soon the males (milters) begin to chase the females. After a day or two of aimless chasing, the spawning-drive begins in earnest. The drive consists of the males pursuing the females to and fro across the aquarium or pond. At this time the fish are oblivious of all else, and, indeed, in a wild state they fall an easy prey to fish-eating birds and other enemies. The drive, which continues for about two or three hours, until the female is stripped of eggs, is an attempt on the part of the male to bump the abdomen of the female and so facilitate the release of the ova. Finally, the female sinks to the bottom of the aquarium or pond. By means of his snout the male lifts the female until she is on top of the plants and almost out of the water. It is now that the eggs are released. They are released in batches (the first batch is best: the last is likely to produce weak fry) and each batch is immediately fertilized by the male. A female goldfish in good condition releases a large number of eggs at one spawning. The number, of course, depends very much on the size of the fish, but in general a medium-sized female goldfish releases from 500 to 1,000 eggs at a spawning, and a large female releases anything up to 3,000 eggs. These figures, however, apply only to a first spawning, and fewer eggs are released subsequently.

An unfertilized egg, as shed into the water, consists of a living protoplasm, and a quantity of yolk, enclosed in protective membranes. The yolk (non-living foodstuff) accumulates at one end of the egg (the vegetative pole) and the protoplasm at the other end (the animal pole). The membranes are pierced at the animal pole by a tiny pore (the micropyle) which is just large enough to admit a single sperm. Naturally, before release the egg is quite small, but on release it swells by the osmotic uptake of water. Meanwhile, if all goes well, a sperm finds its way through the micropyle, which closes behind it, and fertilizes the egg.

The eggs of goldfish are demersal adhesive: that is to say, they sink, and are covered with a sticky substance by which they adhere to the aquatic plants. They are easily recognized. They have the appearance of blobs of gelatine about 1/16th in. in diameter.

Once the female has ejected her spawn, and the male has fertilized it, the brood-fish have played their part. They take no interest in the development of the eggs, which are left to incubate on their own. Indeed, the aquarist who intends to go in for serious breeding must promptly take steps to separate the parents from the aquatic plants to which the eggs adhere. If this precaution is not taken the parents will eat most of the eggs, and later, the newly-hatched fish (larvae).

The drive leaves the brood-fish—particularly the female—exhausted. Some breeders permit them to eat some of their eggs as a stimulant. We consider this unnecessary and undesirable, and in our opinion it serves only to give them a taste of the forbidden fruit. Still, in a wild state spawning is followed by a recuperative period of intensified feeding and rest, so that for a few days after the drive the aquarist should pay particular attention to the feeding and comfort of the parents.

Breeding goldfish, then, is not difficult. If the aquarist is concerned only with raising a few common goldfish every season, all he needs to do is to construct a pond that holds about 500 or 600 gallons of water, plant it thickly with *Myriophyllum*, *Elodea*, and *Fontinalis*, stock it with about eight mature fish, and leave a warm summer and Nature to do the rest. This method, however, will not do for the serious breeder, nor for him who wishes to breed fancy goldfish. For, as we have seen, if the eggs are not protected most of them will be eaten by the adult fish. Then, when the young fish hatch out they are helpless for some time, and during this period only the most active will be able to escape being eaten. Finally, an unprotected pond will contain many natural enemies of goldfish-fry; and any sudden drop in temperature (a not uncommon occurrence during an English summer) will prove fatal to them. If the aquarist wishes to raise the maximum number of fish to maturity, he must take certain precautions to protect the eggs and the larvae.

To breed goldfish successfully outdoors, at least three ponds should be constructed. The first is for spawning (the spawning pond), the second is for rearing the fry (the rearing pond), and the third is for those fish which have grown so big that there is no danger of their being eaten by adult fish, and for wintering all the fish (the wintering pond). The ponds need not be very large, but, to get the best results, they should be at least 10 ft. long and 5 ft. wide. No surrounding ledges need be constructed, as in ornamental ponds, but the bottoms should slope so that there are shallow and deep ends. The bottoms of the spawning pond and rearing pond should slope from a depth of about 6 in. to 24 in.; of the wintering pond, from a depth of about 2 ft. to at least 4 ft., as illustrated in the accompanying sectional diagrams of ponds.

The water must be under control, and the ponds not allowed to overflow. The ponds, therefore, should be fitted with outlets, well protected, and constructed near to a source of good water that can be relied on never to fail. It is an advantage to cover the ponds with fine wire netting, to protect the fish from cats, fish-eating birds, and other enemies. During the winter months the spawning and rearing ponds should be kept empty and thoroughly clean.

This lessens the risk of the many natural enemies to spawn and fry being present during the spring, and the development of poisonous gases.

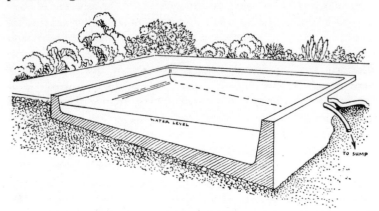

Fig. 45. Sectional View of Spawning and Rearing Pond
(See page 199)

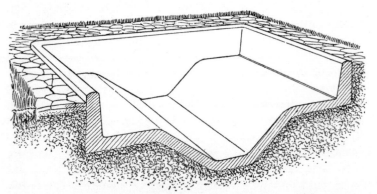

Fig. 46. Sectional View of Wintering Pond (See page 199)

Goldfish breed when they are a year old, and sometimes at the age of nine months. They continue to breed up to the age of six or seven, and there is a record of Fantails breeding at the age of ten.[1] The best breeding age is between three and four. If old fish are chosen four males should be placed with three females; if young

[1] See article 'Breeding the Scaled Fantail' by A. Boarder, in *The Aquarist* (March 1948).

fish, then, four males with six females. It is best for the fish to be all about the same size, but if the females are much bigger than the males then six males should be placed with three females. The female fish should be at least 2 in. long.

In this country goldfish spawn outdoors usually from June to August, but, if the weather is warm, breeding may take place as early as May and as late as September. Early in the summer, therefore, the selected fish should be carefully conditioned. This is most important. Constipation must be avoided, and dried foods should not be given in any large quantity. There is, without doubt, no finer food than earthworms for bringing fish into good breeding condition, and these should be the staple diet. They may be varied with *Daphnia*, bloodworms, *Tubifex*, boiled minced spinach, and oatmeal cooked with scrambled egg and a little cod-liver oil. The brood-fish, in fact, should be fed to repletion on the best possible food. During the conditioning period the water should be kept at a temperature of about 60° F. This has been found to be the best feeding temperature. The fish should be kept under these conditions until the male fish begin to show interest in the females. They are then transferred to the spawning pond, the temperature of which should be slightly higher than 60 degrees. The hardier breeds of goldfish spawn best at temperatures between 60 and 65 degrees, and the increase in temperature helps the spawning act. Rain, or watering the pond, is said to encourage the fish.[1]

The spawning pond should be well stocked with bushy-foliaged plants. *Myriophyllum*, *Elodea* and *Fontinalis* are all suitable and easily obtained in this country. Chinese breeders use large quantities of *Ceratophyllum*, so much so that in China it is popularly known as Goldfish Weed. The plants should not be rooted, but tied in large bunches to wooden rings or pieces of cork, and allowed to float at both ends of the pond; or the plants may be anchored with lengths of string to the banks at the deep and shallow ends of the pond. Breeders call these bunches of plants Goldfish Nests. If sufficient plants cannot be obtained, bunches of long grass, willow roots (favoured by the Japanese breeders) or soft hay will answer the purpose. Plants should never be taken from

---

[1] We have been told by an amateur breeder that he could spawn his goldfish almost to order by drawing water from his pond in a garden-syringe and forcing it back until the air bubbles clung to the fish.

the wild. They are almost certain to contain many enemies to fry, the dreaded *Hydra* in particular. Nothing else should be put in the pond. A planting medium is not necessary, and even snails must be excluded. They are voracious feeders on the spawn of fish.

Spawning usually takes place between four o'clock and nine o'clock in the morning, but sometimes late in the afternoon. Whenever it is thought that the fish have spawned, the bunches of aquatic plants should be carefully examined for eggs. If eggs are seen adhering to the plants, the plants should be transferred to a bucket, which has been half-filled with water from the spawning pond, and taken indoors.

Meanwhile several aquaria, each holding about 12 gallons of water, should have been placed in a greenhouse or a sunny window (for good light is essential), and these should be filled, to a depth of not more than 10 in., with water drawn from the spawning pond. The aquaria should be screened from draughts. The eggs must not be removed from the aquatic plants, but the plants with the eggs adhering to them should be distributed among the aquaria, allowing from ten to twenty eggs to every gallon of water. When the eggs are transferred, care must be taken to ensure that the water in the aquaria is at exactly the same temperature as the water in the spawning pond. Fertile eggs are of a yellowish colour, becoming paler and more difficult to see on the second and third days after release. Infertile eggs, attacked by fungus, turn white and fuzzy, and sink to the bottom of the aquarium. They should be removed at once with a pipette, or their presence will assist the spread of the disease, particularly if the temperature of the water is low.

The period of incubation depends upon the temperature of the water and the condition of the eggs. Japanese breeders incubate the eggs in water at a temperature of 60° to 65° F., and at this heat the eggs hatch in about eight or nine days. Most British and American breeders incubate the eggs in water at a temperature of 70 degrees to 75 degrees, when the eggs hatch in five to seven days. By raising or lowering the temperature, it is possible to hasten or retard the period of incubation, but it is not desirable to do so. Neither a short nor a prolonged period of incubation makes for good fish. Innes very properly points out that the eggs and fry should be kept in a light place protected from temperatures below 60 degrees or above 80 degrees. A temperature about

70 to 75 degrees produces stronger fish than slow incubation, but if the temperature is too high the eggs are liable to be cooked and therefore spoilt.[1] Heat is conducive to the strong and sturdy growth of fry, and to early coloration, and, indeed, most professional breeders keep the water at a high temperature (70 to 75 degrees) until the fry are several weeks old.

Although it is, perhaps, of no great practical value, Shisan C. Chen, as long ago as 1926 made the interesting discovery that if the eggs of goldfish are kept out of water for some time during their early stages of development (that is to say, if the eggs are kept in a moist chamber) and are returned to water one or two days before the time of hatching, they hatch from eight to twenty-four hours earlier than eggs that always remain in the water. Fry hatched in this way may be as normal as those hatched from eggs always in water, but they may be a little premature, though they soon become normal. Chen found that the best form of moist chamber is a specimen-tube (1 in. in diameter and 4 in. in height) covered with a cork partly cut off to allow the free passage of air. A wad of moist filter-paper is placed at the bottom of the tube and another wad at the top. Between the two pads of filter-paper a branch of aquatic plant, with eggs adhering to it, is placed. The eggs are thus suspended in a moist chamber with neither the danger of excessive evaporation, nor that of being flattened by the force of gravity.[2]

The development of the embryo within the egg depends on the period of incubation, which, as we have seen, in turn depends on the temperature of the water. Roughley gives a good description of the embryo in the egg. In an incubation period of five days, the embryo can be distinguished on the second day as an elongated tube, tapering to the posterior extremity, and coiled around the large yolk-sac. On the third day the head is enlarged, and the eyes —as yet unpigmented—can be distinguished. The yolk-sac is much diminished in size, and free at the posterior extremity of the embryo. On the fourth day the eyes are pigmented with black, and the pupils can clearly be seen as circular areas in the centres. Pigment spots can be discerned on the body. The yolk-sac is

[1] William T. Innes, op. cit., p. 70.
[2] Shisan C. Chen, 'The Development of Goldfish, *Carassius auratus*, as affected by being out of water, in distilled water, and in solutions of alcohol' in *China Journal of Science and Arts* (Shanghai, 1926).

The Goldfish

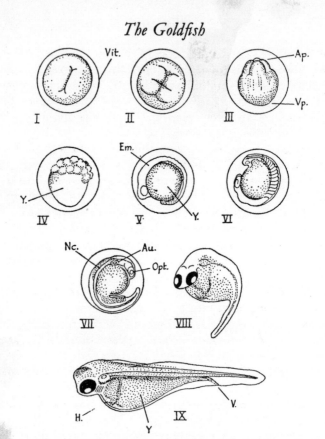

Fig. 47. DEVELOPMENT OF EGG AND EMBRYO
(Modified after Affleck)

(I) First cleavage; (II) Second cleavage, upper view; (III) Second cleavage, side view;
(IV) Advance stage of cleavage; (V. VI. VII) Stages in development of embryo; (VIII)
Embryo immediately after leaving egg; (IX) Larva shortly after hatching.
(ap.) Animal Pole; (au.) Ear; (em.) Embryo; (h.) Heart; (nc.) Notochord; (opt.) Eye;
(v.) Vent; (vit.) Vitelline Membrane; (vp.) Vegetative Pole; (y.) Yolk. (Much
enlarged)

attached only to the lower surface of the head and the anterior
third of the body. The beating of the heart and the flow of the
blood can be observed. On the fifth day the eyes are heavily pigmented, and black pigment spots are scattered over the dorsal
surface of the head and body, and on the yolk-sac. The body is
much elongated, and the yolk-sac much diminished. The contractions of the embryo are more frequent and more vigorous
than formerly, as the pulsations of the heart increase with age (and

temperature). Postulating a temperature of 68·5° F., the pulsations of the heart are 70 per minute at three days old, 81 at 4 days old, and 101 at 5 days old. As the embryo develops, its contractions become more and more restless, until it bursts the egg-membrane in the region of its back; soon its tail is freed; it makes an effort to swim and quickly frees its head.

On emergence from the egg the larva is about one-fifth of an inch long. In general shape it resembles a tadpole. Apart from the large eyes and heart—of which we have already spoken—a brain, ears, and a notochord (the forerunner of the backbone) are present. The dorsal region is greenish in colour, with scattered irregular pigment spots. The rest of the body is translucent. But to the superficial observer the most prominent feature is the yolk-sac, carried abdominally.

At this stage the larvae hang at rest (occasionally labouring for short distances), some to the aquatic plants, others to the sides of the aquarium, still others at the surface of the water. On no account should they be disturbed. If they are they sink to the bottom of the aquarium and find difficulty in rising on account of the pressure. No food need be given to them. At this stage they exist by absorbing the remains of the yolk. Meanwhile the liver develops, and from the upper part of the oesophagus a little outgrowth becomes a glistening silvery sac—the well-known airbladder.

About forty-eight hours after hatching, the yolk has been entirely absorbed and the larva is now known as a post-larva. It is free-swimming; for it is provided with a pair of pectoral fins, and a median fin running along the back, round the tail, and along the underside to the vent. Later the median fin breaks up to form the dorsal, caudal and anal fins. The pelvic fins develop much later.

The little fish now begins to swim in search of the microscopic organisms that are present in all mature water and on which they feed. But in an aquarium this natural food will not last for long and artificial feeding must be given.

It is at this point that most novices fail. The high rate of mortality among newly-hatched goldfish is due mainly to the fact that most inexperienced aquarists rarely supply them with sufficient infusoria during the first two or three weeks after hatching. In this connection Derham writes: 'It is amazing how great is the quantity of infusorians . . . that are consumed by a few baby fish, let alone a tank containing some hundreds of them. A plentiful and continuous supply of microscopic forms of life is the great secret of raising a fair quantity of strong healthy fish, and it is wonderful how much their future growth and strength depends on the amount of correct live food (or suitable substitutes) supplied during the first few weeks.' Innes records that young goldfish eat more than their own bulk in a day.[1]

Actually it is not essential to feed them on infusoria. They may be fed on fine oatmeal, or pea-flour, cooked to a stiff paste and squeezed into the water through a piece of fine muslin. The shape of a goldfish is permanently influenced in its body development in the first few months of its life, and, to some extent, this can be controlled by different methods of feeding. It will be found, for example, that if oatmeal is fed plentifully it helps to build the short round body so greatly desired in some breeds of fancy goldfish. Another artificial food for fry is the yolk of a hard-boiled egg rubbed between the fingers so that it is distributed in the water as a fine cloud. Dealers sell specially finely-graded food for feeding to fry. Hodge and Derham record the raising of a brood of goldfish on a food consisting of 5 parts of dried *Daphnia*, 1 part dried shrimps, 1 part semolina, 1 part fine oatmeal, 1 part dried and crushed brown bread, and 1 part sun-dried earthworms. These ingredients were well mixed, and sifted through fine cheese-cloth. Still, unless the aquarist is breeding for deep round bodies, when, as we have seen, some oatmeal and other starchy foods are desirable, it is best to feed goldfish-fry on infusoria, because a substitute is always a substitute and does not supply the same nourishment as natural food. It has been shown that fry fed on dried foods do not grow nearly so rapidly as those fed on live foods.

There are many ways of cultivating infusoria, and it may be said that almost every aquarist has his own method of making a culture. Austin Watson suggests that a battery of six or seven large jars (such as are used by confectioners) should be filled with old water from an aquarium or pond. In each jar a few lettuce leaves and five or six *Limnaea stagnalis* (Great Pond Snail) are placed. In a fair light the water will, in a day or two, be found full of minute creatures swimming about in clouds.[2] Another method is to use a number of jam jars, or similar vessels, and fill them with warm

[1] W. T. Innes, op. cit., p. 70.
[2] F. Austin Watson, *Aquarium and Pond Management for Beginners* (London, 1933).

water. Into each jar a small quantity of dead lettuce leaves, chopped dry hay, uncooked lentils, or the dried leaves of aquatic plants, are placed. If the jars are kept in a warm, dark place, in about a week's time the water in the jars will be teeming with infusoria. It has been found that banana skins thrown into water and left for a few days will produce innumerable forms of microscopic life. Derham recommends the following method of cultivating infusoria. 'Lay down some lettuces in a place exposed to the sun, and keep them damp. In a very few days the greater part will be reduced to a brown slimy pulp ... get some shallow receptacles and fill them with *old* water preferably from an old water butt, or from a pond in which there is no *Daphnia*. ... Stir in some of the decomposed lettuce and leave for forty-eight hours. At the end of that time you will find, if you examine the culture, myriads of little fellows in every few drops of water.' Derham adds that the culture will be improved if chopped earthworms are rinsed in the water. Red cabbage may be used as a base. One ounce of red cabbage is soaked in 1¾ pints of distilled water. Within twenty-four to seventy-two hours the culture will assume a purple tinge and the water should be acid. But within a week the culture will take on a greenish colour and the water should be alkaline. It is then at its best. Other aquarists recommend putting blood into water; this is known to produce infusoria in plenty. All these methods are good and may be recommended. Our own favourite method is rather more involved. It demands a knowledge of the microscope (every aquarist should have a microscope) and micro-organisms. It has the advantage, however, that we are assured of a pure culture. Water is drawn from an established pond and a drop is examined under the microscope. Desirable organisms (e.g., *Paramoecium*) are picked out with a fine pipette or bristle, and

Fig. 48. SLIPPER ANIMALCULE (*Paramoecium*)
A valuable infusorian.
(Highly magnified)

placed in a jar of water, which has been boiled with some chopped vegetable matter and allowed to cool. The infusoria multiply rapidly. It helps if the drop of water is placed on a piece of well-shredded cotton wool, because the strands of cotton restrict the movements of the organisms, and they may be picked out more easily.

Water containing infusoria should not smell. It should look as though a greyish-white dust is suspended in it. The culture must be kept fresh, and the best way to do this is to aerate the water in which the infusoria are living. Another method is to add a coffee-spoonful of sodium carbonate (washing soda) to every quart of the culture. Infusoria thrive best in soft water. Infusoria have to be fed, and this may be done either by adding to the culture, from time to time, decomposed lettuce leaves, or a teaspoonful of top-soil from the garden. We have kept cultures of infusoria flourishing all the summer merely by emptying the contents of the dip-tube, used for cleaning the bottom of aquaria, into the cultures, and keeping them in a dark and warm cupboard. Decaying plant-life added every few days helps to keep cultures of infusoria healthy.

As we have stated, goldfish-fry eat large quantities of infusoria. One method of feeding the fry is to feed the culture to them two teaspoonsful or more, according to the number of fry, every two hours, and even more often if they will take it readily. A better method, however is to use the drip method of feeding. A jar containing a healthy culture of infusoria is raised above the aquarium. A length of rubber tubing, $\frac{1}{4}$ in. in diameter, is put into the jar and the aquarium as a siphon, and the run of culture from the jar to the aquarium is regulated to a continual drip by means of a pinch-cock. Fresh cultures are supplied in this manner when required. It is of great importance that the culture, however fed, should be at the same temperature as the water in the aquarium, and first strained through very fine muslin. If the culture is not strained there is the danger of polluting the water, and any sudden change of temperature kills infusoria. Breeders who fail to take these precautions, therefore, are simply feeding liquid filth to the fry, and carrion instead of a nourishing live food: of necessity, the result is a loss of many fry. Some German breeders raise infusoria in a filter in the aquarium, so that when the filter is set in motion the infusoria are dispersed into the aquarium.

The appetites of goldfish-fry vary so much that it is impossible to say how much food should be given to them. A general rule with some breeders is to feed the fry five times a day for the first three weeks or so, then three times a day for a few more weeks, then twice daily, finally, at the end of three months, once a day. In our experience the art of raising a brood of fry to maturity is to keep the fry feeding from dawn to dusk. It is important to keep the aquarium free from decomposing particles of food, and any excess of uneaten artificial food. A siphon may be used for removing excess food, provided the precaution is taken to cover the end of the siphon with a piece of muslin to prevent the fry from being sucked up. About once a month it is beneficial to add a little salt to the water, also 1 crystal of potassium iodide to every 2 or 3 gallons of water.

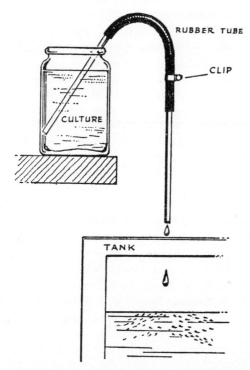

FIG. 49. DRIP-FEEDING INFUSORIA TO GOLDFISH-FRY

Periodically the fry must be sorted. This is essential; for, as the goldfish grow, so they require more and more space, and the more space the better it is for growing fish. As a rough guide, a 12-gallon aquarium, provided that it is planted with oxygenating plants such as *Sagittaria*, *Vallisneria* and *Elodea*, will hold approximately thirty 1-month fry. But this, we must repeat, is only a rough guide, fry are so undeveloped in the body that they can do with proportionately less water than adult fish, at all events for a time. That is to say, eight ¼-in. fry can usually live quite well in an aquarium that is unsuitable for one 2-in. fish. It will be clear, however, that the fry must be sorted from time to time. It is impossible, unless the aquarist has as many tanks as a public aquarium, to raise all the fry to maturity, and the sooner the weaklings are destroyed the better. In fact it is possible to keep more fry than mentioned above in a 12-gallon aquarium, especially if the water is artificially aerated, but it is an established fact that the best fish are those that have been raised in unaerated water, and in which they have ample room. Derham writes that the best Shubunkins raised by him are two or three together in 12-in. or 15-in. bowls, the water in which is never touched or aerated. In any case, artificial aeration is undesirable; partly because it creates a current against which the fry have to swim and so waste their energy, and partly because it stirs up the sediment in the aquarium. If the number of fry and smallness of the aquarium makes artificial aeration a necessity, some steps should be taken to prevent a strong current flowing away from where the air breaks the surface of the water. This is best done by reducing the flow of air to a minimum and placing the diffuser under a large bunch of *Fontinalis*. Fry that are crippled in body, or malformed in finnage, should be destroyed as soon as possible: such fish are not worth the trouble of raising, and rearing them if only to give away is not to be encouraged, since it reflects on goldfish-breeders as a whole. They order these things better in the far east where only the very best fish are allowed to survive. Fry that are growing well should be removed from the aquarium and reared together. If they are allowed to remain with smaller fish they will deprive them of food, and there is the risk that, sooner or later, they will eat the smaller fish. In any case, fry that grow rapidly usually develop into coarse fish of little value. In every brood there is certain to be a number of fry that are weak and delicate, but with well-shaped bodies and good finnage. Although many of these fish will die before they reach maturity, some attempt should be made to rear them. There is the possibility that eventually they will develop into good fish. The best, however, usually develop from among the medium-sized fry. These are they that should be carefully nursed, given the best attention, the best food, and the most room. They will eventually fetch the best price, if the aquarist is interested in the commercial side of breeding, and it is from among them that he will find the most suitable fish to carry on his stock.

At the age of about four weeks the fry are ready to take bigger food than infusoria. Very small *Daphnia* and *Cyclops* ('screened' is the popular term) are the usual foods, and they may be given by placing a quantity in a muslin bag and suspending it in the water. The bag should be left in the water for about half an hour at a time. During this period the smallest of the *Daphnia* and *Cyclops* will escape into the aquarium. The Japanese, who have more patience than Europeans, devote a considerable amount of time and effort to the raising of *Daphnia* and *Cyclops*. Hugh Smith records that they sort them into suitable sizes for the fry with sieves having, respectively, 130, 100, 80, 60 and 20 meshes to the inch.

Modern breeders speak well of Micronematoda (popularly known as Mikro) as a food for goldfish at this stage of their development. Mikro (*Anguillula species*) is a small cylindrical worm related to the threadworms, *Trichina* and other parasitic worms, but is in itself harmless. Mainly it is found in earth and on the roots of trees, but, for a start, a culture may now be obtained from most dealers. Mikro is cultivated as follows. A spoonful of thick, luke-warm, cooked oatmeal is placed in a glass dish, and a small quantity of 'mikro' is added to the oatmeal. The addition of a piece of baker's yeast—about the size of a pea—hastens the development of the culture. Instead of oatmeal and yeast, a sloppy mash of bread and milk may be used. The dish is covered, kept in a warm place (70° to 80° F.), and very soon the culture changes to a thick fermenting jelly, the surface of which is a mass of mikro. Small pieces of wood (about 3 in. long and about ½ in. in cross-section) are arranged criss-cross over the culture, until a couple of layers are clear of the fermenting jelly. In a very short time—even over-night—it will be found that the upper pieces of wood are swarming with mikro free from all impurities. To feed mikro to the fish, the pieces of wood may be dipped into the aquarium, or better still into a feeding-basket, in the bottom of which there has been placed a piece of cotton cloth, as a further precaution against introducing impurities into the aquarium. Although mikro are very hardy (cultures have been known to freeze or dry up without being spoilt), after a time the culture deteriorates. In this event the dish and pieces of wood should be washed in hot water, and a new culture may be started by inoculating a new mess of oatmeal with a small quantity of the old culture. It is considered advisable to have two cultures going, and to restart them on alternate weeks.

About this time, or perhaps a week or two later, the more advanced of the fry should be transferred from the aquarium to the rearing pond. Provided there is no danger of frost the sooner the fry are put outdoors the better. 'There is a magic about outdoors', Derham writes, 'that all the care, food and attention inside cannot compete with.' Apart from the fact that fish in a pond have more room in which to develop, they are provided with valuable foods in the form of small flies and microscopic life which fall into the water. Moreover, the water in a pond is constantly being refreshed by rain and re-oxygenated by wind. Rough handling kills fry almost immediately, and, therefore, the fry should never be netted but captured in what is known as a glass-catcher or glass-net. An alternative method is to ladle out the fry in a cup attached to a length of cane. Great care must be taken to ensure that the water in the aquarium is slowly equalized to the temperature in the rearing pond.

The rearing pond should not be stocked with oxygenating plants. The less plants there are the more easily can the fish be kept under observation, and the presence of any enemies detected. The deeper end of the pond, however, should be planted with one or two water-lilies, or other broad-leaved aquatic plants, to furnish shade and protection for the fish. As well as 'unscreened' *Daphnia* and *Cyclops*, the larvae and pupae of gnats, *Tubifex*, very finely chopped earthworms, and finely-graded dried foods may now be given to the young fish. *Enchytraeus* may also be given provided the worms are first mashed. On no account should *Enchytraeus* be given whole, because its body is covered with small bristles that may cause it to stick in the throat of a small fish and choke it to death. Hugh Smith says that in Japan breeders stock the rearing ponds so thickly with *Daphnia*, *Cyclops*, and other minute forms of life, that the young fish 'have only to open their mouths to obtain all necessary food.' It is undoubtedly the ideal at which to aim.

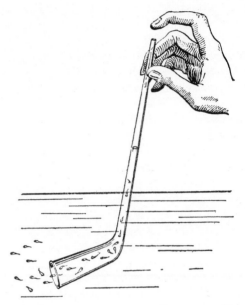

Fig. 50. GLASS-CATCHER FOR CATCHING FRY

By the end of the summer the fish will be ready to be trans-ferred to the wintering pond, provided that no very large fish are kept there, and it is free from predacious insects. Fish less than 2 in. long, however, cannot be wintered outdoors with safety. The wintering pond should be well stocked with aquatic plants. By the following spring the fish will be ready for disposal; the aquarist, of course, retaining the best specimens for himself, to keep up his stock and to be the parents of future generations.

Goldfish may be bred in an aquarium. Indeed, many experi-enced aquarists prefer to breed in aquaria because the conditions are more easily controlled, and spawning can be arranged to take place on the day that it is most suitable to receive the eggs. In fact, by the use of artificial light and heat, it is possible to have broods at any time of the year, even in mid-winter, though we do not recommend breeding in winter unless a good and regular supply of live food is assured.

The breeding aquarium should be as large as possible, and certainly not less than 30 in. long. The centre should be clear of plants, but each end, to an extent of about one-third the length of the aquarium, should be stocked with *Myriophyllum*, *Egeria* and *Fontinalis*. The plants need not be rooted, it is better if they are not, but tied in bunches and sunk with strips of lead. The plants, however, should be so plentiful that the fish have some difficulty in making their way through them. The aquarium should be established some weeks before the fish are introduced, or healthy, clear water from a rainwater-butt or pond may be used. The aquarium should be filled with water only to a depth of about 6 in., and it should be placed in a warm position where it will receive the early morning sun.

A week before the aquarist wishes spawning to take place the males and the females in the stock aquarium should be separated by a glass partition. The light should not be too good. During this period the fish should be fed with plenty of live foods, and chopped and rinsed earthworms. The night before spawning is to take place select the best developed and strongest (not necessarily the largest) male and female that show most interest in each other through the glass partition. The fish will never attempt to spawn that night, at least we have never known them to, but dawn the next day will usually find them spawning. If spawning has taken place, the brood-fish should be returned to the stock aquarium as soon as possible, and certainly before noon, otherwise most of the eggs will be eaten.

If spawning does not take place, it is probably due to the fact that the fish were not ready. They should be returned to the stock aquarium, and the procedure repeated about a week later. Sometimes spawning fails because the male is lazy. In this event some breeders recommend a second male being introduced into the breeding aquarium, but in our experience this avails nothing, and in fact does more harm than good, because the second male seems to spend most of his time eating the eggs instead of fertilizing them. Goldfish are not jealous creatures. There are other reasons why spawning does not always take place. Betts writes: 'Very often a matched pair do not take to one another; for no doubt goldfish have their preferences. [It is probable that there is a certain natural selection even among domesticated animals.] Under these circumstances a feed of very small, crawly earthworms will sometimes set them going. In hot, sultry weather many males are unable to hold the seminal fluid with the result that the desire to drive is not very great. The only way to obviate this is to lower the temperature of the stock tank. Another very annoying characteristic is half-hearted driving. The male will start off with great energy, but quickly tires, and nothing happens. This is generally caused through keeping the fish active during the winter. The best drives are those that follow a healthy hibernation.'[1]

If spawning takes place the fry must be treated as already explained. It must be remembered, however, that if the aquarist has no rearing pond for the young fish he should make no attempt to raise all the fry to maturity. Only the finest specimens in the brood should be kept. Common sense, if nothing more, dictates that it is better to raise about one hundred strong and healthy fish than 1,000 undernourished weaklings. Even so, the aquarist will need a large number of aquaria to raise 100 fry to maturity, though, as the fish grow, wooden tubs, enamelled pans, baths, and similar vessels (which as soon as all danger of frosts has passed should be placed outdoors for the fry to harden and develop) may be pressed into service. They will prove very satisfactory so long as they are made safe for fish, and managed in the same way as recognized aquaria.

In China some of the finest fish are raised in baked-clay pans (kongs), about 3 to 5 ft. in diameter, and 1 ft. or $1\frac{1}{2}$ ft. deep. The Reverend Henry W. Moule has given us an interesting description of a Chinese goldfish-farm some eighty years ago, but doubtless much the same today. Time means no more to a Chinaman than it does to a cat. 'In Hangchow, one of the centres of the goldfish trade in China, there were several places in the Upper City where goldfish were bred and kept for sale. They were all very much alike, but the one I remember best was in Lion Lane. It consisted of an open yard with the owner's cottage at one end, surrounded by a wall of rammed earth and a few trees. There was a small, but fairly deep, pond in which fish were kept, but the most striking feature was the characteristic pans set neatly in rows of groups of four, with space between each group to allow of easy access. These pans occupied most of the yard. In many of the pans the water was green and opaque, but in the majority the water was clear; for the sediment was removed at least once a day by means

---

[1] Leonard C. Betts, op. cit., p. 157.

of a small bamboo pipe used as a siphon. The fish were fed almost exclusively on daphnids (locally known as 'Golden Shrimps') and of which there was an endless supply in the many stagnant ponds in the neighbourhood. Close to the cottage was a well for a water supply, and a few large glazed jars to collect rain-water. Scattered about here and there, were nets, buckets, and all the other tools of the trade. Over the outer gate the words *Chin-yü* were written quite small. Beyond this there was nothing to call attention to the interesting and delightful trade that was carried on behind the plain whitewashed wall. The fish were kept permanently outdoors, and in the winter the water in the pans was sometimes frozen to a depth of 2 in.: in the summer reed mats were thrown over the pans to protect the fish from the burning sun. The fish raised in these pans were what European fanciers now know as Telescopes, Celestials, and Egg-fish.'

We do not recommend this method to British breeders, however, for climatic conditions are very different with us. At Hangchow the months of April and October are always as hot as the hottest months in Britain, and the five months in between are much hotter than anything we ever experience. July and August are hotter at Hangchow than at places like Singapore on the equator. During these seven hot months the fish have the opportunity to put on sufficient flesh to carry them through the severe winter. This is not always possible in Britain, where the average year may be described as four months during which the shade temperature rarely rises above 80° F., and may drop to as low as 60 degrees; and eight months of unreliable weather, with short periods of freezing cold alternating with sharp frosts and muggy days. To some extent it is the same in parts of America. A breeder at Buffalo, who regularly winters Lionheads and Orandas outdoors, expresses surprise that this is not done by British breeders, because the winter climate is much less severe in England than at Buffalo. It may be that the summer at Buffalo is not so hot as at Hangchow, but it is much hotter and more reliable than in England—the sun is more nearly perpendicular. Attempts have been made in this country to winter outdoors the sub-tropical breeds of goldfish, but these experiments have not always proved successful: many of the fish died, and of the remainder most developed and later succumbed to derangement of the air-bladder. If the fish are well fed during the summer months it is not impossible to winter them outdoors, but, even then, climatic conditions play a big part. We strongly suspect that British breeders who tell us that they have successfully wintered the sub-tropical breeds out-doors have ponds which receive as much sun as possible, and are in sheltered and warm districts. It is the English summer, not its winter, that is at fault.

To return from this slight but necessary digression. If success is to be achieved in breeding goldfish, light, warmth and plenty of food are essential. Moreover, there must be no neglect, no crowd-ing and no ill-assortment of sizes. Surplus fish should be disposed of as soon as they reach the saleable size of 1 to $1\frac{1}{2}$ in., and have coloured. To simplify sorting into sizes for the market, many commercial breeders use a method that has much to commend it. The fish are netted out of the water and turned on to a table covered with oil-cloth ruled in 1-in. squares. The fish are then slid through pockets into buckets hanging at the corners of the table. The short time that the fish are on the table does them no harm, though, of course, only common goldfish may be sorted in this way. Fancy goldfish must be sorted while they are in water, because, apart from the fact that the fins cannot be seen properly when a fish is out of the water, they would be liable to damage if numbers of writhing fish were turned on to a table.

An interesting passage on the breeding of goldfish in earthen-ware jars is given in the *Pi Ch'uan Hua Ching* (*Mirror of Flowers*) by Ch'ên, Hao-tzŭ, published in 1688. It deserves more than a passing mention. It is surprisingly modern. 'The Golden *Chi*', Ch'ên Hao-tzŭ writes, 'has long persisted beautiful. In antiquity none were reared in earthenware jars, and not until the Sung [960–1279] did anyone use jars in which to rear them. Now they are generally kept by people as ornaments [pets], and the fish themselves have become a type, called Goldfish. Generally speaking the coloured fish reared in pools and ponds are mostly the black and white variations of *Li* and *Chi*, but those which are of a golden colour are highly valued, and men would not put them meanly into pools. Yet at Shih-ch'êng those who make a living by selling fish gener-ally rear them in pools in order to extend their life. But if fish are in contact with mud they will not be red and bright. They must be reared in jars, and the best jars are those which are pointed at the bottom and wide at the mouth. New jars, which have not yet been filled with water, should always be rubbed with raw yam [modern

Chinese breeders recommended milk] and then, after the water has been poured in, moss [algae] will grow and the water will be alive.[1] In the very hot periods of summer and autumn the water must be changed once every other day, and then the fish will not be scalded and die. . . .

'In readiness for the spawning time in the third month of spring, take several large male shrimps to cover [?] them, and then the young fish produced will all have three or five tails. But half of the claws of the shrimps must first be removed, and then the fish will not be injured. When you see the male fish hurrying round the jar and snapping, that is the time when the female is dropping eggs. She lets the eggs fall on to the weed. Take the weed into the sunshine to see if it has any eggs on it. They are the size of grains of millet and look transparent, like crystal. Take this weed and put it by itself in a glazed earthenware basin, not allowing more than from three to five fingers of water, and put it in a place thinly shaded by trees. If they are completely shaded the eggs will not hatch, nor will they hatch if they are exposed to fierce sunshine. After two or three days the fry will hatch out; but they must not be in the same place as the adult fish for fear they may be eaten by them. After the fry are hatched out take the yolk of a hard-boiled hen's egg or duck's egg, crushed very small with the fingers, to feed them. Next, after ten days take some of the little red insects [*Daphnia!*] which are found in the stagnant waters of canals, to feed them; but it is necessary that the red insects shall have been kept in clear water; and you must not give them too many. After 100 days or more the black ones will gradually change to speckled white, and then gradually to pure white; or first change to pale yellow and then gradually to pure red; and some of them will be parti-coloured—all according to their changes. . . .

'When they are thoroughly domesticated the fish will not avoid the sight of men, and can be called by snapping the fingers, and will come as soon as ever they can see you.

'As to the method of rearing, if the fish turn white and there is floating foam on the water, quickly change it for new water, for fear it may hurt the fish. By taking banana leaves and roots broken very small, and throwing them into the water, it is possible to cure

---

[1] It has been found by experiment that rubbing an aquarium with a raw potato has the affect of greatly increasing the growth of algae.

the fish. But if the fish are thin and come out in white spots, called "fish wind", promptly throw in liquidambar bark, or white poplar bark, and they will be healed. Or take a new brick and bury it in dung and let it remain so for one night; take it out and dry it, and put it into the jar, and this also may cure the "wind". If there are frothy streaks in the water, or they eat the dung of pigeons, the fish are sure to die quickly, so you must use lumps of dung to cure them. If the fish fall ill through eating willow-catkins by mistake, they also may be cured by the use of dung. . . .'

The passage about the use of dung for the control of *Ichthyophthirius* (White Spot) is altogether remarkable. Arthur Derham writes: 'A remark by Bartmann, the well-known German breeder, once tempted the writer to experiment on the lines indicated below. . . . In a tank where fish had been bred freely, and which was "carrying" perhaps too many, an outbreak of white spot occurred, and many fish died. Into this tank was thrown, spread all over, old rotted turves, sifted through a quarter inch mesh. This settled naturally on the bottom, and this was continued for several days until there was a layer about one-and-a-half inches deep at the base. It took about ten days for the water to clear . . . and when it did clear . . . there was no trace of white spot. . . . We treated four tanks in this way, and although white spot has been *introduced* into two of these tanks since, it died out, and no trace of the disease is now seen.' Derham suggests that the turves created a condition inimical to the parasites. He points out, however, that the method failed when other aquarists tried it. In view of what Ch'ên Hao-tzŭ writes, a possible explanation is that when Derham tried his experiment a quantity of dung was introduced with the turves; but this is not to say that we recommend manure in preference to the treatments for ichthyophthiriasis mentioned in Chapter VII.

It sometimes happens that circumstances compel the aquarist to breed in a communal aquarium. The following method may then be used. About one-third of the aquarium is partitioned off with a piece of muslin, or very fine perforated zinc enamel painted, fixed to a frame of well-seasoned wood. The frame should fit flush to the back, front and bottom of the aquarium, and the top stay of the frame should rest on the back and front, so that the frame rises about an inch above the surface of the water. The smaller compartment is well stocked with suitable aquatic plants. When a male and female show signs of spawning they are transferred to the smaller compartment to breed. They are returned to the main part of the aquarium as soon as spawning is over, leaving the eggs, adhering to the plants within the smaller compartment, to incubate on their own. A pane of glass may be used to divide the aquarium, but muslin or very fine perforated, enamelled zinc is better, because it permits the free circulation of water. Moreover, it is not easy to cut a piece of glass to fit exactly against the front and back of the aquarium (though the difficulty can be overcome, to some extent, by cutting the glass a bit short and encasing the edges in lengths of split rubber tubing) and the glass must fit exactly, or the newly-hatched fish will find their way among the adult fish and be eaten by them.

The novice should, perhaps, be advised to confine his first attempts at breeding goldfish to the Common Goldfish, the Shubunkin, and the Comet. The subtropical fancy goldfish, such as the Fantails, the Veiltails, and the like, require more attention, and the fry are rather more difficult to raise to maturity. They are, however, well worth the extra trouble.

If the subtropical fancy goldfish are to breed satisfactorily they require water at a temperature of at least 70° F. Commerical breeders frequently have their hatcheries near a factory, so that the ponds may be heated by steam pipes, and the temperature of the water in these ponds is often raised to as high as 100 degrees. The ordinary man is not so well placed, and, therefore, unless he lives in the south of England and his ponds are in a very sheltered position, he should not attempt to breed fancy goldfish outdoors, but always in an aquarium.

The breeding of fancy goldfish is attended by a considerable amount of luck. In every brood of Veiltails there is invariably a large number of fry with single caudal fins (Nymphs), and Derham records the case of a breeder who 'bought six Veiltails, blue, at five pounds apiece [a considerable price for a fish at the time] from a famous and reliable American breeder who had had a prize-winning stock for years, and in two spawnings from these fish, there was raised *one* only that was blue, and that had the double anals, etc., that denotes the class fish.' Mating fish for colour is something of a speculation; two yellow fish will not necessarily produce all yellow progeny, nor will two red fish necessarily produce all red progeny. Of course, some yellow fish and some red fish will be produced as the result of the matings. It is much the same with the Moor. In the experience of many breeders the best Moors are produced when an all-black Moor female is mated with an all-black Moor male. Naturally all the progeny will not be all-black Moors, but a number will. On the other hand, many breeders advocate mating a male Moor with a rich red female Veiltail. It is claimed that this produces Moors of a richer black. It may be so, but clearly there is a difference of opinion among those best qualified to speak, and, when so many doctors disagree, we would not presume to dictate. Probably the truth is that Moors, like Shubunkins,[1] do not breed true, and, therefore, they may be produced in more ways than one, but which is the best way no one can say, because definite numbers from known crosses are lacking.

In connection with breeding Moors, it is of particular interest to note that Yatsu records that Togawa found that all breeds of gold-fish will turn black if the eyes of the fry are removed, but if the eyes of two-year fish are removed he found that fish with telescope eyes turned black, but those with normal eyes did not; and that Matsui has found that if normal-eyed fish are crossed with tele-scope-eyed fish the majority of the progeny are normal-eyed, but when the back-cross is made many individuals with normal eyes have very much larger eyes than usual, thus showing that, some-how or other, the production of the telescope eye has been in-hibited. Nature, in fact, plays many tricks when it comes to cross-breeding fish. It is to be noticed that when the Lionhead is crossed with the Veiltail the result is the Oranda with a large dorsal fin, but when the Oranda is back-crossed with the Lionhead the result is the Veiltail Lionhead with no dorsal fin.

When choosing brood-fish, therefore, no hard and fast rules can be laid down. But physical vigour, the general form of the body, the character of the finnage and the colour pattern should be con-sidered. Condition is important. The fins should be held firmly, none should be broken, torn, nor bloodshot. The body should be well nourished, without being fat. The scales should gleam. Fish that show the slightest sign of deformity of body or finnage should be rejected as parents. Bad features as well as good ones

---

[1] To obtain offspring all of the Shubunkin type a scaled fish should be mated with a 'transparent' fish. If both brood-fish are of the Shubunkin type only 50 per cent of the offspring will be Shubunkins.

can be inbred and thereby fixed, and, therefore, any deformities in either parent may well be repeated in every fish spawned. This (need we add?) does not apply to temporary injuries, such as a mutilated fin that has not regained its original perfection, or a lost scale. When breeding for characteristic features, such as telescope eyes, divided caudal fin, and the like, the essential features should be present in both parents. They are difficult enough to produce even with perfect fish. When breeding calico fish, in which the blue coloration is much sought after, it is best to mate a deep red with a good blue one. A mating between two blue fish nearly always results in a brood of pale and anaemic-looking fish. In point of fact, fish that are light-coloured should be avoided as parents. The light colours are most persistent (there is a natural tendency that is to say, for fry to be lighter in colour than their parents) and for at least 350 years light-coloured fish have been considered by aquarists to be the least desirable. It is best to choose as parents young and active fish, rather than large, showy ones, and it is important to choose only those that, as fry, grew quickly and changed colour at an early age; for among all domesticated animals there is a tendency to revert to type, and those fish that changed colour slowly, and did not show their characteristic features till fairly late in life, have clearly shown that they are on the downward path. In this connection Mulertt records that fish that colour at the age of six to eight weeks transmit the same tendency on an average, to 98 per cent of their progeny, but those fish that delay changing colour until the second year produce only 5 per cent of fry that will colour in the second year, and, of the remainder, though some will colour in the second year, many will never do so but retain their natural colour all their lives. The general rule, therefore, emerges: always choose as brood-fish the best and healthiest fish available, in which the characteristic features desired in the progeny are pronounced in both parents. But this, perhaps, is a counsel of perfection, and if it is impossible to find a male and female fish both possessing all the required characteristics, the next best thing is to choose a male and female in which some desirable points are to be found in one parent, and the other desirable points in the other parent. By mating a female with good coloration, but with indifferent finnage, with a male with good finnage, but with indifferent coloration, there is a strong probability (we cannot use a stronger term) that some good fish will be found among the progeny; though it is necessary to sound the warning that the aquarist must take into consideration the parentage of the chosen male and female. As we pointed out, there is much luck in breeding fancy goldfish. On several occasions we have been fortunate and found many good fish in a spawning from two inferior fish. Conversely, we have had the unfortunate experience of finding mainly inferior fish in a spawning from two first-class fish. The simple fact is that a breeder always has to risk the chance of many progeny throwing-back. Purchasing a genuine pair of fish from a reliable breeder, and paying his price, does not always prove sound; though the incident recorded on page 220 is probably exceptional, since, in the end, pedigree tells, to the extent, that is, that good fish are always the descendants of good fish. The strain is of paramount importance. All this, of course, is not to deny the laws of Mendel. The geneticist knows the answer, and, doubtless, given time and knowledge of the pedigree, he can predict how two goldfish should breed. But predictions often go wrong, and goldfish are notoriously difficult. Sometimes it seems that alone among the animal and vegetable kingdoms they are a law unto themselves. Or perhaps the truth is that there has been so much cross-breeding that the pedigree of most goldfish is entirely lost. In an attempt to put things right, it was one of the several aims of the Goldfish Society of Great Britain (that came into existence early in 1948) to give recognition to those breeders whose stock might be accepted as of pedigree quality, and to recognize four grades of all breeds of goldfish— specimen fish, first-class fish, brood-fish and commercial fish. As far as we know nothing seems to have come of it.

Heavy feeding is particularly necessary when rearing the subtropical breeds of goldfish, and, as well as infusoria, plenty of cereal food (as described above) and mashed *Enchytraeus*, should be given. This encourages the corpulency that is an essential feature of Fantails, Veiltails, and the like. But although it is impossible to overfeed the fry of fancy goldfish, it is possible to pollute the water by an excess of food, and it is of great importance to siphon out any excess of food every day. Owing to the danger of pollution, Japanese breeders recommend a periodical change of water.

Artificial aeration should be avoided, especially if veil-tailed fish are being raised; compelling the fry to swim against a current (however slight) is not conducive to round deep bodies and drooping lacey fins. Indeed, small containers make for good fin development, and the best Fantails and Veiltails are nearly always raised in containers only just large enough to enable them to live without suffering from a lack of oxygen.

At about the age of six weeks the fry should be about ⅜ in. long and the texture of the scales apparent, so if calico fish are being bred, it is time to sort them out from the scaled throwbacks. Fish with inferior finnage (particularly caudal) should also be among the first to be sorted out. Sooner or later they must go, and it should be sooner, because body-shape and other features of importance cannot be assessed until a fish is several months old.

As soon as all danger of frosts has passed, the young fish may be transferred to ponds, to harden and develop. Subtropical fancy goldfish, especially the calico breeds, will have to be brought indoors by September; they are not sufficiently hardy to endure the cold months outdoors. They must, of course, be acclimatized slowly to the changed conditions. Commercial breeders often keep young fish in lime water for a period, in order to harden the skin. F. L. Vanderplank writes: 'A slightly alkaline water containing dissolved lime is the best for fry. . . . With Shubunkin-fry, and in fact with all goldfish, traces of various minerals in the water more than helps to ensure good colouring of the fish. This can be made up as follows: one crystal each of manganese sulphate, nickel sulphate, and potassium bichromate, and a tiny portion (half the size of a pea) of copper sulphate, dissolved in a quart of tap water, two or three drops (no more) being added to the aquarium [24 in. by 12 in. by 12 in.] fortnightly, after the first week.'[1] A few of the more progressive breeders have tried experiments with tannic acid, and other chemicals, to induce richer coloration.

Fancy goldfish usually spawn three times in one season. The common goldfish, and the more hardy breeds of fancy goldfish, such as the Shubunkin, will spawn even more often. Derham writes: 'In a sunken pond in a heated greenhouse where the temperature is constantly round about sixty degrees Fahrenheit, there will be young Shubunkins all the year round, and contrary to what one would expect the parents grow tremendously and make great fish.'

Fish in breeding ponds suffer from a number of complaints.

[1] See article 'Breed Your Own Goldfish' by F. L. Vanderplank in *The Aquarist* (September–October 1936).

One of the most common, if not the commonest, is spawn-binding, of which we have written on page 186.

Another common complaint is *Saprolegnia* (White Fungus). Goldfish are weakened by spawning, and, however careful the aquarist may be, he cannot avoid a certain shock to the fish when they are transferred from one pond to another or from an indoor aquarium to an outdoor pond. The salt-bath, prescribed on page 182. may be used. But if a large number of fish are affected the progressive salt-bath treatment is not altogether practical. Suitable treatment is to net them out of the water and dip them for half a minute in a brine solution, made by dissolving 1 lb. of salt (not table-salt) in 8 gallons of water.

A disease that manifests itself as white tags on the gill-covers of fry, is, fortunately, not very common. It is brought on usually by overcrowding and incorrect feeding. If the fry are large enough the most suitable treatment is to paint the gill-covers of the fish with a mild solution of iodine and water, or with a solution made by dissolving 3 crystals of permanganate of potash (or 4 drops of Condy's fluid) in a $\frac{1}{2}$ pint of water.

Japanese breeders mention a disease (known to them as *kama*) which affects fry about ten days old. The abdominal wall is thinner than normal and attaches itself to the dorsal side of the abdominal cavity. The fish is thus prevented from eating, and dies. The disease spreads rapidly, even to nearby ponds, and the Japanese recommend destroying the fish and disinfecting the pond. We have no experience of this disease, and from the scanty information available the parasitologist of the Zoological Society of London cannot do more than suggest that it may be caused by a goitre or a tapeworm. Iodine salts added to the water (see page 209) may help if a goitrous thyroid is found.

Kuchigusari is another disease that the Japanese breeders recognize as attacking fish in hatching ponds. The symptoms are a destructive inflammation of the snout, which peels, and the fins of the fish are destroyed. The Japanese say that there is no cure. L. Cura tells us that a disease whose symptoms were similar to *kuchigusari* attacked the fish in his ponds in the early summer of 1944: he threw in a quantity of salt and about half the affected fish recovered. The symptoms suggest that the disease is parasitic, so that immersing the fish in a mild solution of permanganate of potash (see page 140) may be tried.

The Goldfish

Finally, the Japanese breeders mention a disease known to them under the general name of 'Pest'. It affects young fish. The symptoms are black spots on the body and fins. It is very infectious. The symptoms are similar to those of myxosporidia. Ida Mellen cured pike suffering from myxosporidia by immersing them for 1 minute in a bath made by dissolving 10 drops of ammonia in a quart of water. Three or four baths at intervals of three days were given. Goldfish may be given the same treatment.

We have by no means exhausted the subject of breeding goldfish. Indeed, we doubt if anyone could record all the minute details of the art—for such it is—of raising goldfish from egg to maturity. We have written enough to show the general principles, and it will be seen that the breeding of goldfish is not difficult. It is an interesting hobby, if no more. We are not prepared to say that it is a lucrative one. Breeding on a commercial scale necessitates considerable practical experience in the handling of fish, and an appreciable capital. Many scores of large aquaria, as well as large ponds, are necessary to raise to maturity the fry from only one spawning. On the Continent of Europe, particularly in Germany, fish farms are (or, at all events, were before the Second World War) of considerable size. Some of them extend to as much as 7,000 acres. Nor is it for those who are not prepared to work very hard; breeding goldfish in a big way means working from dawn to dusk, sometimes in the hot sun and sometimes in the cold wind, from early spring until the late autumn. There are disappointments to be faced, too. Parasites, outbreaks of contagious diseases, enemies in the forms of dragon-fly larvae, water-beetles, fish-eating birds, and the like, can kill every fish in a pond in the proverbial no-time. Even under ideal conditions, and given ordinary luck, the breeder can rely upon no more than about 30 per cent of the eggs laid resulting in fish surviving long enough to reach a marketable size. We have no wish to deter anyone from taking up goldfish breeding as a profession; but we do wish to make it clear that it is not an easy way of making a living. Fancy goldfish, however, present a brighter picture. It may be that they are no longer worth their weight in gold, but good specimens fetch good prices. Since a hundred fancy goldfish can be reared indoors with no great expense or trouble, a reasonable profit can be made if all goes well.

For centuries China and Japan have led the way in the culture of goldfish. America developed, if it did not produce, the Comet. Germany has given us some interesting hybrids. It is on record that Richter succeeded in hand-spawning a Veiltail Goldfish × Rosy Barb (*Barbus conchonius*). The progeny were perfect barbs with the drooping tail of the Veiltail.[1] The goldfish will cross readily with its colour variations, and now and again it has been known to cross outside its own species. There are records of a cross between a Mirror Carp and a Fantail; and of a Common Goldfish with a Crucian Carp, to produce fertile hybrids. Whether or not Chinese breeders have bred goldfish with Chinese characters on their bodies in a matter of dispute. Certainly 350 years ago Chang Ch'ien-tê wrote: 'Amongst those which I myself bred at my home at one time in the *Kêng-yin* year [1590] there were some with a vermilion *wang* character (王) on the top of the head' (*The Book of Vermilion Fish*, 1596). Although Chang Ch'ien-tê makes no claim to have specially bred these fish, observation shows that there is a tendency for the markings on fish to take definite shapes, and there is reason to believe that, once the facts were known and fish with particular genotypes available, it would not be impossible to breed such fish. Whether the Chinese have succeeded is another matter. Even today, very little is known about the actual colour- and pattern-inheritance in fish, although the genetical possibilities are known.[2] So far as Chang Ch'ien-tê is concerned, faking may be ruled out. He was certainly too big a man to resort to such methods, but faking seems to have been known in his day. In the contemporary *K'ao P'an Yü Shih*, T'u Lung wrote: 'They [the breeders] also produced counterfeits.' Later, faking seems to have been resorted to fairly freely. In the *Mémoire* sent from Peking to Paris, in 1772, there is mention of the *Wên-yü* (Marked Fish) and it is expressly stated that the fish is so called because breeders have found a means of writing a Chinese character on a common goldfish. The author adds: 'A European will have difficulty in recognizing the form of a Chinese character in the colours so irregularly disposed on these little fishes, but it is certain that a Chinaman sees them, recognizes them, and distinguishes them.'

[1] Since some doubt has been thrown on the authenticity of the cross, we point out that it was recorded in *Bird Fancy and Aquaria News* (23 February 1935).

[2] When the Goldfish Society of Great Britain (see p. 223) came into existence, one of its aims was to breed goldfish to a programme, in an endeavour to find out as much as possible about colour inheritance and how certain characteristics can be controlled.

The Goldfish

Faking fish is nothing unusual, and there need exist no doubt that an elaborate character on the body of a fish would be the result of faking. Indeed, the *Mémoire* admits as much; although the author has some misgivings he explains that the *Wên-yü* was obtained by painting the desired character on the fish with a pencil dipped in arsenic diluted in the urine of a tortoise. Yatsu records that even to this day a few unscrupulous dealers increase the commercial value of goldfish by pulling out some of the scales to improve the colour pattern. Hugh Smith writes: 'At Koriyama the practice has existed from very early times of artificially making designs on the backs of fish. This is done by the use of dilute hydrochloric or muriatic acid, and the process consists in a decolorization which leaves the treated parts white. . . . By the use of a brush, glass rod, or stick, the acid is judiciously applied after the skin has been wiped dry. In this way flowers, figures, letters, etc., are produced.' Smith is careful to add that the practice is not common, and not to be commended. There is, however, no fake about the Chinese Telescope, the Japanese Oranda, and the American Comet, and what has been done in China, Japan and America, can be done in Britain. There is a task for someone, and plenty of scope for experiment. As recently as 1934 Shisan C. Chen, by crossing the Blue Fish and Brown Fish, produced a Blue-Brown Fish that breeds true to colour.[1] What man has done, man can do.

Finally, a word must be said about the most satisfactory way of hand-spawning goldfish. The operation is not nearly so difficult as some would have us believe, and it by no means calls for the hand of the specialist. A mature male and female goldfish are placed for from twelve to twenty-four hours (perhaps a little longer) in a medium-sized aquarium, with some aquatic plants. As soon as the female has shed a few eggs, the male is removed and the female taken in the hand and allowed to wriggle. Squeezing her is not necessary, and, indeed, it is not desirable to do so. The wriggling results in the ejection of a large number of eggs, fully as many as are ejected in the normal way. As soon as all the eggs are shed, the female fish is placed aside, the water given a gentle stir, to distribute the eggs over the plants, and the male taken in the hand. By gently squeezing him in the anal region the sperms are ejected and carried by the same wave to fertilize the

[1] Shisan C. Chen, op. cit., p. 70.

eggs. This method almost guarantees all the eggs being fertilized, and it has the further advantage that the brood-fish, not being in the aquarium, cannot eat the eggs before the breeder has time to remove them.

Chapter IX

SHOWING

That thorough inspection of the exhibits by which the instructive purpose of the wonderful collection can be most fully realised.

Daily Telegraph, 14th May 1883

In Chapter II we referred to an estimate that there are about 126 different breeds of fancy goldfish. For the purpose of show, however, the various aquarist organizations, past and present, have never recognized more than the common goldfish and about twenty-five odd of the better-known fancy breeds. The more grotesque fancy breeds, such as the Pompon, the Brocade, and the like, have never yet been recognized for show purposes, and, probably never will be. This, of course, is only to be expected, since, as we have had occasion to remark, the more grotesque breeds are seen but rarely in England, and, when they are, mainly only in the collections of specialists.

From time to time organizations have appointed a Standards Committee to lay down the desired standards and points for each breed of goldfish. The current standards and points are ignored in this book, since they are always open to alteration. There are, in fact, fashions in goldfish, as there are in women's clothes, and, since fashions come and go, the perfect fish of yesterday is not the perfect fish of today, and what today is considered a desirable feature in a goldfish may not be so tomorrow. We intend, therefore, to touch only upon the important matter of selecting and preparing fish for show; to be followed by a few general considerations. Meanwhile we would recommend that the aquarist who intends to show a fish should make himself acquainted with the standards by which the fish will be judged.[1] More we cannot do. Nor would we if we could; for we are not altogether satisfied that

[1] Fish are judged either by the standards published by the Federation of British Aquatic Societies or those published by the Goldfish Society of Great Britain.

230

the present standards, the 'new look' in goldfish, are the ideals at which the breeder should aim.

Goldfish for show must be chosen with great care. The shape of the body and the finnage should conform to the standard laid down by the Standards Committee, and, in the calico types all the colours mentioned in the standard should be present. This is so important that it is usually a waste of time and work to show a fish that fails to conform to the standard, whether of body-shape, finnage, or coloration. Although a common goldfish with a large tail looks attractive, it will be passed over by the judges if it fails to conform to the standard. In the same way it is virtually useless to show a Comet unless its tail looks as though it needs to be supported with bean sticks. The aquarist may consider that such a fish is a freak of nature. Perhaps he is right, but it is, as we say, a matter of conforming to the standard, and if beauty is largely in the eye of the beholder, the beholder here is not the owner of the fish but the Standards Committee.

Symmetry in a fish counts for much, so that the pectoral and ventral fins should be perfectly matched and well balanced. If a fish with a divided caudal fin is to be shown, both fins should be identical in size, shape, and forking. So, too, should a fish with a divided anal fin. In the same way, a fish with telescope eyes should have both eyes the same size; and, so far as possible, the colours of the fish should be evenly matched on both sides of the body. If fish are being shown in pairs, they should be identical in shape of body, finnage, and coloration. In point of fact, provided they are evenly matched, two fish of inferior body-shape, finnage and coloration will be looked upon far more favourably by the judges than one good fish with an inferior one. The former pair may gain an award: the latter hardly ever.

Since pale-coloured goldfish are not thought highly of by aquarists, the colour of the fish to be shown should be deep and even; but it is to be noted that, in their respective classes, pale yellow fish stand a better chance than pale red fish. Silver fish, however, are never worth showing. They fit neither into the red nor the yellow class. If a variegated common goldfish is to be shown, it should exhibit on its body at least two colours, preferably more, and preference should be given to a fish that also exhibits some black.

To sum up, the body of the fish should be of the correct shape and outline, the fins must be perfectly matched and balanced, and the colour, or colours, must be correct down to the last detail.

There is an art in showing a fish. Some fish are naturally good showers: others are the opposite. The art lies in preparing the fish for show. It is by no means unusual for an inferior fish carefully prepared for show to beat a better specimen whose owner, quite obviously, has taken no trouble to prepare it for its ordeal.

An unsteady fish, no matter how handsome it may be, stands very little chance of winning a prize. If a fish constantly darts to and fro in its aquarium, not only are the judges unable to inspect it properly, but they deduct points for faulty deportment. Steadiness in a fish, therefore, is a great asset. 'The steadiness of fishes', Derham writes, 'can be controlled almost to the same extent as can that of birds, and really matters. . . . The method employed with birds, with but little variation, can be used with fishes. About a fortnight before the show, the fish that one intends to exhibit should be put into a small tank, aerated of course, and placed where one is constantly passing, so that he comes to ignore the continual presence and passing of humans.' The aquarium should be screened from other aquaria, so that the fish will become accustomed to being alone. Feeding should be confined to live foods, and earthworms should be the staple diet. As we have seen in Chapter VI, there is no better food than earthworms for getting goldfish into good condition. Plenty of nourishing food is essential, but regular feeding hours should be discontinued. Instead, to quote Derham, 'the habit should be acquired of frequently dropping into the tank a tiny portion of food. If this is done, the fish will practically always be on the *qui vive*, fins erect, and full of life, and showing his paces to the best advantage.' In fine, the fish will be kept on the alert, and an alert fish, thoroughly at home in its surroundings and indifferent to crowds (it is surprising how many people attend fish-shows and peer into the aquaria) will count for much with the judges. The aquarium should be devoid of stones, or any object against which the fish might damage itself; a scale knocked off, or a split fin, is quite enough to prevent a fish from winning a prize. It is inadvisable to feed a fish for at least two hours before taking it to the show; it travels best on an empty stomach.

At many shows the aquaria are lit by electricity, and sometimes they are artificially aerated. It follows, therefore, that if a fish is not accustomed to electric light and artificial aeration, part of the preparation of the fish must be to accustom it to the new conditions. To prove the wisdom of this it is only necessary to remove a fish from a pond, and place it in an aquarium that is lit by electric light and artificially aerated: observe how the fish will mope among the aquatic plants until such time as it becomes accustomed to its new surroundings.

It amounts to this: the preparation of a goldfish for show follows much the same lines as preparing any other animal for show, since it is largely a matter of educating the fish to behave normally under abnormal conditions. We do not say that the careful preparation of a fish for show is a guarantee that it will win a prize, any more than the careful grooming of a glamour-girl will make her an actress, but we do say that it helps.

Goldfish are shown in bare aquaria of the uniform size of 24 in. × 12 in. × 12 in. or less, according to the size of the fish. At some shows the aquaria are set on the bench and filled with water in advance by the stewards, so that all the aquarist has to do is to transfer the fish from the travelling-can to the ready-filled aquarium. At other shows the aquarist has to bring his own aquarium and water with him. This, of course, is the better method, since the fish remains in the water to which it is accustomed, and there is no risk of the fish suffering from a sudden change in the temperature as pH value of the water. If the show is a large one, sometimes there is a special class for the best aquarium-grown plants, or the best aquarium set-up and stocked by the exhibitor himself (furnished aquarium). In this event special care must be taken to filter the water and to stock the aquarium with healthy plants that are artistically arranged; for, of course, the judges will deduct points for dirty water, for incorrect planting (such as burying the crowns of *Vallisneria* and similar plants), for an inartistic arrangement of the plants and rockwork, for introducing jagged rocks that might injure a fish, for an unsuitable planting medium, and the like. Originality should be aimed at. Reproducing a natural stretch of water may be good for ordinary purposes, but to win a prize something more striking is needed. Novel effects can be obtained with different graded planting mediums, and rockwork, and by the use of plants that contrast in foliage. But artificiality is frowned on by most judges, and they look first for an original idea and a feeling for design, form and colour. There must be a convincing geological relationship between the planting medium and the rockwork. The plants must be in character and focus the eye on a centre of interest. Preferably the fish should be all of the same breed, and since the aquarium generally used for this class is 24 in. × 12 in. × 12 in., not more than three 3-in. fish should be introduced. In fine, the aquarium must be planned. Rocks and stones scattered over sand, plants stuck here and there, and two or three fish of doubtful quality, do not make what the Americans have named an aquascape—a barbarism offensive to the ear.[1] We prefer aquascene. Attention to detail is all important. As a general rule there is little to choose between two aquaria set-up and stocked by two experienced aquarists. It follows, therefore, that when it comes to a decision between two aquaria of equal merit the decision may go against the exhibitor whose cover glass is not quite level, or who has perhaps overlooked a few drops of water on the outside of the aquarium.

In America, where they pay much more attention to the decorative aquarium than in England (experts in aquarium management visit houses and aquascene aquaria for a fee), the judges go from house to house and assess aquaria and ponds in their natural surroundings so to speak. But in England this method of judging is rare, and something of a novelty.

A word must now be said on behalf of the judges. Without doubt they are impartial, conscientious, and do their best to make the awards fairly. None the less, when competition is keen and the standard of excellence high, in a world in which the voice of faction echoes more loudly than it should, it is very easy for even the most experienced of judges to overlook the merits of a particular fish. We would not presume to remind our readers that the decision of the judges should be accepted without question, but we would remind them that it is impossible to please everyone.

Many aquarists disapprove of showing. They are, we may say, in good company. We know at least one famous aquarist who strongly disapproves of showing and resolutely refuses to act as a judge. Although he does not say why, and may have good reasons, those who disapprove of showing usually argue that the aquarist with the longest purse must carry off the prizes, and that

[1] The combination of Latin (*aqua*) and Dutch (*schap*) outrages the laws of philology, and the sooner aquascape goes the better.

some cruelty to the fish is involved. Neither argument will bear much weight. No doubt a rich man could carry off the prizes by paying a breeder a very high price for a fish, but no man in his right senses, however rich he may be, is likely to go out of his way to pay an inflated price for a fish in order to win a comparatively small prize. Prizes are usually very small, being governed mainly by entry fees (never very large) and the extent of the show; and though the funds of the organization and the generosity of donors sometimes permits the value of the prizes to be augmented, at the best of times they are never very large. In any event, many an aquarist of moderate means has bred a fish that will carry all before it.

As to the accusation that showing involves some cruelty. The argument is advanced that the fish on show suffer from lack of oxygen, hunger, and the strain of being subjected to a bright light. There is nothing to support this argument: indeed, it is contrary to the known facts. Everything is done at shows to ensure the comfort of the fish. Stewards aerate the water and feed the fish, when necessary, and shade the aquarium of a fish that is suffering from the effects of too strong a light. Moreover, if the show is held in cold weather, some method of heating the water is always provided. Fish on show are very carefully tended during the period that they are on the bench. They are certainly better looked after than those offered for sale in many pet-shops, and those condemned to a life of torture in a small glass bowl on a window-sill in the full glare of the midday sun.

Fish being taken to a show sometimes suffer from the shaking that is sustained during transit. But even here, no cruelty need be involved; nor is it if a proper travelling-container is used, if it is not jolted unnecessarily, and if the water is artificially aerated when the journey is a long one. It has, in fact, been proved, at all events so far as the hardier breeds of goldfish are concerned, that a fish which has become accustomed to being moved rarely suffers any ill effects from the journey, provided reasonable precautions are taken to ensure its comfort.

The advantages of showing are many. It enables experienced breeders to find a market for pedigree fish; it enables novice-breeders to meet experienced breeders, and those with specialized knowledge, and from them to learn much about the art of breeding, and feeding and raising fry to maturity; it brings together aquarists from all parts of the country, and so permits an exchange of ideas at the same time as it creates new friendships; it fosters interest in the hobby and teaches the novice-aquarist to distinguish between a good fish and an inferior one, because, though perfect fish are very rare, even at shows, any fish that wins a prize must, of necessity, be something above the ordinary.

Such, then, are the disadvantages and the advantages of showing, and even if the fish suffered some small temporary discomfort (and we deny that they do) the advantages so much outweigh the disadvantages, that we do not hesitate to give it as our opinion that shows are to be encouraged rather than deplored. We strongly recommend them to novices, if only because they are an admirable way of gaining experience in the handling of fish. We have little patience with the aquarist who tells us that he has at home a more personable fish than any fish in the show; for one thing, we do not believe him. But we have much sympathy with the aquarist who never shows because it is too much trouble to do so; it is the one reason why we ourselves never show a fish.

> 'No, sir, I do not bite my thumb at you, sir;
> but I bite my thumb, sir.'
>
> *Romeo and Juliet*, I, i.

Chapter X

THE GOLDFISH AND ALL THE ARTS

The wise take all knowledge as their province, but
concentrate on what is most important.
The Book of Mencius, vii. 118
Trans. LIONEL GILES

Of all fishes the goldfish is the most ubiquitous. Models of
trout and salmon are often to be seen on ashtrays, inkstands
and paper weights, but these are seasonal gifts designed for the
angler. Not so the goldfish. Like the top model girls in the glossier
weeklies, you see it everywhere: enamelled on cigarette cases and
powder compacts, hand painted on cocktail glasses and lamp-
shades, embroidered on cushions and shawls. You see it in every
likely and unlikely place: indeed, the informative 'Ripley' records
that daring Parisiennes during the reign of Napoleon III wore ear-
rings consisting of small glass globes in which tiny goldfish swam
(*Sunday Express*, 15th September 1944). You see it worked into
the designs of jewellery, rugs, wall-paper, and the backs of play-
ing-cards; sometimes hardly recognizable, but still, the goldfish.

Its very ubiquity presents us with a problem, or rather two
problems. Of necessity we have a bias towards instruction, yet we
remain conscious of a need to please. The combination of originality and quotation is not a happy one, and a descent to a mere
catalogue of facts, some trivial, some not, smells of the lamp and
is even worse. We are in doubt where to begin. We have confidence that the first problem will resolve itself by self-discipline
and pruning, though some quotation cannot be avoided. The
second problem is more easily solved. We remember the admirable advice that the King gave to the White Rabbit in *Alice's
Adventures in Wonderland*: 'Begin at the beginning, and go on till
you come to the end; then stop.'

We must begin just over 900 years ago, in the eleventh century.
The earliest reference to the goldfish in the literature of the world

dates from about the year 1030, when Su Tzŭ-mei (1008–1048) composed his *Poem on the Pagoda of the Six Harmonies*.[1]

> *At the Pine Bridge I waited for the Golden* Chi [Goldfish]
> *All day I lingered late, alone.*

The contemporary poet, Su Tung-p'o (1036–1101), read the verse but could not understand it. 'At first I did not understand these words', he writes, 'until I became Deputy of Ch'ien-t'ang, and then I knew that there were these fish coloured like gold in the pool at the back of the monastery. Yesterday I strolled again above the pool, and threw in cakes and dumplings for a long time. They came out indeed a little, but did not eat, and went in again so that I could not see them again.' It was then that Su Tung-p'o first understood the meaning of 'all day I lingered late, alone', so he said: 'The present time is separated from Su-Tzŭ-mei by forty years, but they are swimming about as of old. This may be called long life indeed.' Some years later Su Tung-p'o returned to see the goldfish, and in *The West Lake Re-visited*, composed either in the year 1089 or 1090, he writes:

> *I love the Golden* Chi *fish of Nan-p'ing,*
> *Coming again I lean on the rail,*
> *And throw them the crumbs of my frugal feast.*

Before the close of the eleventh century, goldfish are mentioned many times in the literature of China. Wên T'ung (1019–1079) mentions goldfish, or Golden *Chi*, in a *Poem*; and Su Tzu-mei, in *Lines in Reply to Tzŭ-lü*, expresses his admiration for the gold-fish in words that have found a place in the *P'ei Wên Yün Fu* (*Dictionary of Quotations*).

> *The Silver* Chi *at dawn is the beauty of fishes.*

The early years of the thirteenth century saw Po Yü-ch'an compliment a painter of fishes in a charming and all too short verse:

> *Over your paper a stream of water flows full;*
> *With two or three fishes set free in it.*
> *Gold scales, embroidered gills, red and white fins;*
> *Restlessly hither and thither they play in the waves.*

[1] The Six Harmonies Pagoda (Liu Ho T'a) near Zakow, outside Hangchow, was built by the local ruler in 971 to propitiate the tide which was very destructive. The woodwork was restored in 1165 and again about 1900, but the very massive brick-work is the same that the eleventh-century poets saw. It is about 170 ft. high,

There follows a number of poems, of which we know nothing except their titles and authors, leading to Hsü Tse-mo, one of China's greatest modern poets, who writes of the last day in the Imperial Palace, and in a pathetic passage describes an unattended collection of goldfish.[1]

The Chinese, and also the Japanese, are very responsive to the delicate phenomena of nature. It is inborn in the oriental character and touches poet and peasant alike. A humble Chinese craftsman will spend a lifetime perfecting his work. A Japanese gardener will spend years looking for a stone of exactly the right size and shape to complete his scheme. But, of course, this responsiveness to natural phenomena has reached a higher development among the poets and painters with their greater understanding and appreciation of form and colour. This expression of the Chinese character reaches almost to perfection in what the author of the *Hsien Shun Lin An Chih* (*circa* 1274) writes of the Ch'ien-ch'ing Hill, with its reed-surrounded Dragon Pool, the home of the multi-coloured goldfish.

'Tsên-liao-tzŭ has the phrase: "This hill with its irregular lofty peaks crowns half the sky." The top has an expanse of a thousand *ch'ing*. It has the Dragon Pool, surrounded with dense beds of reeds and rushes. In the Pool the fish are gold and silver in colour. If one prays for rain there is an immediate response. To the west is the So-lo Cliff, where one tree of the *so-lo* flower [? *Shorea*] grows luxuriantly. The flowers open in early summer, and the scent can be smelt for several *li*. Pyrus, daphne, and *huang-ch'ing*, grow all over the slopes of the hill.

'The poet Hu ... [the name is illegible in the text] of Hsin-an, on being ordered by the Tê-shou-kung to catch gold and silver fish says:

> *The Ch'ien-ch'ing Hill is sixty* li[2] *high;*
> *On it is a cold pool clear and fresh.*
> *Long ago a divine dragon came hither to coil itself within.*
> *Having made the sweet rain to appear;*
> *And all the fish follow it as it sometimes floats,*
> *And sometimes sinks;*

[1] We have, unfortunately, been unable to trace this poem. All our Chinese friends recollect it, but cannot remember when they have seen it. No one ever does.

[2] The *Concise Oxford Dictionary* gives the Chinese *li* as about 633 yards. This makes the hill nearly three times the height of Mt. Everest. But the Chinese, very wisely, measure a hill along the road, and not perpendicularly.

The Goldfish

Gasping, shining brilliantly,
Like suns or moons in the deep;
Shapes and bodies naturally different, all finny;
Either like beautiful jade, or like gold,
Or black, or red, or mottled;
Such as drive the painter to despair.
For how many years they lay hid, and few men knew;
One morning their fame stirred the whole capital.'

We begin to understand better what Winifred Galbraith means when she writes: 'Nature . . . was a passion with these men. The life that ran through rocks and hills and trees ran through men too' (*The Chinese*).

It is all very romantic. But then the goldfish, if not romantic in itself, has a romantic setting. Take only the names that the Chinese have given to the many colour variations that they bred. Some, we know, were chosen with a fine regard for allusion; the Seven Stars is a reference to the constellation known as *Ursa Major*, and the Eight diagrams to an ancient means of divination by the arrangement of lines, whole or bisected. But far more names were chosen as T'u Lung records, according to man's fancy. And what a fancy; what a delightful picture is conjured up when we read of fish that were given such names as Lotus Terrace, Embroidered Coverlet, Eight Melon Seeds, Crane Pearl, Silver Saddle, Red Dust, to mention only a few. Many of these fish were bred in the Goldfish Pool (originally known as the Fish-weed Pool) south-east of the Chêng-yang Gate at Peking. Liu T'ung and Yü I-chêng, the authors of the *Ti Ching Ching Wu Lüeh* (1635), tell us something about this pool. 'Above the Pool was a hall, with a jasper pool at the side. The foundations of the hall cannot now be traced. . . . Every year at the height of summer visitors bring wine-jars and drink here, and toss in cakes and dumplings which the fish gobble up noisely. When the large ones have devoured the dumplings at last they go. . . . All along the north side of the Pool there are more gardens and pavilions than dwelling houses, and to the south it faces the Altar of Heaven;[1] a wide open view all round.' Once horse races were held here every June, if they no longer are.

[1] The Altar of Heaven, open to the sky, on the summit of three terraces all paved with white marble laid in concentric circles. The Emperor repaired here once a year, in winter, to adore with solemn ritual 'The Azure Heaven'. The Emperor claimed to represent man—with Heaven and Earth—in the Divine Trinity.

The Goldfish and all the Arts

The Goldfish Pond is only one of the many thousands of ponds that are to be seen in the far east. Water is a *sine qua non* in every oriental landscape garden, park and temple ground, no matter how small it may be; and feeding the goldfish in the ponds is as much a custom among the Chinese and Japanese as feeding the ducks on the Serpentine, the sparrows in the Luxembourg Gardens, and the pigeons outside the Basilica of Saint Mark, is a custom among Londoners, Parisians, and Venetians. Peter Fleming tells us that he took away at least one memory of Peking which will always give him pleasure. 'It is a picture of one of the many courtyards in the beautiful house in which I was staying. I used to have breakfast there. The boy would bring coffee and scrambled eggs and the local paper and go away. While I ate and read an old, brown, wrinkled man would come shuffling down a narrow flagged path between the shrubs to the pool in the centre of the courtyard. Very meticulously, muttering to himself, he would feed ants' eggs to the frilled elaborate goldfish in the pool. His face was terribly serious' (*One's Company*). The scene is typical of the East, where the goldfish has been the pet of the Orient for centuries. Nowhere in the world is it so important as in China and Japan. No house is complete without a goldfish; sometimes in muddy pond, sometimes in carved ivory and gilded aquarium. The goldfish stall is a notable feature of every large market-place in China and Japan, and just as an English country squire will weigh the merits of one cocker spaniel against another, so a Chinaman will peer into a gigantic bowl of goldfish, and, to quote Sir Osbert Sitwell, 'tally with true virtuosity one golden fin, one sable veil, one protuberant and goggling eye against another' (*Come With Me*). In Japan it is much the same. 'Interest in goldfish', Hugh Smith writes, 'is manifested by all ages and in every class of society, from the humblest peasant to the highest court official. The small boy on a holiday will be made supremely happy by the purchase of a goldfish costing half a cent, while a wealthy connoisseur may give one hundred and fifty dollars for a single pair of fish of select breed.'

The esteem in which the goldfish is held in the far east is charmingly illustrated by Austin Strong. He relates that when he was a small boy living in Honolulu he overheard 'Japanese attachés, dressed like dark butterflies in their national costume . . . telling about the beautiful double-tailed goldfish that the Emperor of

The Goldfish

Japan had just sent to King Kalakaua, and how they had emptied them officially that morning in the lily-pond of the royal Kapiolani Park. They told my mother that they were very rare and belonged to the Royal Family of Japan.' Because the neighbouring children twitted him that his parents were too poor to have goldfish, one day he tip-toed through the gates leading into Kapiolani Park. There, in a beautiful Chinese garden, he came to a lily-pond. 'A moon-bridge arched over the still water', Strong continues, 'and I climbed the incline; on top I lay on my stomach, quaking. . . . I peered down into the pool below, and there I saw them—the noble goldfish of the Emperor of Japan! They were prodigious fellows, wearing feathery fins and tails like court trains, trailing clouds of glory. Quickly I bent a pin, and fastening it to the end of my string, I lowered it into the liquid crystal below. . . . A large, dignified grand duke of a goldfish, attracted by the brightness of the pin, made the stupid mistake of thinking that it was something good to eat and swallowed it. I hauled him up. Hastily I stuffed the fish into the crown of my hat, and jamming it on my head I flew in terror out into the open road.' Then he goes on to tell how his only thought was to keep the fish alive until he reached home. An irrigation ditch ran along one side of the road, so every few moments the fish was given a dip in the ditch, to enable it to survive the journey. 'Suddenly I was in the midst of warning shouts, stamping horses, jingling harness, military commands— a carriage had nearly run over me. An officer leapt from his saddle and stood before me. I was led to a shining victoria. . . .' Inside the victoria sat the king himself. There was no alternative except to confess to the crime. At the sight of the monster goldfish, the king ordered the cavalcade to drive to the nearest horse-trough. A native was sent running for a calabash, and eventually young Strong reached home, sleepy, but still possessed of the stolen goldfish, so 'restoring face to my parents and raising their social standing in the eye of my enemies'. A few hours later he received a large gilt-bordered envelope on which was stamped the crown of Hawaii. Inside was a Royal Grant giving him permission to fish in the Kapiolani Park for the rest of his life. King Kalakaua had signed it (*The Atlantic Monthly*, May 1944).

But we must go back 300 years, to the middle of the seventeenth century, that is, to find what, we believe, is the first mention of goldfish in European literature. Martin Martini (1614–

1661) who was stationed at Hangchow from 1646 to 1650, mentions 'the little gilded fish . . . which the Chinese have for this reason named *Chin-yü*, because the skin glitters, being somehow interwoven with threads of gold—the whole back sprinkled as it were with gold dust. . . . They are a strange sight. The Chinese make much of them . . .' (*Description Géographique de l'Empire de la Chine*). Before the end of the century (1696) we find Louis Le Comte describing goldfish with some detail and not a few inaccuracies. He writes: 'They are commonly of a finger's length, and of a proportionate thickness; the male is of a most delicate red. . . . The female is white. . . . Those who would breed them, ought to have great care; for they are extraordinary tender and sensible of the least injuries of the air. They [the Chinese] put them into great basins, such as are found in gardens, very deep and large. . . .' (*Nouveaux Mémoires* . . .). Almost simultaneously Engelbert Kämpfer, in his *History of Japan* writes: 'The goldfish is a small fish, seldom exceeding a finger in length, red, with a beautiful shining yellow or gold-coloured tail, which in the young ones is rather black. . . . Another kind hath a silver-coloured tail.'

The mid-eighteenth century (1735) saw the publication of Du Halde's *Description . . . de la Chine*. Du Halde touches on goldfish but we need not quote him. His book is a compilation that, at all events in the matter of goldfish, clearly owes much to Martini and Le Comte, though many of the latter's inaccuracies are commendably absent. Soon after the publication of Du Halde's *Description . . . de la Chine*, the first mention of goldfish by an English writer of standing appeared; it was in 1742 that Thomas Gray wrote his *Ode on the Death of a Favourite Cat: Drowned in a Tub of Goldfishes*.[1] The poem, perhaps, is not to be compared with the immortal *Elegy*—nothing can compare with that—but it has given us one memorable and oft-quoted line—though its Grayian origin is rarely recognized—'A fav'rite has no friend'. A few years later we find Horace Walpole mentioning goldfish ten times in his *Letters* between July 1746 and July 1783. His pond ('Po-yang') at Strawberry Hill, was famous for its goldfish. 'They breed with me excessively and are grown to the size of small perch,' he writes to George Montagu on 6th June 1752; and a year later (16th August 1753) he tells Montagu: 'You may get your pond ready as soon as

---

[1] The cat which has earned this unfortunate immortality was Horace Walpole's 'Selima'.

you please, the goldfish swarm. Mr. Bentley carried a dozen to town t'other day in a decanter.'

The story could be continued almost indefinitely; for today we find the goldfish serving as an inspiration to poets and authors the world over. Robert Lynd has given us a charming word-picture of the goldfish. 'Here you have all foreign travel before you in a bottle. Here is a piece of the same world that is inhabited by tropical butterflies and humming birds. There is nothing that can diminish the spell of its strangeness. Never can it seem less than a beautiful alien' (*The Goldfish*). And that great humanitarian, John Galsworthy, reminds us of man's inhumanity when:

> *He bends on Heaven every wish,*
> *Believes the tale of Kingdom Come,*
> *And prisons up the golden fish*
> *In bowl no bigger than a drum. (Pitiful).*

But for what is without doubt the finest full-length poem on goldfish in the English language, and probably in any language, we must turn to Harold Monro's *Goldfish*. We quote the first verse:

> *They are the angels of that watery world.*
> *All innocent, they no more than aspire*
> *To move themselves about on golden fins*
> *Or they can fill their paradise with fire*
> *By darting suddenly from end to end.*

Finally (for we must not permit enthusiasm for quotation to run away with us), the poetic imagery that the goldfish inspires is well expressed by Maurice Baring in *Translations: Ancient and Modern*.

'Fish, fish, fish, fish, fish, little gold fish, who will buy?

' "Who will buy?" cries the old man in the market-place, as he walks up and down between the bookstalls, and the booths where children buy tops and sugar plums.

' "Who will buy?"

'No-one will buy, no-one will buy the little gold fish; for men do not recognize the gifts of Heaven, the magical gifts, when they meet them.'

Of the goldfish in literature little more remains to be said. Few contemporary writers have eulogized the goldfish, and most have relied upon it only to provide them with allusion and simile, or as a peg on which to hang a smart epigram. Some of it, we fear, is neither very appropriate nor very original. In 1939, Ann Stair wrote *The Goldfish*, a novel about a rich woman who visits Soviet Russia. ' "In England, you see," the Russian Olga says, "people live like goldfish swimming round and round in a little bowl; here they have to swim endlessly in a rough sea." . . . But Elise was fingering a ring. *A goldfish in a little bowl*, was that really what she had been all these years? . . .'

We must not omit P. G. Wodehouse's: '. . . how curious it is that goldfish should have acquired a taste for ants's eggs, seeing that in their natural, wild state they could scarcely have moved in the same social sphere, so to speak, as ants.' (*Money in the Bank*); for here, as always with this humorist, there is much truth, and much to make us think, behind the inimitable and inevitable flippancy. Nor must we forget H. H. Munro's ('Saki'). 'I might have been a goldfish in a glass bowl for all the privacy I got.' (*Reginald*), if only because it has passed into legend.[1] But though it deserved congratulations for a week, it has hardly deserved its immortality. And to Sir Osbert Sitwell our applause is due for describing aged clergymen delivering lantern-slide lectures to schoolboys: '. . . another would have no roof to his mouth, while again another would, from time to time, lose his voice altogether and mouth at the assembled school after the manner of a rebellious goldfish' (*Penny Foolish*). It is altogether delightful. Standing in striking contrast is 'Guillaume Apollinaire's' (Wilhelm Kustrowicki): 'Your tongue, that goldfish in the bowl of your voice.' It is remarkable for the imagery it evokes. Let us leave it at that; for few, we think, would subscribe to all the superlatives that Paul Eluard accords it in *This Quarter* (September, 1932).

In the sister art of music the goldfish has inspired a number of leading modern composers. We do not suggest that Saint Saëns had goldfish in mind when he composed *Aquarium*; but there need be no doubt that an aquarium stocked with aquatic plants and several breeds of fancy goldfish inspired Billy Mayerl to compose *Aquarium Suite* for piano and orchestra; the four movements are entitled *Willow Moss*, *Moorish Idol*, *Fantail* and *Whirligig*. To the French composer, Claude Debussy, whose creative genius was so

[1] The epigram, 'As much privacy as a goldfish', has been ascribed to several writers, but Munro appears to have first claim. *Reginald* was published in 1904.

suited to reflecting the moods and mysteries and beauties of nature, we owe a great debt for revealing to us the essential grace and charm of the goldfish, as expressed in his charming piano composition entitled *Poissons d'Or*, from *Images*. All his life Debussy had a love for Japanese works of art, and Leon Vallas records that *Poissons d'Or* was inspired by the contemplation of a piece of lacquer that Debussy owned (*Claude Debussy: His Life and Works*). In lighter vein mention must be made of Sidney Jones's song, *The Amorous Goldfish*, from *The Geisha*. Seventy years ago, when it was composed, it created a sensation. It was whistled by every errand-boy, ground out on every barrel-organ, and sung (with stagey gestures) at every musical evening. It was one of the songs that made him, yet, and despite the revival of *The Geisha* as recently as 1931, who today can remember Harry Greenbank's famous opening lines:

> *A goldfish swam in a big glass bowl,*
> *As dear little goldfish do.*

In the art of the dance, mention must be made of Louis Min-kous's three-act *Ballet fantastique*, *Le Poisson Doré*, composed in 1860; and Mikail Mordkin's ballet *The Goldfish*, produced in America in 1939, with music by Cherepnin (1913) arranged by Fuerst, inspired by a poem of Pushkin. The poem tells of a poor fisherman who catches a goldfish. The fish begs to be spared and in return promises to fulfil every wish. The fish keeps its promise until the greedy wife of the fisherman—not content with being a great lady with great riches—asks to be made queen of the water, with the fish her most obedient servant fulfilling her slightest whim. This was going too far. . . .

> *No response gave the fish to the fisher;*
> *With her tail she but splashed the water,*
> .   .   .   .
> *The old man waited long for an answer*
> *But in vain.*

(Trans. BORIS BRASOL)

When we turn to the graphic arts, one fact stands out above all others: the artists of China and Japan have always made a speciality of painting fishes. For fishes, partly from the multitude of their spawn, and partly because the Chinese words for 'fish' and 'abundance' have the same sound, have by a widespread symbolism become an emblem of fecundity, and in Chinese art paired fishes are an emblem of conjugal felicity. But contrary to what might be expected, the goldfish is not nearly so frequently depicted as the carp. Indeed, the fish on the Chinese stamps of 1897 and 1898 turns out on close inspection to be a carp, and not a goldfish as no less than three writers have claimed. There is, in fact, good reason why the carp takes precedence. In Chinese art the goldfish has no special significance, but the carp from a very early date has been surrounded with legend and symbolism. Originally Chinese, legend and symbolism have been appropriated by the Japanese. There are, therefore, many good reasons why oriental artists should introduce into their pictures fish in general and carp in particular, with the double purpose of pleasing their patrons and the sentiments of the public.

There exists a large number of pictures of goldfish by oriental artists, but the advice that the King gave to the White Rabbit, though it remains good, is of no great help to us; we do not know where the beginning is. We have good reason to believe that the earliest printed picture of goldfish dates from 1607 and is to be found as an illustration in the *San Ts'ai T'u Hui*, but, of course, there are much earlier likenesses of goldfish on paintings and ceramics. Indeed, Nobuharu, of the Ashikaga Period (1335–1573) excelled in painting fish among aquatic plants. In the British Museum there is a very fine painting, by an unknown Chinese artist, of a *Lady and Children Playing with Goldfish*. It is painted in the style of Su Han-ch'ên the Southern Sung artist who began as a court painter a few years before 1127, but is in itself not earlier than Ming (1368–1644) or more probably eighteenth-century. And among the Japanese woodcuts, there is a print by the famous Utamaro (1754–1806) representing a *Child Upsetting a Goldfish out of a Bowl*. Among modern Chinese artists, mention may be made of Jen Po-nien, of the late-Ch'ing (Manchu) Dynasty (1644–1912) who often painted goldfish; of Chi Pai-shih, the Pekinese artist, who was considered to be one of the finest painters of small nature including goldfish; and of Hsieh Kung-ch'an, whose very delicate study of *Telescope Goldfish* was used by Chiang Yee to illustrate an article in *The Studio* under date of April 1937. Finally, the Japanese water-colourist, K. Ito, is well known for his studies of fancy goldfish, two of which are reproduced (unfortunately uncoloured) in Hugh Smith's *Japanese Goldfish*. Many more might be mentioned, but it is not our intention to compile a catalogue.

In the lesser arts of the potter, the carver, the bronze-worker, the tapestry-worker, and the like, oriental artists have used goldfish as decorative motifs from a fairly early date, though they are more frequently found on the porcelain of the Ch'ing Dynasty.

Except for dead fish in still life studies, the academic artists of the west, rarely, if ever, make fish the subject of a painting. Even the once popular bowl of goldfish is rarely seen in pictures (even in the background) painted by western artists. We may except only a few, notably the much-maligned Henri Matisse, who has painted four goldfish in a bowl under the title of *Poissons Rouges* (now in the Museum of Modern Western Art, in Moscow), and who has introduced a bowl of goldfish into several of his paintings and at least one of his etchings.

Whatever may be lacking in the academic artists of the west, it is more than made up for by the work of commercial artists, who, as we have seen, make full use of the decorative goldfish as part of their designs. It is a good sign for those who are interested in the culture of goldfish. It marks the steadily increasing interest on the part of the public in aquarium-keeping. Whatever may be said against commercial interests, at least they are good barometers of public demand.

In the mechanical art of photography there are many outstanding names, and in the closely allied art of the cinema, special mention must be made of Walt Disney, who introduced a coquettish Fancy Goldfish ('Cleo') into his version of *Pinocchio*, and Rudolf Ising the creator of *The Little Goldfish*, an amusing technicolor cartoon produced by Metro-Goldwyn-Mayer.

Interior decorators have for long made use of aquaria of goldfish as part of the decorative schemes of rooms. At one time much of it was unimaginative; but today some of the more progressive interior decorators are obtaining striking and original effects by matching the fish and aquaria to the furnishing of the room. For a room furnished in oriental style, the frame of the aquarium is lacquered in black and scarlet, picked out in gold, stood on an oriental lacquered table, and stocked with veil-tail Moors. For the ultra-modern room, the aquarium is chromium-plated, stood on a chromium-plated stand, and stocked with Comets. For the dining-room, an aquarium of goldfish, instead of a bowl of flowers, is by no means unusual, and, indeed was fashionable among society hostesses in the mid-1930's. It was unfortunate that unmannerly guests used these aquaria for extinguishing their cigarettes, so that numberless goldfish died untimely deaths. But for novelty in dining-room decoration we must look to a rich Indian merchant with whom we dined years ago (1922) at his house in Karachi. An aquarium of fancy goldfish stood on legs; the cutlery, glass-ware and napery were laid on top of the thick plate-glass cover, and we ate our meal with the fish swimming about under our plate so to speak. For the bathroom, tiles with fancy goldfish in natural colours are available, and more expensively, the fish may be painted direct on steam-proof surfaced walls. For sheer originality of goldfish in the bathroom, however, commend us to a certain lady of fashion who out-poppæas Poppæa and her daily bath of she-asses' milk,[1] by taking a cold bath every morning with her pet Fantails swimming about in it. It stands in striking contrast to Francesca Nortynege, a reformer of Dieze, who died in 1902 and left her fortune to her niece with the proviso that, for the sake of decency, she kept her goldfish always clothed in tights.

In jest and anecdote—these too are arts—the goldfish has always been a favourite subject. Indeed, jokes about goldfish are legion. They range from the inevitable story that the Aberdonian has fish soup for supper every time that his wife changes the water in the goldfish bowl, to the unprintable. The present soaring cost of living (thinly disguised as 'inflationary tendency') has given rise to the story that a well-known business man keeps a goldfish in a bowl on his desk to console him: 'It is', he explains, 'the only thing in the office that opens its mouth without asking for money.' Indeed, every topical event finds the humorist ready with an apt remark or sketch, in which the goldfish in the inevitable bowl appears.

Of anecdotes, as distinct from jokes, about goldfish there are many. The owner of every pet-shop and the attendants at every public aquarium have a fund of good stories to tell. For the ignor-ance of most people on the care and management of goldfish has not yet stopped them from airing it. But perhaps we would be advised not to say too much; for if we have now progressed into

[1] Poppaea Sabina the second wife of the Emperor Nero. The story that she bathed daily in milk supplied by 500 she-asses is to be found in the elder Pliny's *Natural History*.

that stage when we know little and know that we know nothing, we too reached it only by first passing through that stage when we knew little and thought that we knew all. Not, we think, that we were ever quite so bad as the malapropist who wrote to the editor of a magazine to ask, among other things, if two pike 10 in. long would be 'alrite in a communist tank with Shoe Bun Kins'.

In the art of gastronomy, the goldfish has played an important part; for, contrary to popular belief, the goldfish is edible. Oriental cooks know many ways of preparing them for the table, and in China and Japan, goldfish, carp, and allied species, are considered great delicacies, and have been for centuries. As long ago as the Han Dynasty (206 B.C.–A.D. 220) the poet Sin Yen-nien tells us that to impress the young and pretty wife of an innkeeper . . .

> *The very gallant officer, the dashing Fung Tze-tu,*
> *He called for wine in tasselled jug, and carp on golden plate.*
>
> (Trans. CHARLES BUDD)

For a description of a meal of goldfish in the far east at the present time we must look to William Plomer. 'After our having walked three *ri*,[1] a brace of tiny goldfish and a doll's salad of moss are the mainstay of supper, together with berries, bits of fern, odds and ends out of the forest, all under-propped with rice and washed down with tea. Why worry? It is a pity that goldfish, when cooked, turn black with surprise' (*Paper Houses*).

Francis Buckland, who ate and enjoyed most things in his time, though earwigs defeated him—they were so horribly bitter—pronounced goldfish as 'tasting like carp, and I cannot say very good eating.'[2] Job Baster, however, thinks differently. He writes: 'Together with some of my friends, I have eaten a few of the larger of these little fish cooked. We have tasted them with various dressings, but they had the best flavour when they had that sauce poured on them which we are accustomed to call egg savoury, and they were much better than carp. Their flesh, when cooked, is not as firm as that of perch, but otherwise it is as light, soft, and tender as the flesh of any other freshwater fish. . . . Fried they were sweeter and more delicate than perch.' The natural food of the Cyprinids gives them a muddy flavour, but this may be removed by keeping the fish alive in running water—or in clean water

---

[1] According to the *Little Oxford Dictionary* the Japanese *ri* is 2.44 miles.
[2] Francis Buckland, op. cit., p. 163.

occasionally changed—for two or three days; by soaking the dead and cleaned fish in a strong salt solution for some hours; or by cooking the fish in vinegar.

A dish of live goldfish is not the sort of thing to please one who is a gourmet by conviction or natural inclination. Yet shortly before the Second World War a number of America's self-styled bright young things attracted undesirable attention to themselves by swallowing small goldfish alive. This disgusting (to us) practice lacked even the merit of being original. Walter Lannoy Brind informs us that: 'a vaudeville clown whom I saw at the old Royal Aquarium in London, fished goldfish out of a globe with his fingers, held them up by their heads, and while their tails wriggled munched them up alive—and then spat out their scales.'[1]

Finally, in the medical art, Li Shih-chên, in the *Pên Ts'ao Kang Mu* (*circa* 1590), offers a cooked goldfish as a cure for chronic dysentery. He writes: 'To check and confine the force of the disease when [the patient] is dying take one Gold-thread *Li* fish weighing one or two catties,[2] as in ordinary cures [?]; use an onion in salt sauce and be sure to add two or three candareens[3] of pepper. When it is well cooked, place it in front of the sick man. If, when he smells it, he wishes to eat, let him eat his fill with the gravy as he pleases, and the root of the disease will then be removed. There is evidence of frequent cures. [Taken from] *I Fang Tsê Yao* by Yang Kung.' A modern medical book recommends astringents and a light diet so, when all is said, perhaps Yang Kung (whoever he may have been; he cannot be identified) may not have been so very far wrong. Certainly we prefer him to those doctors (*dit*) who not so long ago recommended a gudgeon eaten alive as a cure for consumption.

In any event, the proverb 'No-one eats goldfish' is refuted.

---

[1] See article, 'My Tropical Fishery', by W. L. Brind in *The Aquarist* (March–April 1937).

The Royal Aquarium, or Royal Aquarium and Summer and Winter Garden to give it its full name, was London's third public aquarium. It was opened in 1874 by the Duke of Edinburgh (Queen Victoria's second son) and special music was composed for the occasion. As an aquarium it was a failure almost from the start, and music-hall turns were introduced in an attempt to popularize it. Towards the end of its existence it became very notorious, and what had begun with a flourish of trumpets ended in a parade of strumpets. It was closed at the beginning of the present century. The site is now occupied by the Central Hall, Westminster.

[2] A catty is approximately 1·33 lb.

[3] A candareen is approximately 1/10th of an ounce.

Appendix

OTHER FISHES FOR AQUARIUM
AND POND

> Our plenteous streams a various race supply,
> The bright-eyed perch with fins of Tyrian dye,
> The silver eel, in shining volumes roll'd,
> The yellow carp, in scales bedropp'd with gold,
> Swift trouts, diversified with crimson stains,
> And pikes, the tyrants of the wat'ry plains.
>
> POPE, Windsor Forest

Although the goldfish in its many variations is generally accepted as the most handsome and satisfactory fish for the aquarium and garden-pond, there are many others that call for something more than a mere passing mention. This is particularly the case when it comes to stocking a pond. In the opinion of Laurence Wells, the ideal garden-pond contains bottom-feeders, such as loach and tench, to scavenge; fishes that swim in mid-water, such as goldfish and golden rudd, to form a background; surface fishes, such as dace and golden ide, to keep down insects and add animation; and, if the pond is a large one, a small shoal of minnows to furnish interest.[1]

It is very important to notice that this selection has been made with care. It is not all fishes that will live amicably together. Pike, as most people know, are voracious and must not be placed in the same pond as other species; nor would we care to guarantee even two pike being safe together, particularly if one is much larger than the other. Perch and sticklebacks are pugnacious fish and should be kept apart from other fishes. Some fishes, too, notably the bullhead or miller's thumb, cannot be kept in the normal aquarium or pond; they will not live for any length of time in water more than five or six inches deep. Finally, many fishes accus-

---

[1] A. Laurence Wells, *The Observer's Book of Freshwater Fishes of the British Isles* (London, 1941).

tomed to the very cool and highly oxygenated water of swift-flowing mountain streams will soon die if they are transferred to a home-aquarium or ornamental pond.

In the following catalogue, therefore, we mention only those that will live on amicable terms with goldfish and allied species, that will thrive in a large aquarium or garden pond, and that may be fed and cared for in the same way as we have recommended for goldfish. To some extent the catalogue is arbitrary. Many of the fishes that we mention under 'Cold-water Aquarium-fish' can be kept in a pond, and many of those that we mention under 'Pond-fish' can be kept in a large aquarium, at all events if small specimens are chosen. Our distinction is mainly one of size and suitability.

COLD-WATER AQUARIUM-FISH

Bitterling (*Rhodeus sericeus*).
Bleak (*Alburnus lucidus*).
Crucian, or German Carp (*Carassius carassius*).
    Gibel, or Prussion, Carp (var.).
Dog-fish (*Umbra krameri*).
Minnow (*Phoxinus phoxinus*).
    Minnows should be kept away from fancy goldfish with telescope eyes.
Spined Loach (*Cobitis taenia*).
Stone Loach (*Nemachilus barbatulus*).
Weather Fish or Pond Loach (*Misgurnus fossilis*).
    Loaches thrive best in shallow water, certainly not deeper than 12 in.

POND-FISH

Common Carp (*Cyprinus carpio*).
    Golden Carp or Higoi (var.).
    Kollar, or Bastard, Carp (var.).
    Leather Carp (var.).
    Mirror, or King, Carp (var.).
Common Rudd (*Scardinius erythrophthalmus*).
    Golden Rudd (var.)
Common, or Green, Tench (*Tinca tinca*).
    Golden Tench or Schlei (var.).
Dace (*Leuciscus leuciscus*).

Dace need a large pond and well oxygenated water; for their natural habitat is a rather swift-flowing stream.

Ide or Silver Orfe (*Leuciscus idus*).

Golden Ide or Golden Orfe (var.).

Ides thrive best in water round about 45° F.

Finally, there are two small species, which, though usually sold by dealers for tropical aquaria, may be introduced into an aquarium in which fancy goldfish are kept under ideal conditions: we mean an aquarium in which the temperature never falls much below 65° F. They are the Australian Rainbow Fish (*Melanotaenia nigrans*) and the Brazilian Armoured Catfish (*Corydoras paleatus*).

The above list is by no means complete, nor is it intended to be. It is, however, fairly representative of the large number of fishes that may be taken from British freshwaters or bought from dealers. For one reason or another, we have omitted a number of species that are sometimes recommended for aquaria and garden-ponds: notably the barbel, because it grows to a large size and not uncommonly seizes small fish: the gudgeon, because it does a lot of rooting, disturbs the plants, and makes the water cloudy: and the roach, because it is particularly subject to *Saprolegnia* and melanosis.

IN MANY LANGUAGES

... to see the stir
Of the Great Babel ...
COWPER, *The Task*, Book IV

We set out below, in alphabetical order, the name of the gold-fish in a number of languages. The list is not intended as an exhibition of our erudition, and we hope it will not be thought so. We believe that, under certain conditions, it will be of some practical value to the inquiring aquarist.

Our first intention was to include many more languages. Wiser counsel prevailed. If we included Afrikaans, Lithuanian, Welsh, and others that we know, we might be asked why we had not included Amharic, Lappish, Wendish, and others that we do not know. It was, therefore, a question of either including every language in the world, or only the more important ones. Since the former is impractical, if not impossible, we include only the latter. The line had to be drawn somewhere.

Arabic	Samak murjān: Laun dhahabi
Chinese	Chin-yü
Czech	Zlatá rybka
Danish	Guldfisk
Dutch	Goudvisch
French	Poisson rouge: Dorade (de la Chine)
German	Goldfisch
Greek	Chrusopsaron
Hungarian	Aranyhal
Italian	Pesce dorato
Japanese	Kingyo
Norwegian	Guldfisk
Persian	Mâhi-e-talâ-i
Polish	Zlota rybka
Portuguese	Dourada

The Goldfish

Roumanian	Pestele de aur
Russian	Zolotoi ribki
Serb-Croatian	Zlatna ribica
Spanish	Dorado
Swedish	Guldfisk
Turkish	Mercan baligi
Urdu	La machhi: Someri mase

The world over, *A thing of beauty is a joy for ever.* . . .

BIBLIOGRAPHY

Books must follow sciences, and not sciences
books.

BACON, *Proposition touching amendment of Laws*

The books, monographs and periodicals that follow is by no
means an exhaustive bibliography. Nor is it intended to be.
For the most part it represents those publications to which the
present writers are most indebted. Some of the works mentioned
are more advanced than others, some are more exhaustive than
others, and some are better than others, but it is outside our duty
to distinguish one from the other. All are worth reading and may
be recommended with confidence to those who desire to study
further the scope of the present volume.

The date of a work is the date of the edition that we have consulted. It is not necessarily the date of the first or of the most
recent edition.

The name of the publisher of a book is given only if the book
was published during the present century.

Monographs are distinguished by an asterisk.

FOR THE GENERAL READER:
Atkins, E. M.
Goldfish and Other Cold-water Fishes (Atkins, Sanderstead, 1936)
Axelrod, H. R.
Gold Fish Book (TFH Publications, New Jersey, 1954)
Bateman, Gregory C.
Freshwater Aquaria (Bazaar Exchange & Mart, London, 1937)
Berridge, W. S.
All About Fish (Harrap, London, 1933)
Betts, Leonard C.
First Steps in Pond-keeping (Marshall Press, London, 1938)
The Goldfish (Marshall Press, London, 1939)

Boulenger, E. G.
  Fishes (Chapman & Hall, London, 1931)
  Keep an Aquarium (Ward Lock, London, 1939)
  The Aquarium (Poultry World, London, 1933)
  The Aquarium Book (Duckworth, London, 1925)
Brind, Walter Lannoy
  Domesticated Fish (Brind, New York, 1913)
  The Practical Fish-Fancier (Brind, New York, 1919)
Brünner, Gerhard
  Aquarium Plants (Trans.: Gwynne Vevers) (Studio Vista, London, 1966)
Buckland, Francis
  Curiosities of Natural History (Macmillan, London, 1900)
  The Natural History of British Fishes (London, 1881)
  Ibid. Sections edited by L. R. Brightwell (Batchworth Press, London, 1948)
Chen, Shisan C.
  The Development of Goldfish, Carassius auratus, as affected by being out of water, in distilled water, and in solutions of alcohol (China Journal of Science and Arts, Shanghai, 1926)
  Variations in the External Characters of the Goldfish, Carassius auratus (Con. Bio. Lab. Sci. Soc. China, vol. 1: Nanking, 1925)
Churchill, E.
  The Learning of a Maze by Goldfish (Journal of Animal Behaviour, vol. VI, Boston, 1916)
Clegg, John
  Aquatic Insects (Marshall Press, London, 1938)
Day, Francis
  The Fishes of Great Britain and Ireland (London, 1880–4)
Derham, Arthur
  The Breeding of Fancy Goldfish (Marshall's Printing Works, Harlow, 1926)
De Wit, H. C. D.
  Aquarium Plants (Blandford Press, London, 1964)
Duijn, C. Van
  Diseases of Fishes (Water Life, London, 1956)
Edwards, George
  A Natural History of Birds (London, 1751)
  Gleanings of Natural History (London, 1760)

Bibliography

Elwin, M. G.
  First Steps in Aquarium Keeping (Marshall Press, London, 1938)
Evans, Anthony
  Goldfish (Muller, London, 1954)
  Your Book of Aquaria (Faber & Faber, London, 1959)
Fraser-Brunner, A.
  A Home Aquarium on a Small Income (Hutchinson, London, n.d.)
Furneaux, W. S.
  Life in Ponds and Streams (London, 1896)
Gosse, Philip Henry
  The Aquarium (London, 1856)
Günther, Albert C. L. G.
  An Introduction to the Study of Fishes (Edinburgh, 1880)
Hall, C. B.
  The Culture of Fish in Ponds (Min. Agric. Fish. Bull. 12, London, 1936)
Hance, Robert T.
  Heredity in Goldfish (Journal of Heredity, vol. XV, Washington, 1924)
Hems, Jack
  How to Take Care of Your Goldfish (Link House Publications, London, 1939)
Hervey, G. F.
  The Goldfish of China in the XVIII Century (China Society, Sinological Series No. 3, London, 1950)
Hervey, G. F. & Hems, Jack
  The Book of the Garden Pond (Paul, London, 1958)
Hibbert, Shirley
  The Book of the Aquarium (London, 1860)
Hodge, A. E. & Derham, Arthur
  Goldfish Culture for Amateurs (Witherby, London, 1926)
Innes, William T.
  Goldfish Varieties and Tropical Aquarium Fishes (Innes Publications, Philadelphia, 1917)
  Goldfish Varieties and Water Gardens (Innes Publications: Philadelphia, 1947)
  The Complete Aquarium Book (Blue Ribbon Books, London, 1937)

Kirby, William
  The History, Habits, and Instincts of Animals (London, 1835)
Kiskinouye, K.
  *The Goldfish and Other Ornamental Fish of Japan (Natural Science, vol. XIII, London, 1898)
Koh, Ting-pong
  *Notes on the Evolution of Goldfish (China Journal of Science and Arts, Shanghai, 1934)
Kyle, Harry M.
  The Biology of Fishes (Sidgwick & Jackson, London, 1926)
Latimer-Sayer, Derrick
  Teach Yourself Indoor Aquaria (English Universities Press, London, 1965)
Latter, Oswald H.
  Elementary Zoology (Methuen, London, 1923)
Macan, T. T. & Mortimer, C. H. & Worthington, E. B.
  The Production of Freshwater Fish for Food (Freshwater Bio. Ass. Brit. Emp. Sci. Pub. No. 6, Ambleside, 1942)
MacMahon, A. F. Magri
  Fishlore (Penguin Books, Harmondsworth, 1946)
Mannering, Rosslyn
  Fishponds and Aquaria (Cassell, London, 1935)
Matsubara, S.
  *Goldfish and Their Culture in Japan (Proc. Fourth Internat. Congress, Washington, 1908)
Maxwell, Herbert
  British Freshwater Fishes (Hutchinson, London, 1904)
Meehan, W. E.
  Fish Culture in Ponds and Other Inland Waters (Sturgis & Walter, New York, 1913)
Mellanby, Helen
  Animal Life in Freshwater (Methuen, London, 1938)
Mellen, Ida
  *The Treatment of Fish Diseases (Zoopathologica, vol. II, No. 1, New York, 1928)
Mellen, Ida & Lanier, Robert J.
  1001 Questions Answered About Your Aquarium (Harrap, London, 1936)

Bibliography

Mitsukuri, K.
  The Cultivation of Marine and Freshwater Animals in Japan (Bulletin U.S. Bureau of Fisheries: Washington, 1904)
Mulertt, Hugo
  The Goldfish and its Systematic Culture (Cincinnati, 1883)
Niklitschek, Alexander
  Water-lilies and Water-plants (Chatto & Windus, London, 1932)
Norman, J. R.
  A History of Fishes (Benn, London, 1931)
Page, C. N.
  Aquaria (Des Moines, 1898)
Palmer, Ray
  Marvels of Pond-life (Butterworth, London, 1927)
Pennant, Thomas
  British Zoology (London, 1776)
Pereira, R. A.
  The Goldfish (Hong Kong Naturalist, vol. VIII, Hong Kong, 1937)
Perry, Frances
  Water Gardening (Country Life, London 1961)
Peters, C. H.
  Life and Love in the Aquarium (Empire Tropical Fish Import, New York, 1934)
Pincher, H. Chapman
  A Study of Fishes (Jenkins, London, 1948)
Pycraft, W. P.
  The Story of Fish Life (Newnes, London, 1901)
Ramsey, L. W. & Lawrence, Charles H.
  Garden Pools (Macmillan, New York, 1930)
Regan, C. Tate
  The Freshwater Fishes of the British Isles (Methuen, London, 1911)
Richardson, Ernest
  The Bog-garden (Marshall Press, London, 1938)
Roe, Colin D.
  A Manual of Aquarium Plants (Shirley Aquatics, Solihull, 1964)
Romanes, George J.
  Animal Intelligence (Paul, London, 1910)
Roughley, T. C.
  The Cult of the Goldfish (Angus & Robertson, Sydney, 1936)

Roule, Louis
  Fishes: Their Ways of Life (Routledge, London, 1935)
Schubert, Gottfried
  Diseases of Aquarium Fish (Trans.: Gwynne Vevers) (Studio
    Vista, London, 1967)
Smith, Hugh M.
  Japanese Goldfish: Their Varieties and Cultivation (Roberts,
    Washington, 1909)
Sterba, Günther
  Freshwater Fishes of the World (Vista Books, London, 1962)
Thomas, G. L.
  Garden Pools, Water-lilies and Goldfish (Van Nostrand, Princeton,
    1958)
Tricker, W. E.
  The Water Garden (New York: 1897)
Vinden, John S.
  The Pan Book of the Home Aquarium (Pan Books, London,
    1961)
Wachtel, Hellmuth
  Aquarium Hygiene (Trans.: Gwynne Vevers) (Studio Vista,
    London, 1966)
Warburton, Leslie
  Electricity in Your Aquarium (Marshall, London, 1959)
Watson, F. Austin
  Aquarium and Pond Management for Beginners (Cage Bird Fancy,
    London, 1933)
  Fishponds and Home Aquariums (Collingridge, London, 1936)
Weigel, Wilfried
  Planning and Decorating the Aquarium (Trans.: Gwynne Vevers)
    (Studio Vista, London, 1966)
Wells, A. Laurence
  Live Foods for Aquarium Fishes (Marshall Press, London, 1938)
  The Observer's Book of Freshwater Fishes of the British Isles
    (Warne, London, 1941)
Wickler, Wolfgang
  Breeding Aquarium Fish (Trans.: Denys W. Tucker) (Studio
    Vista, London, 1966)
Yarrell, William
  A History of British Fishes (London, 1859)

Bibliography

Yatsu Naohide
Recent Progress in the Studies of Goldfish in Japan (XIIe. Congrés
   Internat. de Zoologie, Sect. IX, Lisbon, 1937)

WORKS IN FOREIGN LANGUAGES:

Bade, E.
   Das Süsswasser Aquarium (Pfenningstorf, Berlin, 1923)
Baster, Job
   Opuscula Subseciva (Haarlem, 1765)
Billardon de Sauvigny, Louis Edme
   Histoire Naturelle des Dorades de la Chine (Paris, 1780)
Blanchon, H. L. A.
   Le Cyprin Doré de la Chine et ses Variétés (Cosmos, Paris, 1912)
Bloch, Marc E.
   Oeconomische Naturgeschichte der Fische Deutschlands (Berlin,
   1784)
Carbonnier, Pierre
   Sur la Reproduction et le Dévelopment du Poisson Télescope (Comptes
   Rendues Hebd. Acad. Sciences, Paris, 1872)
Cuvier, Georges & Valenciennes, Achille
   Histoire Naturelle des Poissons, Vol. XVI (Paris, 1842)
De Schaek, M.
   Histoire du Poisson Doré (Carassius auratus) (Revue Sci. Nat.
   Appliq., Paris, 1893)
François, M.
   Décors Exotiques et Plantes d'Aquariums (Desseaux, Colombes,
   1951)
Kuhn, Franz
   Der Kleine Goldfischteich (Insel, Leipzig, n.d.)
Moreau, Emile
   Histoire Naturelle des Poissons de la France (Paris, 1881)
Pouchet, G.
   Sur les Cyprins Monstreux (Journ. Anat. Physiol., Paris, 1870)
Schreitmüller, Wilhelm
   Zierfische ihre Pflege und Zucht (Müller, Frankfurt-a-M., 1931)
Stansch, K.
   Der Schleierfisch und die übrigen Abarten des Goldfisches (Bib. fur
   Aquarien- und Terrarien-kunde, vol. V, Brunswick, 1910)
Vallot, J. N.
   Ichthyologie Française (Dijon, 1837)

For the Specialist Reader:

Bateson, W.
> *Materials for the Study of Variation, treated with especial respect to Discontinuity in the Origin of Species* (Macmillan, London, 1894)

Chen, Shisan C.
> **The Inheritance of Blue and Brown Colours in the Goldfish, Carassius auratus* (Journal of Genetics, vol. XXIX, Cambridge, 1934)

Cocking, T. Tusting
> *pH Values, What They Are and How to Determine Them* (British Drug Houses, London, 1938)

Matsui, Y.
> *Genetical Studies on Gold-Fish of Japan* (Journal of the Imperial Fisheries Institute, vol. XXX, Tokyo, 1934)

Pearl, R.
> *Modes of Research in Genetics* (Macmillan, New York, 1915)

Ryder, J. A.
> **The Inheritance of Modifications Due to Disturbances of the Early Stages of Development, especially in the Japanese Domesticated Races of Gold-carp* (Proc. Acad. nat. Sci., Philadelphia, 1893)

Periodicals:

> *Amateur Aquarist* (London, 1924) continued as *Amateur Aquarist and Reptilian Review* (1924–8) continued as *Aquarist and Pond-keeper* (1928–41; Brentford, 1946 *et seq.*)
> *Aquarium* (Philadelphia, 1932–59; Norristown, 1959 *et seq.*)
> *Petfish* (London, 1966 *et seq.*)
> *Tropical Fish Hobbyist* (New Jersey, 1952 *et seq.*)

In conclusion, special mention must be made of Bashford Dean's *Bibliography of Fishes* (American Museum of Natural History, New York). It has proved invaluable in enabling us to trace many of the books, monographs and articles mentioned.

INDEX

Get a thorough insight into the index, by which the whole book is governed and turned, like fishes by the tail.

SWIFT, *Tale of a Tub*

Index

Index